# MOTIVATION

# A Systematic

## Reinterpretation

DALBIR BINDRA

Associate Professor of Psychology
McGill University

THE RONALD PRESS COMPANY   •   NEW YORK

The Library of Congress has cataloged this book as follows:

Bindra, Dalbir.

Motivation: a systematic reinterpretation. New York, Ronald Press
Co. [ᶜ1959]

p.   illus.   22cm.

1. Motivation (Psychology)

BF199.B5                          158.734                          59–6101 ‡

Library of Congress

# Preface

This book attempts to provide a systematic presentation of the variety of experimental findings emerging from recent research in the area of psychology labeled motivation. I have aimed at writing it in such a way that the undergraduate, given occasional guidance, will not find it too difficult and the graduate student and research worker will not find it too elementary. Since the discussions are based on the results of both animal and human experiments, this work will also provide the necessary background for students interested specifically in human motivation and personality and in comparative psychology, and will be useful to those concerned with general behavior theory. Finally, it is my hope that this book will present an up-to-date, coherent treatment of motivational phenomena that will interest social and clinical psychologists, neurophysiologists, and workers in other related disciplines.

For reasons which can be left to the historians of psychology to unravel, the study of motivation has assumed increasing importance over the last two decades and has come to command a considerable portion of the research energy of psychologists. One need only cite the experimental controversies arising from various aspects of "drive theory," studies of the effects on behavioral development of variations in experiences of infancy, and the remarkable advances in neurophysiology and physiological psychology. *The Nebraska Symposium of Motivation*, an annual publication since 1953, testifies to the rapid flow of research on the problems of motivation. It has been these developments that prompted me to undertake a systematic interpretation of the facts and problems in this field.

Before I had gone far into this venture, it became clear that the area of motivation in current psychology is not defined by any unique physiological or psychological process, but only by a class of phenomena. These "motivational phenomena," as they might be termed, include the behavioral aspects of exploration, fear, hunger, sex, and the like. It is true that phenomena of this type show certain features that are not evident in perceptual and learning phenomena; nevertheless, it would be incorrect to say that those features are unique to motivational phenomena. The whole weight of recent evidence and theory tends to link learning, perceptual, and motivational phenomena by common principles and processes. Thus, clearly, motivational phenomena must be described and interpreted in terms of the same concepts, principles, and processes that have been, or could be, employed in dealing with other categories of behavioral phenomena. As far as possible, that is what I have attempted to do.

One feature of my approach is that concepts such as "instinct," "drive," and "need" are not employed as (hypothetical) explanatory constructs. Rather, various phenomena are interpreted in terms of a few general processes which can be closely linked to manipulable variables. I have also tried to follow a consistently objective point of view; subjective terminology and concepts are avoided as far as can be done without omitting important problems. Within such a general framework, I have asked specific empirical questions and have attempted to answer them in the light of experimental research. Some of my discussions are, admittedly, tentative, and I certainly do not expect the reader to agree with all the specific analyses and interpretations proposed here. However, it is my hope to be able to persuade him that the general systematic position adopted in this book offers a consistent and fruitful way of approaching a diversity of motivational phenomena.

Since my main concern throughout has been with questions of a fundamental nature, I have organized the discussion of the various phenomena around certain general concepts and processes. The reader will, therefore, not find separate chapters on the familiar topics of exploratory activity, specific hungers, sexual responses, emotional behavior, and conflict. Rather, various aspects of each of these and other phenomena will be found throughout the book, in the chapters dealing with the processes to which they are relevant. For example, certain aspects of hunger behavior are discussed in the chapter on the description of motivational phenomena, while its other aspects are discussed in chapters on sensory cues and blood chemistry. The reader who wishes to study any of these phenomena in more traditional fashion can do so by employing the detailed entries for each phenomenon in the index.

I have profited greatly from the comments of my colleagues and students at McGill University, who were ever ready to read and criticize the manuscript throughout its preparation. In particular, frequent discussions with S. Fillenbaum, D. O. Hebb, and W. E. Lambert helped me to clarify and better formulate my ideas on various issues. Many psychologists at other universities were also kind enough to read critically the whole or various portions of the manuscript. The work has been much improved through their suggestions. I am particularly grateful for the detailed and extensive comments of R. J. Audley, F. A. Beach, P. H. R. James, G. Mandler, and P. S. Siegel, and especially to J. McV. Hunt, general editor of the series of which this book is a part. Mrs. Cynthia Wimer advised me on literary matters, and Miss Joyce Blond helped me in the preparation of figures. Mr. N. Spinner assisted in the proofreading, and Miss Jane Stewart in the long and exacting job of preparing the index. Finally, I should like to register my gratitude to Miss Beverley Houghton who, with patience and skill, typed numerous drafts of the manuscript and prepared the final copy.

Montreal                                         DALBIR BINDRA
   January, 1959

# Contents

# MOTIVATION

## A Systematic

### Reinterpretation

# Chapter 1

# The Problem and
# the Present Approach

This book deals with the area of psychological investigation called "motivation." Psychology has not yet reached the stage where its subject matter can be divided into well-defined and theoretically meaningful sections. Thus the dividing lines between its currently recognized main areas, such as perception, learning, and motivation, are far from clear. Rather, these areas are identified and distinguished from each other only on the basis of the types of phenomena and theoretical questions that have traditionally been included in them. The phenomena that are discussed under the rubric of "motivation" include the behavioral aspect of hunger, sex, exploration, play, fear, anger, and the like. The type of general theoretical issues raised in this area is represented by questions such as these: Why are organisms active at all? Why do organisms behave as they do? What are the processes that underlie the initiation, direction, and termination of different types of activity? It is these types of phenomena and theoretical questions that roughly delineate the field of motivation in modern psychology.

The recognition of "motivation" as a conveniently identified area of psychology has at times given rise to the misconception that some unique "motivational processes" are responsible for motivational phenomena, and that these processes are different from those that operate in other, "nonmotivational," activities. Undoubtedly, it is true that motivational phenomena have frequently drawn attention to certain features of behavior that are less dramatically manifested in perceptual and learning activities. However, this fact does not necessarily imply that the processes underlying motivational activities on the one hand and perceptual and learning activities on the other are basically different; nor that the general principles governing them are different; nor that the theoretical questions raised by them are dissimilar. In fact, the processes, principles, and questions that have generally been discussed with reference to perceptual and learning phenomena seem to apply just as well to motivational phenomena, and vice versa. For example, as we shall see, there is every reason to believe that the learning principles involved in the acquisition of perceptual responses and in the acquisition of motor, verbal, and problem-solving skills are essentially the same as those that operate in the acquisition of "motivational responses," such as eating, exploring, and fighting. Again, the problem of "stimulus generalization" is no more relevant to conditioning and perceptual equivalence than it is to exploration, sexual responsiveness, fear, and other motivational activities. Similarly, the general problem of the role of periodic variations in blood chemistry in determining behavior, which has been analyzed mostly with experiments on motivational activities, is just as important, though normally not as evident, in the contexts of perceptual and learning responses. Thus, as will become increasingly clear in the course of this work, it makes little sense to define the area of motivation as the study of "motives" or of some kind of a unique motivational process; it can be meaningfully defined only as the study of motivational phenomena.

The purpose of this book is to formulate, within a general systematic framework, specific and empirically meaningful questions about motivational activities, and to attempt to answer them in the light of available experimental evidence. With only a few exceptions, the evidence will be selected from the studies of the behavior of mammalian species, and the discussion will be conducted at a level of generality that would make it applicable likewise to the rat, man, and other mammals. As may be expected from the considerations in the last paragraph, an attempt will be made to describe and interpret motivational phenomena in terms of the same concepts, principles, and processes that are, or can be, employed in the areas of perception and learning as well. Such an attempt will also help to bring out the relevance of the analysis of motivational activities to theoretical questions that are currently discussed almost wholly with reference to other types of behavioral phenomena.

This chapter provides a sketchy historical perspective for the current discussions of motivation, defines the main problems, and outlines the approach adopted here.

## CURRENT IDEAS IN HISTORICAL PERSPECTIVE

Until two centuries ago, almost all attempts to explain behavior made use of the animistic concept of soul. Descartes was perhaps the first philosopher to explore systematically the possibility of answering questions about behavior without reference to soul. He considered animals as machines and postulated fluid spirits, rushing through the nerves, as the dynamic or driving agents that moved these complex machines. He found it difficult, however, to apply this model to the behavior of human beings. While maintaining that many human acts were mechanical in nature, like those of animals, Descartes resorted to the concept of soul to account for "rational acts" which involve judgment, choice, or will. This practice of interpreting animal behavior in terms of one set of concepts and human behavior in terms of other, radically different, concepts was not finally discarded until Darwin's influence had become widespread.

In *Origin of species* (1859), while talking about the anatomical and physiological continuity between the animal and human species, Darwin implied that there is also a corresponding continuity in their behavior. This idea was explicitly developed by him in a later book, *Expression of emotions in man and animals* (1872). From this point on, the study of animal behavior gradually came to be regarded as a clue to the more complex, but essentially similar, behavior of the human species. Comparative psychology became as respectable a study as comparative anatomy and comparative physiology. More and more biological concepts crept into the discussions of both animal and human behavior. It was in the course of this intellectual ferment that the early animistic concepts were replaced by "instincts" as the dynamic agents responsible for "moving" organisms to different kinds of activity. Though the concept of instinct had been a part of intellectual thought for centuries (*see* Beach, 1955), and though Freud (1910; 1st ed. 1905) had used it in a psychological context, it was McDougall (1912; 1st ed. 1908) who formally introduced this concept, with its newly acquired biological overtones, into the main stream of psychological theorizing.

THE INSTINCT DOCTRINE

McDougall developed his famous instinct doctrine within a general metaphysical framework of "purposiveness." He emphasized the purposive nature of behavior and postulated instincts as the fundamental "motives" which moved organisms toward particular ends or goals. An *instinct* was for McDougall a biological process that was innate rather than dependent on learning. He characterized it as an emotional impulse or striving which predisposed the organisms (1) to notice significant stimuli, and (2) to make approach or avoidance movements in relation to those stimuli. Thus the "pugnacity instinct" was an emotional impulse to fight which manifested itself in fighting when exposed to appropriate stimuli, and the "instinct to escape" referred to a fear impulse and tendency to run away from a threatening situation. At first, McDougall (1912; 1st ed. 1908) thought he could account for all behavior in terms of about a dozen instincts, but thereafter he felt compelled to change the number and the items in the list from time to time. By 1932 his list included eighteen "native propensities": food-seeking, disgust, sex, fear, curiosity, protective or parental propensity, gregariousness, self-assertion, submission, anger, appeal, constructive propensity, acquisitive propensity, laughter, comfort, rest or sleep, migratory propensity, and a cluster of specific bodily needs —coughing, sneezing, breathing, elimination (McDougall, 1932, Chap. 7). To account for the varieties and complexities of observed behavior, he suggested ways in which these instincts or innate propensities could be modified, compounded, and integrated into more complex functional units.

For a while the concept of instinct seemed to have become quite popular in psychology and related fields. Many psychologists, including Thorndike (1913), Dewey (1917), Woodworth (1918), and Watson (1914, 1919), adopted and made extensive use of it in discussions of the various aspects of animal and human behavior.

But this was not to last. Specific criticisms of the instinct doctrine started accumulating after Dunlap's (1919) general attack entitled "Are there any instincts?" Since there was no way of directly observing the processes called instincts, Watson (1930) argued that the instinct concept was an easy and ever-ready substitute for true explanations of observed activities. To say that the animal fights because of the instinct of pugnacity, or runs away because of the instinct of fear, is merely to give a redundant description of the observed activity—description which would be complete even if one said only that the animal fights or runs away. Sociologists like Bernard (1924) complained that the supporters of the doctrine were unable to agree on the exact number of instincts to be postulated. They also pointed out that the activities, such as maternal love and acquisitiveness, to which the various instincts referred were too complex and variable from culture to culture to be considered as innate; as sociologists viewed it, they were acquired by the individual from his social environment. Many psychologists wanted proof that the so-called instinctive activities were really unlearned before they were willing to consider them innate. Kuo (1928) and Watson (1930) argued that, instead of accepting instinct as an explanatory concept, an attempt should be made to determine in each case the relative roles of learning and innate factors.

Three things seem to have emerged from all the controversy that revolved for over twenty years around the concept of instinct. First, comparative and physiological psychologists started analyzing the processes underlying the activities that were attributed to instincts. Migration, nest building, maternal behavior, sexual responses, and many other complex patterns of behavior were experimentally analyzed in a variety of species. These studies revealed some intriguing humoral, perceptual, and, sometimes, experiential factors as the bases of the complex activities (*see* Morgan, 1943; Beach, 1951). For example, nest building in rats was shown to be related to the mechanism of temperature regulation, migration in birds to gonadal development, and obstacle avoidance in bats to the echoes of sounds they produce during flight. Studies of this kind seemed to take away some of the mystery of such activities, and it became obvious that, though there were undoubtedly innate components in them, the concept of instinct was too broad to serve as an adequate basis for explaining them. Such analytic studies are still continuing.

The second outcome of the controversy over the concept of instinct was the gradual acceptance of the term *instinctive behavior*. This term came to be used simply as a descriptive label for activities of the type that McDougall and others had sought to explain in terms of the concept of instinct. These activities (e.g. hoarding of food and other objects, maternal behavior, nesting, and the like) involve complex sequences of responses, are quite stereotyped, seem to occur in all normal members of most mammalian species, and apparently occur without specific learning. However, the use of the adjective "instinctive" to describe such activities no longer commits one to any particular interpretation regarding whether they are in fact innate or learned. Certainly, the notion that they can be explained in terms of unitary, innate processes, called "instincts," has been widely discarded by psychologists.[1] So

---

[1] Some ethologists, particularly Lorenz (1950) and Tinbergen (1951), have sought to reintroduce, without much reference to the earlier psychological work, the concept of instinct as an explanation of such species-specific behavior. Bindra (1957) pointed out that, at least so far as psychological thought is concerned, these attempts have met with little success. We shall

as completely to avoid the connotations of the term "instinctive," the more recent phrase *species-specific behavior* will be used here to refer to such activities.

The third child of the instinct affair was the concept of *drive*. The analyses of various instinctive activities always reached the point where it seemed necessary to postulate some other ultimate, innate driving agents. Thus, even if maternal behavior, for example, could be shown to result from the integration of cleaning the pups, nursing, and other acts, and could not be interpreted as the outcome of a single unitary instinct, the origin of the cleaning, nursing, and other component acts still needed to be explained. The concept of drive attempted to do this by postulating the existence of some simpler innate agents. Thus, the concept of "homeostatic" or *primary drives*—hunger, sex, pain, and the like—crept into the psychological literature, replacing the unpopular "instinct." The drives resembled instincts in that both were considered to be the primary, innate basis for activities of all types, no matter how complex. As Lashley (1938) pointed out, the drive, in many respects, was not unlike its parent, the instinct.

However, as an explanatory tool, the concept of drive did show two refinements over that of instinct. For one thing, the concept of drive, for the most part, did not carry any question-begging purposive implications with it. For another, drives were regarded as "more elementary" than instincts. This fact left the way open for attributing to learning the observed individual and cultural differences in maternal behavior, aggression, gregariousness, and other similar activities that had been labeled "instinctive." It seemed more reasonable to say, for example, that maternal behavior was somehow "built up" from elementary processes called drives than to consider maternal behavior itself as unitary and irreducible to simpler processes. Thus, drives gradually replaced instincts

discuss some specific aspects of the interesting empirical work of this group of naturalists in appropriate chapters. For an evaluation of the theoretical concepts of ethologists, see Lehrman (1953) and Hinde (1956). An attempt to bridge the gap between ethological and psychological research has been made by Thorpe (1956).

as the primary dynamic agents and have since continued to play an important role in psychological theorizing.

## THE DRIVE DOCTRINE

While the concept of drive has appeared in psychological discussions for about forty years (*see* Young, 1936, for the history of the concept), the drive doctrine in its present form is most closely identified with the names of Mowrer, Hull, Miller, Dollard, and Spence. Agreement on the nature, number, and functioning of drives is far from unanimous among drive theorists themselves, and, of course, they all have modified their positions from time to time. The typical position, if there is one, seems to be that four *primary drives* exist:[2] *hunger, sex, thirst,* and *pain*. Objects or events that reduce primary drives (food, sexual activity, water, and escape from noxious stimulation) are called *primary reinforcers*. The essence of the drive doctrine can perhaps be summarized in the form of two propositions: (1) Organisms act only to reduce their drives; thus all activities are to be interpreted as direct or indirect attempts at drive reduction. (2) Activities that are accompanied by a reduction in drive are strengthened, and such drive reduction is a necessary condition for learning to occur. Admittedly, a system of behavior study that is still developing and is so complex cannot be stated in two propositions without gross oversimplification. However, for our present purposes, we need pay attention only to the most general aspects of this system; we shall have occasion to examine many specific hypotheses of drive theorists in later chapters.

The main problem that drive theorists had to face was, of course, one of showing how various complex activities could be built up from hunger, sex, thirst, and pain drives. The answer to this was provided in the evidence (*see* Miller, 1951, for review) showing that new or *secondary drives* and *reinforcers* could be acquired through the association of irrelevant stimuli (objects, activities, and events) with primary drives and reinforcers. Wolfe (1936) demonstrated that chimpan-

---

[2] Some psychologists, like Spence (1944, p. 61), prefer to consider drive simply as a convenient construct having no substantive reality.

zees could be made to learn and perform new tasks with inedible tokens as the (secondary) reinforcer, when the tokens had previously been associated with a primary reinforcer (grapes). Anderson (1941) showed experimentally that stimuli associated with food deprivation could play the same (secondary) drive role in the learning of a maze as food deprivation itself. And Mowrer (1939) showed that innocuous stimuli could be associated with pain and could thus produce "fear" in the absence of the primary pain stimuli.

Theoretically, there was no limit to the number of secondary drives and reinforcers that could develop through association with the primary drives and primary reinforcers. Thus, it was argued that any activity could be attributed to the operation of primary and secondary drives and reinforcers. This point of view was developed particularly by a group of psychologists at Yale University. Miller & Dollard (1941) interpreted certain aspects of social behavior in terms of the secondary drive and reinforcing values of verbal and other social stimuli. Mowrer (1948) and Dollard & Miller (1950) applied this orientation to the problems of neurosis and psychotherapy. The work of the Yale group represents perhaps the most ingenious and painstaking attempt to interpret all behavior, no matter how complex, in terms of the concepts of primary and secondary drives and reinforcers. The contributions of drive theorists to the experimental and theoretical psychological literature have undoubtedly been of remarkable magnitude and merit. However, within the last decade or so, dissatisfactions with certain aspects of the drive doctrine have begun to be voiced.

## The Current Controversy

Criticisms of the drive doctrine have centered around the fact that it seeks to link all the varied observed activities to four or five primary drives. Nissen (1954) has argued that many simple acts and complex activities are unrelated to the so-called primary drives. He says:

The fact that much behavior is so patterned as to realize major homeostatic goals does not mean, however, that all activities are thus organized into goal-directed series of units or acts. Observation of animals and people in "free," and even in highly "structured," situations indicates that much time and energy is taken up by brief, self-contained, often repetitive acts which are their own reason, which are autonomously motivated, and which are not to be interpreted as being small contributions to some remote, critically important aim. The organism scratches itself, stretches, shakes its head, grunts or chirps, looks around, examines an irrelevant item of the environment, picks its nose or its teeth, rocks back and forth, shifts its position, twists a paper clip out of shape, cracks its knuckles, doodles, looks at a picture on the wall, and so on *ad infinitum*.[3]

This point is elaborated by Nissen (1953) with reference to certain observations of chimpanzee behavior. In this study, Nissen worked with five male and five female post-adolescent, but sexually naive, chimpanzees. He paired every male with every female, and observed the behavior of each pair a number of times. Observations were made only when the females were in heat and thus, physiologically, were sexually receptive. Nissen spent roughly 100 hours in these observations. He estimates that, had he been observing sexually sophisticated chimpanzees, roughly 200 copulations would have occurred in this time. However, not a single copulation occurred in the course of his observations of these five pairs. These animals were nevertheless quite active during the observation periods. They engaged in all types of individual and social activities, including most of the acts that normally would be part of the mating pattern. Though a drive theorist will likely ascribe these diverse activities to sex drive, Nissen points out that there is no justification for such an interpretation. "The only excuse for doing so is *our* knowledge (a) that with other, experienced, male-female pairings the sex act would occur, and (b) that, with continuation of the prevailing conditions for a long enough time, the sex act most probably will occur . . ." (1953, p. 293). But these considerations do not in any way support the view that all activities during the observation periods were related to sex drive. Take grooming, for

[3] H. W. Nissen, The nature of the drive as innate determinant of behavioral organization, in M. R. Jones (Ed.), *Nebraska symposium on motivation* (Lincoln: University of Nebraska Press, 1954), p. 314.

instance. Chimpanzees often scratch, clean, and caress each other; and such grooming is often considered to be related to sexual drive. Nissen points out that grooming in chimpanzees occurs before sexual maturity, it occurs not only in male-female pairings but also in male-male and female-female pairings, and it occurs more often after mating than before mating. These characteristics of grooming argue against its being considered a secondary drive, acquired by being associated with sexual activity. Nissen concludes that "the behaviors legitimately and descriptively named sex, hunger, thirst, and so on are relatively infrequent, isolated events in the flow of behavior; their motivation demands explanation no more, and no less, than do the many [other] activities. . . ." (1953, p. 294).

Hebb (1955) also has raised similar objections to drive theory. Referring to his own investigations of emotional behavior in chimpanzees, he points to examples where the observed behavior cannot be accounted for in terms of hunger, sex, thirst, and pain drives, and their associated stimuli. In one of his experiments, Hebb (1946a) exposed laboratory-reared chimpanzees to a variety of stimuli with which they had had no previous experience. The stimulus objects and events included a doll, cast of a snake, skull of a monkey, anesthetized chimpanzee infant being carried by the experimenter, and the like. Some of these objects, such as the snake-cast and anesthetized chimpanzee, frequently evoked "fear" behavior (avoidance) on the first occasion that the animals were exposed to them. Hebb points out that the observed avoidance behavior cannot be explained in terms of prior association with noxious stimulation (or in terms of "innate" mechanisms —see Chap. 4). Because the animals had been reared in the laboratory, one could be certain that the chimpanzees had never experienced these particular stimulus patterns and pain together. Nor had the chimpanzees any previous exposure to the stimulus patterns. (Of course, all the subjects had seen other chimpanzees before, but none of them had seen an anesthetized chimpanzee—prostrate, limp, and inactive.) Thus, Hebb argues that "spontaneous fears" of this type do not result from secondary drives, acquired through association with primary noxious stimuli. Addressing drive theorists, he asks:

What is the drive that produces panic in the chimpanzee at the sight of a model of a human head; or fear in some animals, and vicious aggression in others, at the sight of the anesthetized body of a fellow chimpanzee? What about fear of snakes, or the young chimpanzee's terror at the sight of strangers? One can accept the idea that this is "anxiety," but the anxiety, if so, is not based on a prior association of the stimulus object with pain.[4]

The implication of Nissen's and Hebb's arguments is simply that the range of behavioral phenomena is too vast to be forced into a simple classification of the drive or instinct variety. As a theoretical scheme, the drive doctrine with less than a half dozen primary drives appears bound to misinterpret behavioral data.

Drive theorists can, and often do, answer this criticism in two ways, but not to the entire satisfaction of their critics. One way is to argue that all the above-mentioned phenomena in fact result from the operation of secondary drives or secondary reinforcing stimuli so subtle and complex that their operation cannot be easily demonstrated. This amounts to a proclamation of faith in the drive doctrine and does not constitute an acceptable argument. Rather, drive theorists need to demonstrate that secondary drives and reinforcers do in fact underlie the type of experimental findings listed in the preceding paragraphs. Until such demonstrations have been made, the use of secondary drives and secondary reinforcers as explanatory concepts must remain open to question. Meanwhile the concepts of secondary drives and reinforcers, as employed by drive theorists, have themselves been criticized. Thus, Nissen (1954) has shown how the assumption of secondary drives in certain cases leads one into logical difficulties, and Schlosberg & Pratt (1956) have found the concept of secondary reinforcer, within the framework of the drive-reduction interpretation of learning, to be untenable on empirical grounds.

[4] D. O. Hebb, Drives and the C.N.S. (Conceptual Nervous System), *Psychol. Rev.*, **62**, 245.

The other way out for drive theorists is to add to the number of primary drives so as to cover a larger range of behavioral phenomena. Though drive theorists themselves have, in general, been hesitant to increase the number of primary drives, other psychologists have done so. Thus, Harlow and his colleagues (*see* Harlow, 1953), as well as Berlyne (1950, 1954) and Montgomery (1953, 1953a, 1953b), have found it expedient to postulate a primary but nonhomeostatic drive to account for some aspects of the exploratory activity of animals. They have shown that the opportunity to explore in the absence of any reduction in pain, hunger, or sexual excitement can serve as a reinforcer. In order to make this finding fit the drive-reduction interpretation of reinforcement, they have attributed the reinforcing effects of exploration to a reduction in an "exteroceptive drive." This new primary drive has been variously designated as *exploratory drive*, curiosity, or manipulatory drive, and exploratory activity is assumed to reduce this drive. This method of adding to the number of primary dynamic agents is no different from the way in which instinct theorists tried to save the instinct doctrine. The shortcomings of this method are the same whether applied to the concept of instinct or that of drive. It is equally ad hoc in both cases.

The second main proposition of the drive doctrine has also been challenged in recent years. There seems to be growing evidence that drive reduction is not as important a condition of learning as has been supposed by drive theorists. For example, experiments by Harlow and his colleagues (*see* Harlow, 1953) have shown that an *increase* in drive can serve as a reinforcer for learning in certain cases. This point will be discussed in detail in Chapter 5. For the present, let us simply note that this apparently reasonable tenet of the drive doctrine has not remained unchallenged.

Drive theorists have not been disheartened by these criticisms. They seem to have come back with renewed energy to make explicit and sometimes to modify their basic postulates in order to meet the criticisms. For example, Brown (1953), observing certain inconsistencies in current discussions of secondary drives, has redefined the concept of drive. He now attributes only an *energizing* function to drives, denying them any capacity to *elicit* any specific directed pattern of response. Making one or two additional assumptions, Brown (1955) has also defended the important role ascribed to drive reduction in reinforcement.

The ingenuity of drive theorists in answering objections and devising crucial experiments has been remarkable. If one ignores the many specific hypotheses of drive theorists and looks upon the drive doctrine as a model or framework for approaching the problems of motivation, it has been most fruitful by way of stimulating research. Thus, the current criticisms of the drive doctrine do not so much show that it is "wrong," as they point to the desirability of devising alternative, competing frameworks for the study of motivation. It may be that an alternative approach can deal with behavioral data at least as well as the drive doctrine and may perhaps be as fruitful in stimulating research.

## THE PROBLEM AND AN APPROACH

Starting with a formulation of what has been regarded as the problem of motivation, this section sets forth some features of the general approach to the problem to be adopted in this work.

### THE PROBLEM OF MOTIVATION

Implied in the concept of drive (and instinct) is the notion that the organism would not be active at all were it not for the operation of one drive or another. This implication is misleading and contrary to fact. As Hebb (1949) has pointed out, the organism is active all the time, even when it is asleep and all its drives, as they are usually listed, are fully reduced. The organism is always active because the nervous system is always active; the nervous system is always active simply because it is living matter, and activity or irritability is one of the prime characteristics of life. The answer to the question, "Why is the organism active at all?," therefore, lies not in the operation of hunger, sex, thirst, and pain drives but rather in the biological properties of living tissues that make up the organism. This question poses a problem for physiology and biochemistry, not for psychology. The psychological problem of motivation is quite a different one.

If one observes the behavior of an animal in its familiar surroundings, one is likely to be struck by the effectiveness with which it manipulates and adapts to its environment. It feeds, protects, and amuses itself in what appears to be a fairly efficient way. Each response systematically follows, or is accompanied by, others in such a way that the animal usually manages to effect an adaptation in relation to changing objects, events, and other classes of sensory stimulation. The activities of animals seem almost always to be aimed at some particular consequences, directed toward some "goals." In common-sense language we say that behavior tends to be "purposive" or that animals "have purposes." It is this "purposive" or "moving-in-the-direction-of-goals" aspect of behavior that is the dominant feature of the phenomena that are termed motivational, and that has been generally considered to present the core of the psychological problem of motivation.

Thus, Tolman (1932) in his *Purposive behavior in animals and man* emphasized the "directedness" feature of behavior as the one pivotal to understanding behavior. Similarly, Young (1936) defined "motivational psychology" as the study of conditions which arouse ("move") and regulate (direct) the behavior of organisms. Similarly, a currently popular definition of motivation makes it the study of the factors that underlie the initiation, direction, and termination of various activities. Here the terms "direction" and "termination" both imply some sort of consequence or goal with respect to which a given activity is directed and terminated. Within the same general framework, McClelland *et al.* (1953) have stated that ". . . one of the important ways in which motivated behavior may be identified is in terms of the *coordination* of responses or in terms of some kind of a response *sequence*, which terminates when the organism arrives somewhere with respect to a source of affect. The terms approach and avoid-

ance imply a sequence of responses which has a *goal* . . ."
(1953, p. 38). In view of this consensus, it appears reasonable
to proceed on the assumption that the core of what is usually
called the problem of motivation lies in the "purposive" or
goal-directed aspect of behavior. This feature is also to be
found in perceptual and other "nonmotivational" activities, but
it is particularly evident in motivational phenomena.

The psychological problem raised by the goal-directed aspect of behavior can be stated in the form of two related
questions. In most general terms, these two questions constitute the essence of the problem. The first general question is
concerned with the *origin* of directed activities. How are responses patterned into complex, "purposive" activities? What
factors determine their development in the animal's repertoire? The second question concerns the *occurrence* of directed activities. How is it that certain types of directed
activities occur at a particular time and others do not? What
specific factors affect the frequency, rate, and timing or periodicity of the various classes of directed activities? These
two questions incorporate all the problems that are usually
discussed under the heading of motivation. The first question
incorporates the problem of purpose, goal direction, and instinctive behavior, the issues of the nature and number of
"primary drive behaviors" (eating, drinking, etc.), and the
problem of reinforcement or "pleasure and pain." The various
problems connected with the phrase "strength of motivation,"
which refers to the frequency, manner, and certain other features of the occurrence of an activity, are incorporated in the
second question. Broadly speaking, the present work assumes
that all the traditional and current issues in motivation are
special cases of the above two questions, and it attempts to
find answers to these questions with reference to motivational
phenomena.

## INADEQUACY OF "MOTIVE" AS AN EXPLANATORY CONCEPT

The common-sense "explanations" of motivational phenomena consist merely of verbally linking a given activity
with one or another of certain states or events that are cul-

turally recognized as "goals" or "ends." As Koch (1956) has pointed out, any given behavior is made intelligible to common sense when the form "X does Y in order to . . ." is completed. Thus, one says that X eats in order not to be hungry, X fights in order to protect his wife, X joins a club in order to be respected, X goes to a movie in order to amuse himself, and X takes a drink in order to relax. Though such statements are culturally accepted accounts of behavior, they do not constitute explanations in any scientific sense.

Unfortunately, psychological discussions of motivational phenomena have not yet fully emerged from the basic assumptions of the common-sense view. This criticism, made earlier by Skinner (1953), has recently been restated explicitly by Koch (1956). He points out that, in general, psychological theorists have proceeded by classifying the culturally recognized goals into orderly classes. They have then postulated or assumed the existence of some sort of systems within the organism to correspond to the classes of goals. Such end-determining systems have been called desires, motives, urges, wishes, wants, needs, instincts, demands, drives, and so on. These postulated entities have then been defined in terms of certain functional properties and elaborated upon by linking them to certain real or presumed biological processes such as homeostasis, tension reduction, pleasure, and pain. As we have seen, the main shortcomings of this approach lie in the ad hoc way in which the end-determining entities (e.g. instincts) are postulated, and in the tenuous line of arguments with which the exceptions to any specific interpretations are handled.

The main feature of the point of view adopted in this book is that it is unnecessary and futile to postulate drives, motives, instincts, or any other end-determining systems in order to account for the various motivational phenomena. From this point of view, it becomes pointless to define terms such as "motive" and "drive," and no attempt will be made to do so here, except in referring to their usage in the works of other authors. However, this is not meant to imply a general condemnation of all postulated concepts in dealing with behavioral phenomena. Rather, the only point here is that no postulated system or process that corresponds directly and only intuitively to observed phenomena is likely to be of much value in interpreting them. Even when the postulated entities are defined in neurophysiological terms, as they should be (Krech, 1950), they provide nothing more than redundant descriptions if they only reflect behavioral data. The general rule to be employed here is that postulated processes should not merely echo the phenomena which they are presumed to explain, but should emerge from some sort of experimental analysis of the phenomena.

However, in discarding the traditional approach of postulating goal-determining entities, we should not at the same time discard the idea that one of the central problems of motivational phenomena lies in the goal-direction aspect of behavior. Koch (1956), going beyond his valid criticisms of the traditional approach, seems to have made the error of arguing against the idea that it is possible to talk meaningfully and objectively about the goal-direction aspect of behavior. We shall adopt the position of refusing to postulate goal-determining entities as explanatory concepts, but shall recognize that it is possible to raise meaningful and significant questions in terms of the concept of goal direction. Though no longer fruitful as an explanatory concept, it remains useful as a descriptive one.

It is true that the usual quantitative measures employed for behavior description are not always suited for describing the goal-direction aspect of behavior. Yet the observed behavior is often easily describable, at least roughly, in terms of a certain goal or aim, which seems to give meaning to the whole pattern of activity. For example, suppose a chimpanzee under observation handles the water faucet in its cage, drinks water and then holds some in its mouth, goes and sits near the entrance to the cage, "solicits petting" from a laboratory attendant, holds the hand of the attendant, spits water at him, and then runs to the rear of the cage. In this case, even if we described each response in terms of some quantitative measure—*time* spent handling the faucet, *amount* of water ingested, *activity level* during selected time samples, *frequency* of waving to the laboratory attendant, *accuracy* of water-spitting, and *speed* of running to the rear of the cage—even if we had all these measures, the goal-directed aspect of the chimpanzee's behavior would still remain excluded from such a description. The layman would say that spitting at the attendant is the aim of the chimpanzee's behavior, and it is undoubtedly difficult to translate such a statement into some objective, scientifically meaningful terms. However, this difficulty is not insurmountable, as will be shown in Chapter 3.

## The "Empty Organism" vs. the Neurophysiological Approach

Questions about motivation can be examined and answered by adopting either of the two opposing approaches to the study of behavior. These are the "empty organism" or strictly empirical approach of Skinner (1938, 1953) and the neurophysiological approach, as outlined by Hebb (1951). According to Skinner, the primary task of psychology is to establish functional relations between behavior and the conditions that affect it. He opposes the use of theoretical ideas concerning the neural processes underlying behavior. He is not against considering brain conditions as independent variables so long as they can be directly observed, but he is opposed to postulating hypothetical neural processes as explanations of observed behavior. Skinner feels that behavioral generalizations or laws can be, and should be, made without any reference to unobserved neural mechanisms or any other type of hypothetical constructs.

Hebb, on the other hand, is in favor of "neurologizing." He starts with the assumption, which is a reasonable and widely accepted one—one with which even Skinner would not disagree—that corresponding to every response there exists in the brain a neural integration or process. The observed responses are considered as resulting from the stimulation or firing of the corresponding neural integrations. This assumption is old enough in psychology. However, Hebb has gone on to elaborate on the nature of the (hypothetical) neural integration.

His speculation is that the neural integrations consist of a combination of spatially organized units, called *cell assemblies*, and of temporally organized sequences of cell assemblies, called *phase sequences*. He has attempted to interpret the phenomena of perception, learning, and motivation in terms of these hypothetical constructs. His program calls for gradually refining and specifying the properties of these theoretical concepts, so that they would not only account for the known facts of behavior, but would also suggest and logically imply new relations and ways of classifying behavioral phenomena.

It is true that the adoption of either the Skinnerian or the Hebbian attitude toward the problem of motivation will lead to different formulations of the two sets of questions mentioned above. The nontheoretical approach of Skinner would ask for defining the various classes of responses and then studying the factors (independent variables) that affect their development and probability of occurrence. From the functional relations generated by such studies would emerge behavioral laws or generalizations. The theoretical (neurophysiological) approach, on the other hand, would postulate two sets of neural processes; one ("neural integration," for example) corresponding to the responses under consideration, and the other determining the "release" or firing of the neural integrations. According to this view, it would be the interaction of these two hypothetical neural processes that produce the various observed activities of organisms. Empirical questions would thus be formulated so as to enable us progressively to refine and elaborate theoretical neural processes and their interactions.

Now, in the present context, the refinement and elaboration of concepts means nothing more than ascribing precise properties to the hypothetical neural constructs and then changing these properties so that deductions from them would better correspond to the observed behavioral relations. Such refinement and elaboration must be based either on advances in neurophysiology (for example, the discovery of new connections or pathways in the brain, or new knowledge of the workings of the neuron) or on the observed new functional relations between behavior and various internal and external conditions (independent variables). Clearly, then, the approaches of Skinner and Hebb overlap with each other at a crucial point. To the extent that knowledge of functional relations between behavior and independent variables can contribute to the refinement of hypothetical neural constructs, the two approaches have something in common. They both depend upon empirically determined functional relations of observed behavior. In the present work the main concern is with describing and discussing empirical relations; however, theoretical constructs will be used where they are of obvious value in linking empirical findings or suggesting lines for further research.

PLAN OF THE BOOK

The ten chapters of this work follow a fairly simple plan. Chapters 1 and 2 constitute a general introduction to the remainder of the book. The brief historical review and the outline of the present approach presented in this chapter is followed in Chapter 2 by descriptions of certain commonly discussed motivational activities. Since the scope of this book is defined in terms of the problems posed by motivational phenomena, their description in the second chapter provides background information for the more analytic studies reported in the later chapters.

The first three of the remaining eight chapters deal in one way or another with the *development* of motivational activities in the repertoire of animals. Chapter 3 examines the problem of objectively describing goal direction as a feature of behavior and goes on to discuss the general condition, namely reinforcement, which leads to the development of goal-directed activities. Chapter 4 examines the role of reinforcement in the development of some instances of species-specific behavior and of the other motivational activities described in Chapter 2. The nature of reinforcement itself is discussed in Chapter 5.

The last five chapters are concerned with the factors determining the *occurrence* of the various motivational ac-

tivities that exist in the animal's repertoire. The first of these
factors, habit strength, is dealt with in Chapter 6. The following chapter is concerned with the role of stimulus situation, including "stimulus generalization" and "conflict," in
the occurrence of any given activity. Chapter 8 discusses
"level of arousal," and Chapter 9, blood chemistry as factors
determining the occurrence of activities. The last chapter
deals with the problems of behavioral cycles and "functional
autonomy" and goes on to indicate a way of applying the
general approach adopted in this book to the study of human
motivation.

Currently, "motivation psychologists" appear to be concerned more with the problem of the occurrence of activities
("strength of motivation") than with that of the way in
which various activities first develop in the repertoire of animals. Thus, those primarily interested in the contemporary
issues of motivation can move directly from Chapter 1 to
Chapter 5.

The reader should bear two things in mind. First, this work
is concerned with a systematic reinterpretation of the area
of motivation. Therefore, many old and familiar experiments
and issues are placed in new contexts, with no attempt to
relate them to the theories and formulations which initially
prompted them. Of the many implications of any given investigation, only those that bear upon the specific questions
asked in this book are discussed; this precludes the discussion
of other implications, sometimes even those that the investigators themselves were interested in. Second, since this work
focuses on general processes rather than on particular phenomena, discussions of the various aspects of a given phenomenon will be found scattered in different chapters. For example, aggressive activities are described in Chapter 2, their
development is discussed in Chapter 4, the problem of "displaced aggression" is dealt with in Chapter 8, and the relation
of hormones to the incidence of aggressive behavior belongs
to the subject matter of Chapter 9. Those interested in complete discussions of particular phenomena should look for the
relevant entries in the subject index.

# Motivational Phenomena

The phenomena called "motivational," which define the scope of this work, include activities such as eating, drinking, approaching, escaping, attacking, exploring, copulating, maternal care of the young, and the like. It is these and similar activities that are sometimes labeled "drive behaviors" and that have traditionally been interpreted in terms of "instincts," "drives," or some other "primary motives." These activities are almost always to be found in the repertoire of the normal adult mammal and in that of some infra-mammalian species too. Of course, the particular form and the degree of complexity of these activities varies considerably from species to species and individual to individual, and we shall have occasion to examine these differences. However, our primary interest here lies in those features of motivational activities that are shared by most mammalian species, including man. The most common and widely investigated of the motivational activities will be described in this chapter. In later chapters the various psychological questions posed by them will be discussed in the light of experimental evidence. Thus the present chapter is designed to provide a general background for the discussion of specific theoretical questions in the remainder of the book.

## CLASSIFICATION OF MOTIVATIONAL PHENOMENA

Before undertaking a description of the various types of motivational activities, it seems appropriate to consider some aspects of the problem of classifying these activities. A consideration of this problem will help to clarify the confusion that often surrounds this subject.

## "Emotional" and "Motivated" Activities

Many of the phenomena to be discussed in this chapter are sometimes categorized under the rubrics of "emotional behavior" and "motivated behavior." The term *emotional behavior* is used as a collective name for the behavior of anger, fear, joy, and the like, and *motivated behavior* as a general label for the phenomena such as hunger behavior (food seeking and eating), sex behavior, and drug addiction behavior. Now, although emotional behavior and motivated behavior are often treated as if they were distinct classes of behavior, they are not so in fact. Over twenty years ago, Duffy (1934, 1941, 1941a) painstakingly started to examine the various criteria that had been suggested as the differentiating marks of emotional and motivated behavior—criteria such as the physiological mechanisms involved in the response, degree of "arousal" or energy mobilization, and "organization" or goal-directedness of behavior. She found all such differentiating criteria to be inadequate, for they failed to set apart unequivocally the phenomena which, conventionally, are grouped together either as emotional behavior or as motivated behavior. For example, the increase in arousal found in emotional behavior (e.g. fear and anger) is also present in sexual activity and other cases of motivational behavior. Similarly, the type of visceral responses, and the thalamic and cortical structures, involved in the various instances of emotional and motivated behavior have not been shown to be different.

Unfortunately, Duffy's arguments for discarding emotional and motivated behavior as classificatory categories in psychology did not until recently draw the attention they deserved. Even now, however, degree of goal direction is frequently suggested as a criterion for differentiating between emotional and motivated behavior. For example, Young (1943) defines emotional behavior as disorganized behavior, that is, behavior lacking goal direction. Similarly, Leeper (1948) and McClelland *et al.* (1953) have defined motivated behavior in terms that would identify it with goal-directed behavior. Bindra (1955) has argued that a distinction between emotional behavior and motivated behavior on the basis of degree of goal directedness is untenable. His argument is based on the similarity between the development of emotional behavior and the development of motivated behavior. In order to make the argument concrete, let us consider in detail the development of goal direction, first in an instance of "emotional" behavior and then in an instance of "motivated" behavior.

*Emotional behavior.* Hebb reports the following observations made on chimpanzees:

The experimenter, disguised with a grotesque false face and a change of clothing, approached each animal's cage wearing heavy gloves and acted the part of a very aggressive individual. . . . The first response by a number of animals was a generalized excitement and marked autonomic activity. An animal might be "friendly" and viciously aggressive, almost in the same breath, or show erection of hair and scream and yet solicit petting. Attack, flight, and the friendly pattern alternated unpredictably. As the stimulus was repeated over a 5-week period, the autonomic activity decreased and one or other of the various patterns dominated. Eventually each animal's behavior became predictable, but it appeared often to be a matter of chance whether the original disturbance would develop into fear, aggression, or (less often) friendliness.[1]

Considered developmentally, this analysis indicates that on the first few trials the animals were excited and their reactions were haphazard, lacking direction with respect to the experimenter; on later trials the responses were sustained and goal-directed, with little sign of aimless activity. Observations of this kind have been made before. For example, Sherman's work (1927) on "emotional development" in the human infant led him to stress the emergence of specific response patterns from an undifferentiated "aimless activity of most of the musculature." The above investigation of Hebb is reported here in some detail to show that, under suitable conditions, a similar course of development can also be seen in the adult animal. Essentially the same sequence of development appears in the following description of "motivated" behavior.

[1] D. O. Hebb, On the nature of fear, *Psychol. Rev.*, **53**, 271.

*Motivated behavior.* A need for morphine was established
by Spragg (1940) in four chimpanzees by giving them injections of the drug. When morphine was withheld from these
addicted animals for a day or so they showed, in addition to
the physiological withdrawal reactions, rather undirected general activity: pacing about their cages, crying, screaming, and
so on. Although withholding the drug evoked this disturbed
behavior within only a few weeks of the beginning of the
experiment, the animals did not show any tendency to "look
for" injections of morphine until later. It was several weeks
before they exhibited evidence of "desiring" morphine, at
which time they tried to pull the experimenter into the injection room, adopted the injection posture, handled the injection paraphernalia, and showed other signs of wanting an injection. Here, too, as in the "emotional" example, we find the
gradual emergence of goal-directed acts from responses which
initially were neither sustained nor directed. Such observations have often been made in connection with feeding in the
neonate; the present study shows how the same developmental
pattern can be observed in the adult when an artificial
"hunger" is created by withdrawing a drug on which the
animal has been made physiologically dependent.

It is clear that this sequence of development, from aimless
activity, or with fluctuation of aim, to goal-directed responses,
is not peculiar to behavior usually labeled emotional (anger,
fear, etc.) but can be observed also in so-called motivated
behavior (e.g. hunger and thirst behavior). It appears that in
both cases we are dealing with a developmental continuum
ranging from aimless activity to goal-directed acts. To sum
up, our developmental analysis suggests that contrary to what
is usually implied, we cannot distinguish between emotional
and motivated behavior (as conventionally labeled) in terms
of goal direction. That is to say, the degree-of-goal-direction
dimension cuts across these traditional categories, and cannot
be employed as a differentiating criterion.

In view of the above considerations it becomes apparent
why some psychologists, for example Young (1949a) and
Leeper (1948), could get involved in a controversy over

whether emotional behavior is goal-directed or not. Young looks upon emotional behavior as primarily disorganized or lacking in goal direction and defines "emotion" as "acute disturbance or upset" (1943, p. 51). Leeper, however, considers emotional behavior as goal-directed, stating that "emotional processes . . . arouse, sustain, and direct activity" (1948, p. 17). One suspects that the two authors do not mean the same thing by emotional behavior. It seems that Young's "emotional behavior" refers to the early stage of development, involving aimless activity, whereas Leeper is talking about a later stage in the development from aimless to goal-directed behavior.

This interpretation of the Young-Leeper controversy can be supported by experimental findings. For example, in one of his studies, Hebb (1946) observed Tom and Dick, two young male chimpanzees, who occupied a strategic position in the Yerkes Laboratory. They could see the experimenter approaching before the experimenter could observe them. On the first day of the experiment, an unfamiliar test object evoked considerable undirected excitement in both chimpanzees. But on later trials with the same stimulus, on observing the approaching experimenter, Tom and Dick would walk to the rear of the cage and sit calmly near the back wall of the cage. In deciding whether the behavior of Tom and Dick is goal-directed or aimless, the crucial factor is the stage or trial at which it is observed: on initial trials the behavior is undoubtedly aimless, but on later trials it is goal-directed.

*Conclusion.* Since no one has yet proposed any criterion which is generally applicable and which meaningfully differentiates between the traditional categories of emotional behavior and motivated behavior, we shall recognize no distinction between the phenomena assigned to the two categories. Whether the activities under investigation are those traditionally discussed as "motivated" (e.g. sexual activity and food-seeking) or as "emotional" (e.g. fear and aggressive attack) is of no consequence for our purpose. Similarly, whether the stimulating conditions used in a study are those conventionally labeled "emotional" (e.g. "frustration," exposure to an unfamiliar situation, and "stress") or "motivating" (e.g. food deprivation and hormonal imbalance) also is irrelevant from the point of view adopted here. It is true that conditions that evoke motivated behavior appear to be mostly internal, whereas those that evoke emotional behavior seem mostly environmental. However, as will be seen later, both these types of response patterns are determined by both internal and environmental conditions and can be controlled by manipulating either one of these sets of conditions. Thus both the traditional categories are subsumed here under the rubric of "motivational activities."

## CLASSIFICATION OF ACTIVITIES

Theoretically, there are two general ways of defining an activity. It can be defined in terms of the effector action itself or in terms of the effects produced by such action. For example, blinking as an act may be defined in terms of contractions of the eyelid muscle fibers, or it may be defined simply as a quick closing and opening of the eyelids. Whether or not the eyelid closes can be determined by appropriate apparatus arrangements without any reference to the contraction of the muscle fibers that are involved in closing the eyelid. For psychological purposes, activities are almost always defined in terms of operations other than those involving the effector action itself. Thus, acts such as blinking, sniffing, biting, bar pressing, attacking, and eating are defined not in terms of effector action but in terms of some effects produced by their action. It should be noted that the specific effector actions involved in an act are of little importance in the definition of that act. For example, if bar pressing as an act is defined in terms of a certain pressure on the bar, it makes no difference in the definition of this act whether the animal applies the requisite pressure to the bar by its right paw, its left paw, or by sitting on it. The effector actions in these three alternative modes of bar pressing are quite different, but the act, as defined, is the same. Admittedly, this is not the most precise way of defining activities, but, in the present state of our ignorance of the mechanisms which make different effector actions "equivalent" for a particular end result, there is no other psychologically meaningful way of defining activities.

Thus, the only meaningful basis for distinguishing between various classes of motivational activities is in terms of stimulus objects or events around which they are organized, or with respect to which they may be said to be directed. Food seeking and eating are connected with food substances, sexual activity with sexually stimulating objects, exploratory activity with unfamiliar stimulus patterns, and so on. The actual effectors involved in these various activities overlap considerably; they all normally require certain fairly common responses of limbs, head, and neck. However, described conjointly in terms of the responses and their relation to environmental stimuli, different categories of motivational activities can be reasonably well distinguished from each other. As indicated above, this method of categorizing activities is employed in all areas of psychology and is not peculiar to the classification of motivational phenomena.

For the purposes of this work, the common motivational activities have been categorized as follows: "general activity" and exploration, withdrawal and aggressive activities, eating, drinking, and sexual activity, and maternal behavior. The general problems raised by these motivational phenomena will be discussed in the following chapters.

## GENERAL ACTIVITY AND EXPLORATION

Before turning to specific classes of activities, activities which are clearly organized with respect to some specific classes of environmental objects or ends, we shall describe the main features of "general activity" and exploration.

### General Activity

The term *general activity* usually refers to indices of over-all activity of animals during a given time interval. Interest is focused not on the incidence of a given class of response, but on the extent to which the animal makes *any* type of response. The indices of general activity most commonly employed in studies of the rat, for example, are obtained from the stabilimeter and the activity wheel. In the stabilimeter setup, the animal is placed in a cage that is delicately balanced on a central pivot. The movements of the animal tilt the cage slightly in different directions, and these tilts are recorded by appropriate pneumatic or electrical arrangements. The total number, or extent, or both, of the tilts are taken as an index of the animal's general activity. The activity wheel typically consists of two parts. One part is like an ordinary living cage; the rat eats, drinks, and sleeps there. This living part opens into a drum which rotates around a fixed horizontal axle whenever the animal walks or runs on its inner surface. Usually, the animal can freely move from the living part of the apparatus to the drum, and back, and the total number of revolutions of the drum in a specified time interval is taken as the activity score of the animal.

Though the investigator interested in general activity is usually not directly concerned with the specific responses which contribute to activity scores, some responses nevertheless must necessarily be involved whenever the organism is active. The specific responses involved, of course, would depend on the method of obtaining activity scores. In the stabilimeter type of device, for example, any movement of the animal (e.g. scratching, climbing, walking) which is strong enough to shake the cage or to shift its center of gravity is represented in the activity score. In the activity-wheel index, on the other hand, it is the speed and duration of walking which determine the activity score; responses other than walking and all the responses in the living part of the apparatus do not contribute to the score.

One of the major findings in such studies of general activity is that animals show fairly consistent variations in activity over periods of a day or more. The rat, for example, is normally much more active at night than during the day. This diurnal cycle has been observed by Richter (1922) and Hunt & Schlosberg (1939). Richter also reports shorter cycles of activity in the rat, each consisting of short bursts of activity every few hours. However, Hunt & Schlosberg consider the short bursts of activity throughout the day as too irregular to be called cycles. The diurnal variations in activity are accompanied by similar variations in eating and drinking. The problems raised by such behavioral cycles are most complex and intriguing—they will be dealt with in Chapter 10.

## EXPLORATION

In the normal course of living, organisms are constantly exposed to new objects and situations, and some of their responses become organized around the novelty aspect of the environment. Activities that typically occur in response to what is novel in the environment constitute *exploratory activity*. Thus, while general activity is defined in terms of the over-all responses of the organism during a given time interval, exploration refers to the incidence of only certain classes of acts, which are selected by the investigator on the basis of their association with, or relevance to, novel environmental stimuli.

Exploration is generally quantified in such terms as the frequency of approaching and sniffing a novel object, orientation movements of the head, the extent of perambulation, and time spent in looking at or manipulating (novel) stimulus objects. These measures can be illustrated by some recent investigations. Berlyne (1955) employed an exploration box with a small alcove in one corner. The stimulus objects were placed in the alcove. By means of a photoelectric-cell arrangement, Berlyne was able to record the frequency of the rat's approaches to the stimulus object and the duration of each approach. Butler & Alexander (1955) studied visual exploration in monkeys. They inserted a small door into one wall of an opaque cage. The animal could open the door and peep through it for as long as and whenever it wanted. The frequency and duration of door opening was taken as a measure of visual exploration. Montgomery (1951), Thompson & Heron (1954), and Adlerstein & Fehrer (1955) used the extent of perambulation as an index of exploration. They marked off the exploration area into a number of small squares, and the number of squares entered by the animal in a given interval of time was taken as the exploration score of the animal. These measures of exploratory activity have been found to be sensitive to such experimental conditions as the complexity and strangeness of stimulus objects.

The above descriptions show that the actual responses (walking, standing, sniffing, etc.) involved in the measures of general activity are to a large extent those that are also involved in the measures of exploration. It seems that the main difference between general activity and exploratory activity, as they have been commonly defined, lies not so much in the specific responses involved as in the focus of attention of the investigator. When the investigator is interested in the responses of the organism in a new ("exploration") situation or in relation to a novel stimulus, he is likely to call the activity "exploratory"; otherwise he is likely to call it "general activity." Therefore, it should not surprise one to find that the variables that affect a given measure of one of these activities also affect in a similar way certain measures of the other.

Berlyne (1955) has shown that exploratory activity increases when the animal is exposed to an environment presenting numerous and complex rather than few and simple stimuli, and decreases during successive exposures to the same situation. Welker (1956) has found that younger chimpanzees explore more than the older. Thompson (1953) and Adlerstein & Fehrer (1955) report that hungry rats explore more than sated rats, but both hungry and sated animals show a similar decrement in exploration with increasing familiarity with the situation. Montgomery & Monkman (1955) have demonstrated that "fear" induced during an exploration test reduces exploratory activity. In another study, Montgomery (1955) observed less exploratory activity in the dangerous, elevated alleys than in the safer, enclosed alleys. These conditions affecting exploration have been or very likely can be shown to affect general activity in the same way (*see* Munn, 1950, for specific references).

PROBLEM SEEKING AND PLAY

Human beings not only explore and find solutions to problems with which they are presented, but they also seem actively to seek problems. Whether one's stated aim is to advance knowledge, as in science, or to entertain, as in the arts, or to amuse oneself, as in solving crossword puzzles, seeking problems is a common human activity. Hebb & Mahut (1955) have shown that problem seeking can occur in lower animals as well. They observed that when a hungry rat is offered two routes to food, one direct and the other longer and with blind alleys, the animal has a marked tendency to take the more difficult route. Dember, Earl, & Paradise (1957) have also found that, when given a choice, rats prefer a pathway of greater stimulus complexity to the one to which they are accustomed. An experiment by Havelka (1956) demonstrated this even more clearly. He gave hungry rats a choice of obtaining food from either of two equally familiar situations. However, in one situation the food was always to be found in the same location, whereas, in the other, the position of the food was not only at a greater distance from the starting point, but was varied from trial to trial so that the animal had to search for it. Havelka found that some animals consistently preferred the complicated, variable-goal situation to the simple, fixed-goal situation.

Both Hebb & Mahut and Havelka argue that the behavior of these animals is something more than exploratory activity. Exploratory activity is known to decrease rapidly as the animal becomes familiar with a new situation. However, their animals were quite familiar with the experimental situations and yet they chose the more difficult solutions to the problems presented by the maze; furthermore, their animals switched to the easy, direct solution as soon as the variable-goal situation was changed to a fixed-goal one. Therefore, these authors consider the behavior of their rats to be *problem seeking* rather than merely exploratory. Obviously, many further studies of such behavior are needed before one can give an exact description of the essential features of problem seeking and of the factors that affect it.

The so-called "play activities" also seem to belong to the same category of activities as exploration and problem seeking. The concept of play is not, of course, a psychological one. It is a common-sense label for a variety of activities such as a cat chasing and clawing a ball, a dog retrieving objects, monkeys chasing each other or "following the leader," a chimpanzee imitating other chimpanzees or human beings, and a man working out a crossword puzzle. The main feature that seems to be common to all exploratory and problem-seeking activities, including play, is that they are not evidently and directly connected with eating, drinking, and other activities obviously necessary for survival. As Schlosberg has pointed out, what is commonly called play is behavior that "seems useless in the eyes of an observer" (1947, p. 229). It is not a meaningful category of behavior, for the term "play" is commonly applied to any of a variety of types of behavior, as long as the behavior is incomplete or inadequate with respect to the goals that are commonly considered to be related to survival. Schlosberg attributes the occurrence of such incomplete and inadequate responses to generalization of responses from other activities, changing thresholds for the occurrence of different responses, and to the fact that certain sequences of responses may be reinforced accidentally. As one ascends the phylogenetic scale, such responses seem to become more and more complex and occupy an increasing proportion of the animal's time. Systematic investigations of these responses have started only in recent years (*see* Beach, 1945, Hayes & Hayes, 1952, and Welker, 1956a, 1956b), and much remains to be learned about their origin and the factors that influence them.

## WITHDRAWAL AND AGGRESSIVE ACTIVITIES

### GENERAL DESCRIPTION

Many activities of organisms can be described as being aimed at terminating an existing stimulus situation. An animal can change any existing situation either by withdrawing from (escaping or avoiding) it or by manipulating it in such a way as to change the stimuli that make up that situation. Roughly speaking, the former method of changing the stimulus situation characterizes what we shall call *withdrawal activities*, and the method of manipulatively altering the situation we shall consider as a characteristic of *aggressive activities*. (The term "aggression" is used here quite broadly and refers to all attempts at altering a situation, whether or not the attempt involves an "attack" on or mutilation of some aspect of the situation.)

The common-sense terms "fear" and "anger" should not be confused with withdrawal and aggression. Common sense often employs words such as "anger," "fear," "joy," "disgust," and "boredom" to describe behavior. These terms are quite unsatisfactory for the purpose of scientific analysis. For one thing, they are vague. As commonly used, they may refer sometimes to subjective states as experienced, sometimes to behavior, and sometimes to hypothetical processes underlying observed behavior. For another, even when they are intended to refer only to behavior, they are loosely applied. For example, common sense will describe the same instance of an act of attack variously as (1) "anger," if the animal has been frustrated in some way, (2) "irritation," if the animal is known to be hungry, or (3) "sexual advance," if the attack is directed toward a female in heat. This loose and ambiguous usage of common-sense terms results from the fact that, as intuitive labels, they refer not only to the observed behavior itself, but also to certain presumed "causes" of that behavior. That is to say, they describe more than observed behavior itself. For this reason they are often inadequate for psychological purposes. Of course, in practice, the common-sense intuitive labels form the background against which more rigorous definitions develop, and excessive concern with preciseness may lead one to ignore some insightful ideas. Nevertheless, for psychological analysis we must employ, as far as possible, descriptive terms that refer only to acts defined in terms of unambiguous operations. The terms like "fear," "anger," and "joy" are too vague for this purpose.

Though withdrawal and aggressive activities are quite easy to distinguish from each other, they nevertheless quite often are closely associated. Consider, for example, a dog chasing a cat. The cat tries to increase the distance between the dog and itself (withdrawal). If the cat is cornered, it may claw or otherwise attack the dog (aggression), and then leap away in another direction (withdrawal), and so on. The cat rapidly fluctuates between withdrawal and aggression; however both these types of activities can be said to be aimed at altering the existing situation in a way that would eliminate the dog. Thus, though the specific responses involved in withdrawal and aggression are quite different, they nevertheless can be looked upon as related to the same end of altering the existing stimulus situation.

### SPECIFIC RESPONSES INVOLVED

There is hardly any limit to the specific responses that may be involved in withdrawal and aggressive activities. One reasonable general statement that can be made about the responses concerns the increase in their variety as one goes from the lower to the higher species. In the rat, withdrawal almost always involves the acts of walking or running away from the given stimulus situation, and aggression almost always involves scratching or biting. In the dog, barking, growling, and other quasi-attack acts, in addition to biting, are often employed to alter a situation. In chimpanzees, hitting, biting, temper tantrums, sulking, begging, and various combinations of friendly behavior and attack are among the common components of aggressive activities. At the human level, verbal acts such as "I am sorry," "Get out of my way," are added to other, more overt, responses that are employed to alter any given situation. Thus we see that there is an increase in the number of classes of aggressive and withdrawal acts as we go up the scale of evolution.

Another general statement that can be made concerning the specific responses involved in such activities is that, while each animal does have a variety of withdrawal and aggressive acts in its repertoire, it employs some of these acts much more frequently than the others. Thus, some animals ("cowards") habitually withdraw and others ("adventurers") habitually show aggressive behavior in order to alter a situation.

SITUATIONS EVOKING WITHDRAWAL
   AND AGGRESSIVE ACTIVITIES

According to Watson (1919), the stimuli that evoke withdrawal and aggressive responses do so either because they are
unconditioned stimuli and are innately connected to those responses or because they have acquired this potency through
repeated association with such unconditioned stimuli. Undoubtedly, many aggressive and avoidance activities of the
normal adult animal are evoked by stimuli which have acquired the capacity to evoke those responses. However, there
is considerable evidence against the implications of Watson's
view. Hebb (1946a) has shown that chimpanzees react by
escape and avoidance to stimuli that are neither innately connected to such responses nor have ever been associated with
pain or any other possible source of noxious stimulation. Melzack (1952) has observed similar "spontaneous fears" in the
dog. He found that escape and avoidance responses could be
aroused in home-reared dogs by innocuous objects such as a
human skull, a mask on a familiar person, a toy electric train,
and a 12-in. balloon. Melzack considers "strangeness," rather
than prior association with painful stimulation, to be the essential feature of these "fear-provoking" stimulus objects.
Studies of the nature of stimuli that arouse aggressive responses also show that certain stimuli are capable of evoking
aggressive acts without any prior association with any "restriction of movement" which, according to Watson, is the
unconditioned stimulus for aggressive responses. Unexpected
noise and frustration (i.e., obstruction in the path of an antic-
ipated goal) often evoke aggressive responses. Here again, it
seems that "strangeness" of the stimulus objects or of some
feature of the total stimulus situation is the crucial feature of
the stimuli that "spontaneously" evoke aggressive responses.

It appears reasonable to conclude that there are two types
of stimulus patterns that evoke aggressive and withdrawal reactions: (1) Conditioned stimuli which have acquired their
potency for evoking the responses through prior experience.
This category would account for a large number of the aggressive and withdrawal responses of adult animals. (2)

"Strange" or "unexpected" stimulus patterns whose strangeness or unexpectedness undoubtedly depends upon the accidents of earlier experience, but which have never before been specifically associated with the response.

## EATING, DRINKING, AND SEXUAL ACTIVITIES

### EATING AND DRINKING

In eating and drinking the animal transfers food and water to its mouth, and licks, chews, and swallows. The transferring of food and water to the mouth may be achieved by movements of the lips, teeth, and tongue, or by the use of forelimbs. The most commonly employed measures of eating and drinking include frequency of daily feedings, amount eaten and drunk, and rate of ingestion. There appear to be considerable species differences in all these aspects of feeding. Chewing and swallowing responses probably also show some variation from species to species. Cudding is quite common in the group of mammals called ruminants. Unfortunately, there are hardly any detailed studies of the various aspects of normal feeding, and nothing more can be said about this important activity here. However, we shall have occasion in later chapters to discuss the factors that affect eating and drinking.

Even when food and water are available continually, animals typically feed more at certain times than at others. A clear-cut diurnal eating and drinking cycle in the rat, with more feeding during night than during day, has been reported by Siegel & Stuckey (1947a), and a similar drinking cycle has been found by Young & Richey (1952) and Stellar & Hill (1952). Stellar & Hill estimate that rats drink about 78 per cent of their daily water intake at night. Though diurnal feeding cycles have been observed by many investigators, there appears to be no confirmation so far of Richter's (1927) finding of shorter cycles of eating and drinking throughout the day. Rats do eat and drink every few hours, but that these bursts of feeding occur at regular intervals cannot be stated with confidence at present.

## Sexual Activity

By sexual activity here we mean behavior that involves specifically the genital function or is closely linked with that function. There is no generally accepted classification of sexual activities. For our purposes we shall adopt a convenient, though rough, categorization in terms of the type of stimulus objects that initiate the activity. Thus, we recognize heterosexual activity or coitus, homosexual activity, and sexual self-stimulation. There are, of course, other types of stimuli that can initiate sexual activity, but they are not dealt with here in order to simplify our discussion.

Unfortunately, we still lack any precise descriptions of sexual behavior as it is displayed by males and females of various species. The animal whose sexual behavior has been most extensively studied is the rat, but even here we have a reasonably complete description for only the male. The following description, therefore, presents the heterosexual responses of the male rat only. It is based mostly on the work of Beach (1947, 1956). The painstaking work of Beach and his colleagues over the last two decades has delineated the dimensions along which fruitful analysis of the sexual behavior of other species, particularly mammalian, may be carried out.

*Coitus.* Beach (1956) thinks it reasonable to divide the complete masculine coital activity into two phases. These may be called the "sexual excitement phase" and the "copulation phase." The excitement phase consists of increase in excitement, establishing contact with the female, mounting the female, and effecting an erection of the penis. The copulatory phase consists of the initial intromission, followed by repeated dismountings and intromissions until orgasm (indicated by ejaculation).

The *sexual excitement phase* typically starts immediately after the receptive (estrous) female becomes accessible to the male. Some males may establish contact, mount, and effect an intromission within 10 seconds; this may take some minutes in others. It appears that the male starts copulation within about 10 minutes or not at all. Sexual excitement diminishes unless the copulation starts within a fairly short time. Beach interprets this fact in terms of habituation: continuous exposure to olfactory and other stimuli coming from the female leads to a reduction in their capacity to evoke excitement. However, once copulation has started, the animal typically copulates until orgasm.

The *copulation phase* starts with the first intromission. The animal dismounts after the first intromission, engages in autogenital cleaning, and then remounts the female and effects another intromission. This alternate intromission and genital cleaning continues until orgasm. The interval between successive intromissions varies between 30 and 60 seconds, but appears to be quite consistent for any given animal. Usually, it takes the animal from 8 to 15 intromissions to achieve orgasm. After the first orgasm, the animal shows a loss of sexual responsiveness for a few minutes. This period of unresponsiveness is greater after each successive orgasm; that is, with continued access to the female, the interval between an orgasm and the initiation of the next coitus increases progressively. However, at the same time, there is a slight sensitization of the "orgasm response," so that the animal requires less time to achieve orgasm in the succeeding coituses than in the first one of the series.

Beach (1956) feels that there are no major evolutionary changes in the copulatory phase of coitus as one ascends the phylogenetic scale from rat to man. But this is not true in the case of the sexual excitement phase. Approaching the receptive female, mounting, and erection occur quite predictably in the male rat; however, in higher mammals, especially in primates, sexual excitement is quite labile and appears to be more dependent upon factors other than the stimuli emanating from the receptive females. A male chimpanzee may not be excited by one receptive female but, a moment later, may be excited by another. Similarly, a human male may be consistently impotent with one female but not with another. At the same time, in both men and women, sexual excitement may be brought about by stories, pictures, fantasies, and other symbolic factors. Another point noted by Beach (1947) is that, in a large number of species studied, the male appears to be more subject to the influence (both facilitatory and inhibitory) of extraneous environmental factors than the female. [Beach attributes this intersex difference to the more important role of cerebral cortex (and, therefore, presumably of learning) in the sexual behavior of the male than in that of the female. The greater cerebral control of sexual behavior in the male has been demonstrated by extirpation studies.]

The most consistent feature of the sexual pattern of the female rat seems to be the lordosis response. This consists of arching the back and elevating and exposing the genital area. Typically, lordosis is evoked when the male mounts and clasps the receptive female from the rear, or when it places a paw on the female's back. A definite orgasm, coincident with the peak of sexual excitement, has not been observed in the female rat or in any other infrahuman female. There seem to be no other reliable statements that can be made about the female sexual responses.

*Homosexual responses.* Masculine and feminine sexual responses do not belong exclusively to one sex. Carpenter (1942) has reported that male monkeys can be seen to display both masculine and feminine sexual roles. Sometimes, the males alternate with each other in adopting the feminine sexual postures. The female monkeys also display masculine sexual responses. Such bisexual behavior is also found in other animals. For example, receptive female rats often mount other rats, and male rats are known to display lordosis when they are mounted by other, usually highly dominant, rats. It is clear that both masculine and feminine sexual responses can occur in both males and females. It appears that the adoption of the masculine or feminine role depends, to a certain extent, on the dominance of the animal; dominant animals appear more likely to mount and less likely to be mounted than the submissive ones.

When an animal of one sex mounts another animal of the same sex or is in some other way sexually stimulated by it, the behavior of the mounting or sexually stimulated rat may be called homosexual. Both male-male and female-female homosexual contacts have been noted in a variety of mammalian species, and they likely occur in all. There seems to be an increase in homosexual activity as one moves from the lower to the higher mammals. However, animals, including chimpanzees, normally prefer heterosexual to homosexual contacts when given the choice. Homosexual activity in preference to heterosexual coitus occurs in some cases in the human species. According to Kinsey *et al.* (1953), the consistent preference shown by some men and women for homosexual activity is attributable, apart from the reinforcing effects of prior homosexual activity, to the codes governing sexual behavior in restricted social groups.

*Sexual self-stimulation.* Masturbation has been noticed (*see* Ford & Beach, 1951, and Kinsey *et al.*, 1953, for review) in a wide variety of mammals, from the rat to man, and it is likely that it occurs in almost all mammalian species. In general, masturbation is more common among males than among females. Males may masturbate to the point of orgasm. It is possible that the greater incidence of masturbation in the male results from the reinforcing effect of orgasm, which is likely to be greater than that of sexual stimulation not accompanied by orgasm. Similarly, the greater incidence of masturbation in the human male than in the human female (Kinsey *et al.*, 1953) may also be attributed to the fact that sexual stimulation leads to orgasm more dependably in men than in women.

Techniques of masturbation vary considerably from species to species and animal to animal. The male usually stimulates the penis orally, by rubbing it against other animals and objects, or, as in many primates, with its forelimbs. The female also masturbates by rubbing her genital regions against miscellaneous objects or parts of her own body. In the human female the most frequent technique involves the manual rhythmic manipulation of the clitoris and labia minora (Kinsey *et al.*, 1953).

## MATERNAL BEHAVIOR

Females of nearly all mammalian species provide warmth, nurse, and otherwise foster the development of their offspring. Such activities, collectively labeled "maternal behavior," have been studied more extensively in the rat than in any other mammal. Therefore, a description of the maternal behavior of the female rat is most suitable for illustrating the main features of the activities by which mammals care for their young.

## MATERNAL ACTIVITIES OF THE FEMALE RAT

The care of the offspring involves in the rat at least four discrete types of activities: nesting, behavior at parturition, retrieving, and nursing. When these activities occur at appropriate times, and in proper temporal order, they appear to be so closely linked together that their distinctness is often ignored and they are collectively described as "maternal behavior." However, as we shall see, the factors determining each of these activities are different and they are better understood when treated as distinct categories of activities. The following descriptions are based mostly on the works of Kinder (1927) and Wiesner & Sheard (1933).

*Nest building.* Under appropriate conditions both male and female rats build nests. Richter (1927) has reported an inverse relation between general activity and the amount of nest building; Kinder (1927) also has found that female rats tend not to build nests during estrus, when they are particularly active. However, Wiesner & Sheard (1933) do not report any relation between general activity and nest building. It appears that whether such a relation is found depends on the specific environmental conditions under which the observations are made, and on the particular measures of general activity and of nest building employed in the investigation. A relation between environmental temperature and nest building has been demonstrated by Kinder (1927); within certain limits, the lower the temperature the greater the building activity. Morgan (1943) has proposed the plausible hypothesis that the increase in nest building during pregnancy is attributable to the lowered metabolism and body temperature during that state. Glandular changes during pregnancy are, according to Morgan, responsible for the difficulty in maintaining normal metabolic rate and body temperature.

Nest building in the rat typically involves simply carrying the available nesting material (paper, straw, hay, etc.) to the cage and placing or pushing it into one corner. If the material is available in large pieces, the rat may bite it and shred it into fine pieces. The material thus forms a fluffy pile; as the rat repeatedly sits on the pile, a central depression is formed. The building activity is not terminated by any particular shape or size of the nest. Sometimes, when no nesting material is left, some rats eagerly transport food and other transportable objects to the nest; other animals make only a rudimentary nest or none at all. Some rats move their whole nest, bit by bit, from one corner of the cage to another, and continue to do this on successive days. As the above description shows, there are marked individual differences in nest building. Even some of the pregnant females do not always build a nest either before or after parturition. When nest building is instigated by pregnancy, the activity is maintained only for a limited period. Typically, the animal lets the nest disassemble within 10 to 20 days post partum.

*Behavior at parturition.* As soon as a fetus is delivered, and sometimes while it is still passing through the vaginal orifice, the mother starts licking its own vaginal orifice and the fetus. She quickly eats the fetal membrane, biting off the umbilical cord in the process. Since typically several minutes elapse between the delivery of successive fetuses, the rat has sufficient time to complete the "cleaning" operations on one fetus before the next one is delivered. The placenta is also devoured by the mother. Sometimes, having finished the placenta, she also eats a part or the whole of the fetus.

Wiesner & Sheard (1933) have noted that nulliparous females do not lick or eat the membranes of the fetuses offered to them. They also observed that, when fetuses were delivered by Caesarean section and were offered to females who had delivered and cleaned their own litters a few hours earlier, they typically did not lick or eat the membranes of the Caesarean fetuses. These facts suggest that the fetus-cleaning activity of the female rat is closely connected with parturition itself, and is probably an extension of the increased vaginal licking that occurs during the delivery of the fetus.

*Retrieving activity.* The mother rat brings the young pups together in one place, in the nest when she has made one. When she moves the nest or leaves it, she is likely to retrieve all the pups, typically one at a time, to the new habitat. Typically, she grasps the pup with her teeth, carries it along, and deposits it in the nest. If the pups are removed from the nest or are placed just outside the cage, the animal is likely to start retrieving them at once. As the pups grow older and begin to stray away from the nest, the mother first tries to keep up retrieving, but gradually, as retrieving becomes more and more difficult, she stops doing so.

Wiesner & Sheard (1933) have observed that some rats, who nursed and reared their litters successfully, did not show the retrieving response at all. They have also noted that some virgin female rats will retrieve newly born pups with as much eagerness as multiparous females. These facts suggest that retrieving may not be an intrinsic part of the complex of maternal activities; it appears rather to be an activity which is controlled by factors other than those that determine behavior at parturition and nursing. However, there is a striking resemblance in the manner in which rats retrieve young pups and the manner in which they collect nesting materials (and food —*see* Chap. 4).

*Nursing.* Successful nursing seems to depend as much on the activity of the pups as it does on that of the mother. The puerperal female simply crouches over the young pups, and it is the pups that crawl around, find the nipples, and hang on to them. A litter sometimes dies of starvation because the mother does not crouch over the pups. Nursing can be successful only if the mother sits still at least for some time. Wiesner & Sheard (1933) suggest that the relative immobility typically found in the lactating female is only an aspect of the general decrease in spontaneous activity found in the puerperal female.

The careful observations made by Wiesner & Sheard (1933) point up a number of interesting facts about maternal behavior in the rat. First, there exist remarkable individual differences in the exact ways in which the various component activities are carried out by different animals. Second, the same animal may also behave differently at different times. For example, a rat may eat its first litter but rear the second one, or vice versa. Third, none of the component activities, nest building, retrieving, and so on, seem to be fixed patterns of specific responses; rather, the exact manner in which the animal builds a nest or retrieves or nurses depends upon the characteristics of the stimulus situation. The activities adapt to changing circumstances. Fourth, the various component activities appear to be independent of each other. Some animals build a nest but do not retrieve; others do the reverse. Some clean the fetuses but do not nurse them. Fifth, these various activities are not peculiar to the puerperal female, but are also sometimes found in the virgin female and even in the male.

These facts point to the inadequacy of any simple interpretation of what for convenience is called "maternal behavior" in terms of a single "maternal drive." As Wiesner & Sheard have pointed out, any one-factor hypothesis cannot account for the various distinct activities described above. We must look separately for the specific factors that are responsible for each of nest building, cleaning, retrieving, and nursing.

## Maternal Behavior in Other Species

Although there are no detailed comparative studies, it appears that, like sexual behavior, maternal activities become more variable and less predictable as one ascends the phylogenetic scale.

Yerkes (1943) reports that the experienced chimpanzee mother handles the infant as soon as it has emerged from her body, and places it on her abdomen. The infant clings to her, as it does to a paper towel or any other similar surface. The mother then cleans the infant by the typical grooming procedure seen in all adults, and nurses it. The inexperienced chimpanzee mother, on the other hand, may or may not care for the offspring in such a systematic way. She may avoid and circle around the infant, as most animals do in response to a strange object. In the course of exploring it, she may touch it and examine it, without grooming or nursing it. Eventually, she may let the infant cling to her and nurse. Yerkes comments: "Whether in nature a mother ever abandons her first-born and lets it perish from neglected and rough treatment is doubtful. Probably if other adult members of the band were within reach they would lend a hand and by their interest and actions inspire confidence in the fearful or perplexed young mother" (1943, p. 68). This suggests that the successful rearing of the young in certain primates may depend upon the existence of some form of group life, the presence of experienced adults in the group, and social communication of some kind. Those human mothers who are feeble-minded, and are thus unable to benefit by prior verbal instruction, are probably also unlikely to take effective care of their first-born without help from others.

Once the primiparous female chimpanzee starts nursing the infant, she readily becomes quite attached to it. After only a few days, the mother and infant usually become inseparable, and the mother resists attempts at forcible separation. Yerkes (1943) has pointed out that the mother usually looks at the infant periodically and keeps it within easy reach. An experienced mother starts systematic care of a new infant right from the moment of birth.

Normally, presumably, the infant nurses so long as the mother is lactating and is approachable. Under laboratory conditions, Yerkes (1943) reports a case in which nursing continued into the third year. Such prolongation of lactation and nursing has also been reported in many human societies (see Whiting & Child, 1953).

The isolated observations noted above point to the complexity of maternal behavior in primates. However, there is at present a lack of the type of detailed studies that would enable one to make meaningful phylogenetic comparisons of maternal behavior and to specify the evolutionary changes in the various components of maternal behavior.

## DOMINANT FEATURES OF MOTIVATIONAL ACTIVITIES

The motivational activities described above draw attention to certain features that are more or less shared by all of them. First, they appear to be purposeful or goal-directed activities. By observing an animal for a certain length of time it is easy to say, for example, that it is "looking for food," for it ignores objects and events that do not fall into the category of food. Similarly, activities such as nest building, attacking, escaping, and exploring can all be recognized as such by the planned, purposeful way in which the animal executes them. Second, the various motivational activities seem to emerge from a state of high excitement, lacking goal direction. Thus, the low excitement–high excitement variable seems to be closely related to motivational activities. Third, these activities show in a dramatic fashion the control on behavior that is exercised by internal and external conditions. For example, external situation remaining the same, a female chimpanzee will typically copulate only when it is in estrus. And, equally important, the same female in estrus may receive one particular male but not another. Nest building can be induced both by the (internal) state of pregnancy and the (external) condition of lowered environmental temperature. Cyclic variations, found in some motivational activities (e.g. eating, drinking, general activity) are a special case of the control on them exerted by certain internal and external conditions. (*see* Chap. 10.)

As suggested earlier, the above features of behavior are not peculiar to the activities labeled "motivational." However, these features are undoubtedly most dramatically evident in these activities. It is perhaps this fact that has led to such activities being treated as a distinct class of phenomena and has given rise to the erroneous idea that some unique processes (instincts, drives, motives, etc.) are involved in them. Though concerned with motivational activities, the following chapters employ descriptive and interpretive concepts that can be used in dealing with perceptual and learning phenomena as well.

# Chapter 3

# Goal Direction

As we have seen, one of the central problems associated with motivational phenomena is presented by what is commonly called the purposive nature or the goal-directedness of behavior. The exact description of the goal-directed aspect of activities thus becomes one of the fundamental problems in the psychological study of motivation. The first part of this chapter attempts to show how the purposive features of behavior may be described in objective, explicit, and psychologically meaningful terms. The second part deals with the process underlying the development of goal direction in mammalian behavior.

## SUBJECTIVE AND OBJECTIVE MEANINGS OF PURPOSE

To avoid confusion, it is necessary to distinguish between the common-sense and the psychological meanings of "purpose."

### Purpose and Goal Direction

Common sense considers "purpose" to be an entirely subjective concept. For the layman, purpose is synonymous with an experience of intention or a preconceived plan to do something. If purpose is to be defined only in this subjective sense, the scientist cannot give it objective meaning or study it. For us purpose must somehow refer to certain objectively observable aspects of behavior. To avoid confusion, psychologists

51

have adopted the term *goal direction* to refer to the purposive aspect of observed behavior, leaving the term *purpose* for the common-sense subjective connotations of intention or consciousness of some aim.[1]

## STATEMENTS BY MCDOUGALL AND TOLMAN

Perhaps McDougall (1923) was the first psychologist to propose an objective meaning for the purposive aspect of behavior. Actually, McDougall treated purposive striving as a completely subjective phenomenon and linked it to his metaphysical principle of purposivism. However, he did list certain objective features of behavior as the evident correlates of (subjective) purpose. These features included persistence and variation of activity, and its termination when the goal is reached. Soon after McDougall's statement, Tolman (1925) defined goal direction or goal seeking in purely objective terms and successfully took this concept out of the controversial context of McDougall's philosophic views. Tolman wrote as follows:

When a rat runs a maze, it is to be observed that his running and searching activities *persist until food is reached*. And it appears that his persistence is the result of the physiological condition of hunger. We do not know whether the rat, in so "persisting," is "conscious"; we do not know whether he "feels a purpose" (to use the terminology of the mentalists); but we do know that, given (1) the physiological condition of hunger and given (2) the objective conditions of the maze, the rat thus *persists until the food is reached*. It is this purely *objective* fact of persistence until a certain specific type of goal object is reached that we define as *goal seeking*. And as thus defined, a goal seeking is a wholly objective and a wholly behavioristic phenomenon. There is nothing "mentalistic" about it.[2]

Tolman's statements of this kind were probably responsible for establishing the current objective usage of the term "goal

[1] If we accepted the verbal report (which is observable behavior) of a subject as a clue to his private experience, we could study the relation between experienced purpose and goal-directed behavior. For example, we could study the relation between the verbally stated purpose of giving up smoking and the actual behavior with respect to cigarettes. However, questions about such relations are not relevant to our present task. Here we are concerned only with goal direction as a feature of observed behavior.

[2] E. C. Tolman, Purpose and cognition: the determiners of animal learning, *Psychol. Rev.*, 32, 285–86.

direction" or "goal seeking." However, his statement is not explicit enough; it suffers from two obscurities. First, it does not present a general enough definition of "goal": What is it that makes the goal a goal? Second, it does not tell us the precise meaning of "goal seeking."

## WHAT IS A GOAL?

What psychologists ordinarily refer to as goals belong to the general category of objects and events called "incentives." Of the various types of sensory stimulation to which organisms are continually exposed, some are more effective in altering the organisms' activities than are others. An *incentive* may be regarded as an object or event that is presumed to affect an organism's behavior radically and reliably. Thus food, onset or termination of an electric shock, approach to "home," sexual stimulation, sudden loud noise, and the like are incentives because their effects on behavior are likely to be more marked and dependable than those of other environmental events (e.g. mild noises or changes in illumination) that do not affect behavior radically or reliably.

In most psychological discussions, the term "goal" refers to an object or event that terminates an on-going activity of the organism. And it is often implied that, once the goal has been reached, the organism rests in peace at least for some time. This implication is somewhat misleading. Organisms are always active—both before and after reaching a goal. Consider a hungry rat in a cage. The rat can be observed to be quite active: it walks around (W), sniffs (S), sits motionless for a while (M), grooms itself (G), and so on. If we record the individual acts occurring at the end of each of a number of consecutive intervals of x seconds in the order in which they occur (WSGSWGGSW, etc.), then we obtain a sequential description of the animal's behavior, a record of the animal's course of action. Now, suppose the rat discovers a dish of food in one corner of the cage. At this point the animal does not stop acting; rather, what we observe is simply a change in the animal's course of action. It begins to eat (E). After the rat has eaten for some time, its course of action changes again. It begins to walk around, yawn (Y), groom itself, and so on. We can describe these changes in the course of action as follows:

W W S W S M G G W S Food is presented S S E S E E E E E E E
          W W G Y W G M M M

In this example, which can be easily duplicated in the laboratory, it is clear that the rat does not stop acting either when the food is found or when it has been consumed. The food neither made the animal active in the first place, nor did its consumption make the rat inactive; the food only *changed* the course of action of the animal. If food in this illustration is a good example of what we ordinarily call the goal, then we can state that goals belong to the general category of objects or events that radically change the course of action of the organism.

However, what we ordinarily call a goal is something more than an incentive; a goal is a special class of incentive. An incentive becomes a goal when it is treated as a goal; that is, when it is selected, arbitrarily, as the focus or "anchor" with respect to which the behavior of the organism is described. A moment's reflection will show that whether an object (e.g. food) is described as an incentive or as a goal depends only on whether the investigator has selected it as the reference point for the description of behavior. Thus, when we say, for example, that food is the goal for a hungry animal, we are asserting that (1) we know that food is an incentive for the animal, and (2) *we* have chosen to describe the behavior of the animal in relation to food rather than with reference to any other object or event. A *goal* is thus *an incentive that is chosen by the investigator as a reference point for describing observed behavior.*

The choice of the reference point—called goal—is completely arbitrary and has reference only to the investigator's mode of analysis, not to the animal's intention or any other subjective state. Of course, on the basis of his past experience, an investigator normally knows what objects and events are likely to serve as incentives under what conditions, and his choice of a particular object as the goal is determined by this knowledge. Thus, when the animal is known to be hungry, the investigator usually considers food as the goal; when the animal is on an electrified grid, the investigator considers termination of the electric current as the goal. However, the fact that whether an object or event does serve as an incentive depends upon the animal's make-up and its momentary state does not alter the basic fact that a goal is an incentive that the investigator chooses to consider as the reference point for the description of behavior.

If the incentive is a reward (e.g. food) we can talk of the goal being positive; if a punishment (e.g. electric shock), the goal can be said to be negative. In discussing goal-directed behavior it is customary to describe the organism as "moving toward the goal" or "reaching the goal." Such a statement is correct when it describes a situation involving a positive goal. However, in the case of a negative goal, the corresponding description would be "withdrawing from the (negative) goal." Now, it is quite arbitrary whether we describe a given behavior as approach or withdrawal behavior; whether it is approach or withdrawal depends on the objects or events which we have chosen to call the goal—with respect to which we have chosen to describe the behavior. A rat in a familiar maze, for example, can be said to approach the food or to avoid the blind alleys. In describing behavior with respect to any particular object or event it makes no difference whether we have a positive goal or a negative goal in mind. As Nissen (1954) has pointed out, all statements in terms of approach can be translated into those of withdrawal, and vice versa. For the sake of convenience, in the following pages the term "goal" is employed to mean only positive goals. However, the statements apply just as well to negative goals. It should be noted that these statements do not deny that positive and negative incentives (rewards and punishments) may influence behavior in quite different ways (*see* Chap. 6), but only state that, so far as the description of behavior is concerned, approach and withdrawal are simply the obverse of each other.

## MEANING OF GOAL DIRECTION

Ordinarily, when we describe behavior as goal-directed or adaptive, we have in mind one or both of two different types of situations. The first involves the presence of a number of different modes of behavior which are (known to be) connected with one and the same goal. Thus, we say that a cat's behavior is adaptive when we have evidence that it can reach a given goal by a variety of different courses of action. If, for some reason, one course of action proves unsuccessful (e.g. if one path to the goal is blocked) or is likely to prove unsuccessful, the cat follows another course of action to the same goal. The second variety of situations called adaptive is one in which the organism's behavior in some way corresponds to variations in the goal itself. Consider a cat chasing a rat. If the rat runs to the left, so does the cat; if the rat dashes to the right, the cat also leaps in that direction; if the rat walks into a tiny hole, the cat puts its paw into the hole or anticipates and "waits" for the rat's emergence from it. The cat's behavior in this case is goal-directed in the sense that the cat's course of action follows and anticipates, or, in general, corresponds to the variations in the location of the goal (rat).

A moment's reflection will show that both these types of situations have one important feature in common, and this feature is the essence of goal-directed behavior. In both cases the course of action of the organism with respect to the given goal changes with variations in the goal itself or in the location of the goal, and it changes in a way that, on the whole, increases the probability that the organism will reach the goal. In the first example above, the cat, when faced with an obstruction, changes its course of action to one that would be more effective under the changed circumstances. Similarly, in the second example, the cat responds to the variations in the stimulus situation (location of the rat) by changing its own behavior to a potentially more effective course of action. We can employ Sommerhoff's (1950) concept of *appropriateness* to designate this essential feature of what we ordinarily refer to as adaptiveness of behavior. In general terms, appropriateness of behavior refers to the characteristic of adjusting to changing circumstances by changing one's course of action in such a way that it is likely to be effective in reaching the goal.

Thus we can say that an organism's behavior is appropriate with respect to a given goal to the extent that the organism shows an effective course of action for the various *possible* changes in the circumstances surrounding the goal. By "circumstances surrounding the goal" is meant the stimuli that, for the given organism, are connected with the goal in some way or another. Thus, for a rat which has had considerable training in the Skinner box, the walls of the Skinner box, the lever, the food trough, as well as the smell and sight of food, are all stimuli connected with the goal (food). For such an animal, variations in any one of these stimuli would constitute a change in the circumstances surrounding the goal.

Now, we can define *appropriateness* as *the extent to which the organism adopts effective courses of action in response to variations in the stimuli connected with the goal.* This definition can be clarified with reference to an example. Suppose we have a given organism, $O$, a specified goal, $G$, and a specified experimental situation. Let us designate the stimuli that in $O$'s experience have been connected to $G$, as $Sg$, and variations in these stimuli as $Sg1, Sg2, Sg3$, and so on. Finally, let $R$ stand for the acts or course of action of $O$, and $R1, R2, R3$, and so on, for the variations in the course of action. Now, we can illustrate the meaning of appropriateness with reference to the following diagram:

$$Sg1 \cdot \cdot \cdot \cdot \cdot \cdot \cdot R1 \cdot \cdot \cdot \cdot \cdot \cdot \cdot \cdot G$$
$$Sg2 \cdot \cdot \cdot \cdot \cdot \cdot \cdot R2 \cdot \cdot \cdot \cdot \cdot \cdot \cdot \cdot G$$
$$Sg3 \cdot \cdot \cdot \cdot \cdot \cdot \cdot R3 \cdot \cdot \cdot \cdot \cdot \cdot \cdot \cdot G$$

The statement that $O$'s behavior in this situation is appropriate means that if $Sg1$ occurs, then $O$ responds by the corresponding effective response, $R1$; if $Sg2$ occurs, then the organism gives the effective response, $R2$; and so on. The extent to which each variation of the stimuli connected with the goal ($Sg1, Sg2, \ldots$) elicits an effective course of action ($R1, R2, \ldots$) indicates the degree of appropriateness of the particular sample of behavior. It should be clear that the concept of appropriateness is applicable only to a sample of behavior which represents repeated trials under conditions of controlled variations in $Sg$. Thus, it is meaningless to say that any one act is appropriate; we can only say that a sample of behavior obtained under prescribed conditions is more or less appropriate than another sample of behavior similarly obtained.

The concept of appropriateness is, of course, quite different from that of *stereotypy* proposed by Miller and Frick (1949). Their concept refers to the extent to which *any* sequence of responses is repeated in a given sample of behavior. Appropriateness, on the other hand, refers to the extent to which the *effective* sequences occur in a given sample of behavior. Thus, behavior that is highly appropriate may, under certain circumstances, also be high in stereotypy, but all highly stereotyped behavior will not necessarily be high in appropriateness. For example, in the above example, if the animal repeated one and the same response ($R1$ or $R2$ or $R3$) no matter what variations of $Sg$ were presented, its behavior would be scored high on stereotypy but low on appropriateness. But if variations in $Sg$ were repeated in exactly the same order (e.g. $Sg1, Sg2, Sg3, Sg1, Sg2, Sg3, Sg1. . . .$) again and again and, in each case, the animal responded with the effective response ($R1, R2, R3, R1, R2, R3, R1, . . .$) its behavior would be high in both stereotypy and appropriateness. Stereotypy and appropriateness describe different aspects of behavior; they do not necessarily covary, directly or inversely.

## OTHER CONNOTATIONS OF GOAL DIRECTION

The concept of goal direction does not refer only to appropriateness of behavior. Rather, in its current psychological usage, it signifies a number of distinct characteristics of behavior which, individually or in combination, are said to make a given sample of behavior more or less goal directed. "Persistence" and "searching" are two additional criteria that are also often employed in assessing the extent of goal direction. *Persistence* describes the rate or duration, or both, of the given effective courses of action. The greater the rate, or the duration for which a given minimum rate is maintained, of certain specified courses of action, the more goal directed the behavior is said to be. "Searching" refers to the hyperactivity often shown by animals when they are exposed to the stimuli associated with a previously experienced goal. The organism is usually said to "search for" or "anticipate" the goal. Thus, if on a given test a rat, previously trained in a Skinner box, finds no pedal in the box, it is likely repeatedly to go in the corner where the pedal used to be and, in general, to act as if it is reacting to the missing pedal. The frequency and duration of such responses defines what for the lack of a better name may be called *searching*.[3]

Whereas, in what we ordinarily refer to as goal-directed behavior, variations in appropriateness, persistence, and searching often go together, this is not necessarily the case. It is easy to visualize situations in which these three features of behavior will vary independently. For example, suppose a rat shows completely appropriate behavior with respect to a specified goal of obtaining food in a given situation. Now, it is likely that while the appropriateness of the rat's behavior with respect to food remains constant from day to day, its persistence would change depending on whether the animal is tested hungry or sated. Similarly, if the rat is tested after 12 and after 24 hr. of deprivation, the appropriateness and persistence will probably remain the same under the two conditions of deprivation, but the duration of searching may well be much greater after 24-hr. deprivation. It appears reasonable, therefore, to consider appropriateness, persistence, and searching as distinct features of behavior, though under many conditions they may show covariation.

Goal direction is thus a multidimensional concept. Appropriateness, persistence, and searching as defined above can be looked upon as some of the dimensions that are involved in judging behavior as more or less goal-directed. "Goal direction" thus becomes a general label referring to any one or more of the dimensions of appropriateness, persistence, and searching.

[3] Lorenz's (1950) term "appetitive behavior" probably describes the same aspect of goal-directed behavior. Searching also appears to be the phenomenon that has led Seward (1953) to postulate "tertiary or goal-instigated drives."

One last point. Two or more phenomena that are descriptively the same may result from fundamentally different processes. Cooperation in ants and cooperation between national governments can probably be described in terms of the same descriptive concepts, but the mechanisms underlying these two instances of cooperation are obviously fundamentally different. Similarly, our descriptive concepts of the various aspects of goal direction will fit the "behavior" of a guided missile, the "behavior" of a phototropic plant, as well as the "behavior" of a "food-seeking" rat or man. However, the processes involved are undoubtedly different in the three cases. In the following section we shall be concerned with the processes underlying the development of goal-directed behavior as it occurs in mammals like the rat and man.

## HOW BEHAVIOR BECOMES GOAL-DIRECTED

This section deals with the problem of the development of goal direction in behavior. How do appropriate, persistent, and searching activities emerge in the behavior of animals? We can approach the present problem by considering in detail cases where behavior is initially not goal directed but becomes appropriate, persistent, and searching. It would then be possible to analyze the factors responsible for producing goal direction in behavior.

SOME EXAMPLES

The ideal way to study the development of goal-directed behavior would be to observe its emergence in organisms whose existing repertoires lack directed patterns of response. The best one can do by way of approaching this ideal is to observe the development of goal direction in the behavior of the neonate. Strange as it may seem, hardly any investigator has concerned himself with such a study. True, normative studies like those of Gesell (1934) have sought to determine the age levels at which various integrated responses appear in the normally reared human infant, but for the most part such studies have not been concerned with the exact course of development or the conditions that affect it. As such, we can safely exclude them from the present discussion.

Somewhat closer to the data of interest to us are the observations of, for example, Marinesco & Kreindler (1933; quoted by Munn, 1955) on the human infant. In a conditioning procedure, they exposed the infant to a metronome followed by an electric shock to one limb. They noted that, to begin with, all four limbs of the infant responded to the shock in a diffuse and generalized way. With repetition of the shock, however, a specific and directed anticipatory response, involving only the shocked limb, replaced the earlier generalized movements. Similar observations can be made on the human infant in a reward situation. The infant shows an increase in general activity just before the normal feeding time. Initially, its responses appear to be random with respect to the feeding bottle and other stimuli associated with feeding. However, after repeated feedings in a consistent manner, the infant begins to show responses directed at grasping the bottle and bringing it to the mouth. These responses seem to emerge as a result of the repeated exposure to the feeding situation. Unfortunately, we lack systematic experimental investigations aimed at determining the exact conditions which lead to the emergence of such directed activities in the infancy of mammals.

Because of the paucity of detailed studies on the development of goal-directed activities in the neonate, we must turn to investigations involving adult animals. However, it is not easy to observe the emergence of goal-directed behavior in the adult animal. The adult already has numerous directed acts in its repertoire, which are usually adequate for meeting the demands of most situations to which it is normally exposed. But it is possible to place the adult animal in a situation so contrived that the animal has no ready responses for it; the development of *new* directed acts can then be studied even in the adult. We shall consider two examples of such development.

First, consider an adult, food-deprived rat in a Skinner box for the first time. It sniffs, walks around, stands and sniffs again, grooms itself, and so on. In the course of this activity it happens to press the pedal, which releases a pellet of food. The rat then walks around, discovers the food pellet, sniffs it, walks around some more, and finally eats the pellet. If the animal is left in the box and is observed again after an hour or so, its behavior is quite different. It systematically and rapidly alternates between pressing the pedal and eating the released pellet. The rat has thus acquired a goal-directed act sequence. The pedal is no longer pressed accidentally in the course of the varied responses; rather, pedal pressing has become an integrated and "deliberate" act. It is clear that, by arranging the events in the animal's environment in a particular way, we can develop directedness in its behavior.

Second, imagine an organism, say a dog, being introduced into a new world—an unfamiliar, noxious situation. This world consists of, let us say, a shuttle box, either of the two sides of which can be electrified. Further, assume that in this world a buzzer buzzes for 10 sec. every three or four minutes, and each buzz is followed immediately by a fairly strong electric shock lasting about a half minute. Let us arrange this world in such a way that the dog can escape the shock for at least part of the half-minute shock period by crossing over to the other, nonshock side of the shuttle box; and it can completely avoid the shock by crossing over during the 10 sec. signal (buzzer) period, before the shock is turned on. Brush (1956) has described the changing course of the animal's behavior in a situation of this kind. First it explores its new environment, circling the perimeter and sniffing. As the signal is turned on for the first time, it may listen attentively and look around. Then, when the shock is turned on, it is likely to howl and scramble about the compartment. It may urinate and defecate. Finally, in the course of this commotion, it may accidentally cross over into the unelectrified compartment of the box. As this experimental procedure continues, the shock following the buzzer every few minutes, the animal is likely to begin escaping the shock by crossing over as soon as the shock is turned on. If the shock is not too strong, nor too mild, and if certain other conditions are optimal, the animal is most likely eventually to start avoiding the shock by crossing over during the signal, before the onset of the shock. Within a few hours, the dog may be found to be completely adjusted to its new world, moving in a coordinated and nonchalant way from one side of the shuttle box to the other as soon as the buzzer is turned on. A "deliberate" or goal-directed act has thus been added to the dog's repertoire. At the same time, other responses that characterized the dog's behavior on its initial confrontation with the box cease to be prominent in the situation. Had the events in this hypothetical world followed a different course, undoubtedly some other goal-directed activity would have emerged. For instance, if the shock had been so arranged that it could be neither escaped nor avoided, the animal might eventually have consistently "tensed up" on hearing the buzzer, remaining in the same position throughout the duration of the shock. The exact act that develops in a new situation thus depends, among other things, on the nature of the events in the situation.

Two Tentative Generalizations

Having considered two representative examples, what general statement can we make concerning the development of goal direction in behavior? The term "learning," in its descriptive or empirical sense, well describes the events that result in the development of goal-directed behavior. It appears that the type of learning involved here can be best designated as, to use Thorndike's (1905) phrase, the "stamping in" of certain responses and the elimination of others. In simplest terms this means that, in a given situation, the probability of occurrence of certain responses increases over that of other responses. The term "reinforcement" is generally used in connection with the processes that are responsible for this selective stamping in of responses. The nature of reinforcement will be discussed in Chapter 5. Here our concern is only with the way in which the general learning process plays a necessary role in the acquisition of goal-directed activities. Tentatively, this role can be stated in the form of two related generalizations.

*Generalization 1.* This generalization states the role of experience (the term "experience" refers to the relatively permanent effects of past sensory stimulation) in the development of goal-directed behavior. *Some degree of repeated or continued exposure to a situation is a necessary condition for the development of activities that are goal-directed with respect to some feature of that situation.*

It is clear that while this generalization makes some exposure a necessary condition for the development of goal direction in behavior, it does not necessarily make exposure a sufficient condition. That is to say, exposure to a situation may or may not lead to the emergence of goal direction; however, whenever goal-directed behavior does develop in a situation, some prior experience with that situation must have taken place.

One other point about the generalization should be noted. Whereas it makes exposure to a stimulus situation essential for the development of goal-directed behavior, it does not necessarily require a great deal of exposure. Sometimes, the behavior with respect to some feature of a given situation may become directed with only a short exposure to the situation. The phenomenon of "imprinting," as described by Lorenz (1935), has drawn attention to this possibility. The main feature of the phenomenon is that in certain species, particularly of ducks and geese, a newly hatched bird will begin to follow a moving object (e.g. another bird or an experimenter) after only a brief exposure to it. The bird is said to be "imprinted" because, according to Lorenz, the following response is irreversible or, at least, difficult to extinguish. For the present discussion, the important point is that the goal-directed following response appears with a minimum of experience in the situation.

Some recent experiments on imprinting by Ramsay & Hess (1954) and Jaynes (1956) suggest that it is reasonable to interpret imprinting as rapid *acquisition* of goal-directed responses. Jaynes' experiment provides data directly relevant to the present discussion. He studied the "following and approaching" responses of 18 domestic newly hatched chicks.

The observations were made in a 10-ft. alley. A cardboard stimulus (goal) object was moved irregularly in the alley, and the time spent within 1 ft. of the object was recorded for each 5-min. period during a ½-hr. test. This time measure (in sec.) was called the imprinting score. Clearly, it is a

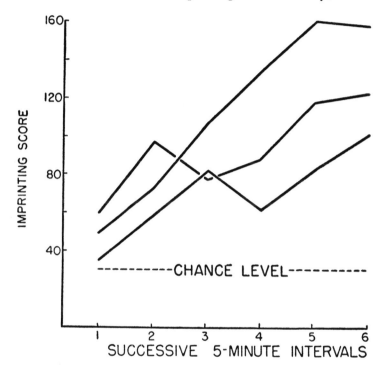

Fig. 1. Development of Imprinting

Three typical curves for the development of imprinting on the first day of life during a ½-hr. session. Scores are the number of seconds spent within a foot of the moving object during a 5-min. interval. (*Source:* J. Jaynes, Imprinting: the interaction of learned and innate behavior: I. Development and generalization. *J. comp. physiol. Psychol.,* **42,** 203.)

measure of the extent to which the animal reacts (by following and approaching) to the variations in the location of the goal, that is, a measure of appropriateness. Jaynes' results for these animals on the first day are presented in Fig. 1. It shows that initially the appropriateness (imprinting) scores were close to the chance level, but very quickly, within a half hour of continued exposure to the situation, the scores increased reliably above the chance level. Jaynes found that on successive days this increase continued until, on the fourth day, the animals spent roughly 80 per cent of the test time close to the (moving) goal. Such a rapid progressive increase from very low to high imprinting scores as a consequence of repeated experience with a moving imprinting model has also been observed by Hinde, Thorpe, & Vince (1956) in coots and moorhens. For the present discussion, the significance of these experiments lies in the demonstration that goal direction may develop quite rapidly under certain conditions. It appears that the moving imprinting stimuli served as incentives and led to positive reinforcement of the following response.

This reinforcement interpretation of imprinting is supported by a finding of Hess (1957). He exposed newly hatched ducklings to the model of a duck for 10 min. Though this exposure time was kept constant for all ducklings, some of them were made to follow the model for 1 ft. only, while others had to follow it for 12.5, 25, 50, or 100 ft. After this imprinting period, the ducklings were tested for imprinting—following the duck model. Hess found that increasing the distance over which the duckling had to follow the model during the imprinting session increased the imprinting strength. That is, the following response is strengthened in proportion to the animal's activity in the presence of the model; exposure without activity is not sufficient to increase the strength of the following response. In their experiments, Hinde, Thorpe, & Vince have also noted that imprinting "occurs when the bird follows the moving object" (1956, p. 241). These findings parallel the results found in the typical learning experiment so closely that it seems reasonable to interpret imprinting as the rapid acquisition of the reinforced (following) response.

Looked upon in this way, the crucial questions in interpreting the imprinting phenomenon concern the efficacy of certain stimuli as reinforcers. Why should a moving cardboard stimulus, or a model of a duck, or the experimenter be sufficient to reinforce the following response? Are there any species differences in the type of stimulus patterns that will reinforce this response? Why is imprinting observed only in certain species and not in other, closely related species? While speculations about some of these questions are presented in later chapters, much more research is needed before any final answers will be forthcoming.

*Generalization 2.* This generalization describes the way in which experience or learning leads to the emergence of activities that are directed with respect to a given goal. *Behavior becomes goal-directed by virtue of the fact that certain movements or component responses (occurring in a matrix of general activity) that are accompanied by a given goal are selectively strengthened or reinforced. This selective reinforcement leads to an increase in the frequency of reinforced movements, so that they appear to constitute an integrated, goal-directed response.*[4]

This generalization requires clarification. One can proceed by discussing it with reference to each of the three dimensions of goal direction mentioned in the last section. Take appropriateness first. It refers to the extent to which an organism gives an effective response each time there is some significant variation in the stimuli connected with the goal. This means that the organism must learn what variations in the situation are significantly related to the goal, and it must also learn the different courses of action which are effective for these variations. That is, if an organism's behavior is directed with respect to a goal, it must have learned a variety of alternative effective courses of action in relation to that goal. Now, one must ask by what process alternative effective responses in relation to a given goal develop. The answer provided by our generalization is *reinforcement.* Alternative effective responses in relation to the same given goal develop by virtue of their being reinforced in the same way. In other words, the responses or courses of action that are reinforced by the

[4] Unlike Hull's (1943) reinforcement postulate, this generalization does not attribute reinforcement to drive reduction or any other specific mechanism (*see* Chap. 5).

same goal come to serve as alternative effective responses with respect to that goal. For example, a rat trained in a Skinner box may press the pedal with its left paw, its right paw, or with its head, and it may do so by approaching the pedal from the right or by approaching it from the left. The various combinations of these modes of pressing the pedal become equivalent because all of them are reinforced in the same way —by the release of the food pellet. As Skinner (1938) has pointed out, such equivalences of the various courses of action do not develop if no latitude in the form of the reinforced response is allowed to the animal. If the animal is reinforced only when it approaches the pedal from the left and then presses it with its nose, the various courses of action mentioned above will not become equivalent. This is the basic method employed in forcing the animal to differentiate its responses. Thus, when we say that an organism has a set of courses of action effective with respect to a particular goal, we are referring to the fact that the organism has a set of courses of action all of which have *previously* been reinforced by the same goal. Of course, normally the set of interchangeable responses learned in one situation is employed by the animal in other, similar situations. The factors that determine the extent of such "generalization" or transfer will be discussed in Chapter 7.

Consider persistence next. With respect to persistence, the problem is simply one of stating the factors that make the effective courses of action occur at high rates for long durations. The generalization above suggests the answer that increased persistence in behavior results from the reinforcing effects of a given goal on the effective courses of action. It is well known that the rate of response is a function of number of reinforcements. It should be noted that the generalization does not exclude the role of factors other than prior reinforcement (e.g. deprivation, environmental stress, changes in blood chemistry, and the like) in determining the rate and duration of the effective courses of action.

That leaves searching. According to the present generalization, searching increases by virtue of the fact that the given goal reinforces all goal-related responses. A hypothetical example given by Skinner (1953) illustrates this point clearly:

> The fact that operant behavior seems to be "directed toward the future" is misleading. Consider, for example, the case of "looking for something." In what sense is the "something" which has not yet been found relevant to the behavior? Suppose we condition a pigeon to peck a spot on the wall of a box and then, when the operant is well established, remove the spot. The bird now goes to the usual place along the wall. It raises its head, cocks its eye in the usual direction, and may even emit a weak peck in the usual place. Before extinction is very far advanced, it returns to the same place again and again in similar behavior. Must we say that the pigeon is "looking for the spot"? Must we take the "looked for" spot into account in explaining the behavior?
>
> It is not difficult to interpret this example in terms of operant reinforcement. Since visual stimulation from the spot has usually preceded the receipt of food, the spot has become a conditioned reinforcer. It strengthens the behavior of looking in given directions from different positions. Although we have undertaken to condition only the pecking response, we have in fact strengthened many different kinds of precurrent behavior which bring the bird into positions from which it sees the spot and pecks it. These responses continue to appear, even though we have removed the spot, until extinction occurs. The spot that is "being looked for" is the spot which has occurred in the past as the immediate reinforcement of the behavior of looking. In general, looking for something consists of emitting responses which in the past have produced "something" as a consequence.[5]

Thus, what we call searching refers to a variety of precurrent responses that have been reinforced by their close association with the specific instrumental acts and the goal. Such "searching responses" are probably acquired by an animal in a variety of situations and come to form a part of his stable repertoire of responses. It may be that it is these responses, acquired in connection with specific goals, that form the basis of systematic exploratory activity observed in many animals.

The above paragraphs should have clarified the meaning of the second generalization, which attributes all aspects of goal direction, including appropriateness, persistence, and searching, to the *prior* reinforcement by a given goal of those re-

[5] B. F. Skinner, *Science and human behavior* (N.Y.: The Macmillan Co., 1953), pp. 88–89. By permission of The Macmillan Co.

sponses that were, in the given situation, related to (contiguous with) the goal.

Evidence in support of this generalization comes from numerous studies of instrumental conditioning. In almost all these studies the experimenter seeks to develop goal-directed behavior in the animal. The technique consists simply in reinforcing the animal at certain crucial points in its general activity. It is almost always noticed that, before the animal develops the desired directedness, there is considerable increase in the incidence of responses that are in some way related to the goal. For example, if the response desired of a rat is that of alternating between the food bin and pressing the pedal that releases the food, it will be seen that, before appropriate behavior appears, there is considerable increase in the movements toward the food bin and the pedal, touching the pedal, looking in the food bin, and other goal-related responses.

The way in which certain bizarre responses can be made to appear in the repertoire of animals also illustrates the role of selective reinforcement in the development of goal-directed activities. A rat in a Skinner box, for example, may continue to press the pedal with its head or by making a turn before approaching the pedal, if this is the response for which the animal happens to be reinforced on the first few trials. This is seen clearly in the development of what Skinner (1948) has called "superstitious behavior." The method involves reinforcement, not of any particular act or act sequence, but on an arbitrarily chosen schedule. For example, a hungry pigeon may be given a piece of food at the end of successive 15-sec. periods, without any reference to the behavior of the bird. If this procedure is carried on for some time, the pigeon may begin to perform certain acts with increasing frequency. One bird may start standing on its right leg, another may repeatedly turn quickly in a small circle, and yet another may cock its head in a certain way again and again. Thus, the animal ends up repeating certain acts which happened to have coincided a few times with the reinforcement, even though the reinforcement follows an arbitrary schedule and is in no way dependent upon what the animal does. Once such a "superstitious response" begins to occur more frequently than other responses, its further reinforcement becomes even more likely, for, being more frequent, it is more likely to be occurring at the time of reinforcement than any other responses.

Observations supporting the second generalization have also been made in a quite different area of investigation. Children reared in different cultures speak different languages. Osgood (1953, p. 684) has shown that infants are capable of producing the sounds of all languages. However, we know that it is impossible for most adults to produce certain sounds characteristic of languages other than those of their mother tongues. The sounds that children do learn to combine into goal-directed linguistic activities are those that are reinforced by adults. Osgood's observations show that before an infant begins to talk its mother tongue, the frequency of occurrence of the component sounds increases and that of "nonfunctional" (nonreinforced) sounds decreases.[6]

These studies show that the development of goal-directed behavior does involve, as a first step, an increase through reinforcement in the probability of occurrence of goal-related responses. As mentioned before, the above two propositions concerning the development of goal-directed behavior are not "laws" but merely tentative generalizations to serve as a basis for further discussion and empirical work.

[6] It would be interesting to determine if the development of species-typical songs in birds, which is being studied extensively by Thorpe and his colleagues (see Thorpe, 1956), can also be interpreted in terms of selective reinforcement of the component sounds that any given species is capable of emitting.

# Chapter 4

# Development of
# Motivational Activities

The two generalizations stated in the last chapter attribute an essential role to experience and reinforcement in the development of goal-directed behavior. The generalizations also make these two related conditions sufficient for the development of directed activities. Thus, in essence, the two generalizations state that *continued or repeated exposure to and reinforcement by a given goal must produce goal-directed activity and, conversely, goal-directed activity cannot develop without the operation of these two factors.* The above statement can be considered as a learning hypothesis of goal-directed behavior. It denies the existence of innately goal-directed acts; though, of course, the possibility of innately determined reflexes and movements is left open. This chapter considers some of the implications of the hypothesis; the first section deals with the question of the innateness of species-specific (the so-called "instinctive") activities, and the second section of the chapter discusses the development of the motivational activities described in Chapter 2.

## IS SPECIES-SPECIFIC BEHAVIOR INNATE?

Our hypothesis obviously does not allow for the interpretation of species-specific activities as "innate" acts. The species-specific activities, such as "hoarding" and maternal behavior in the rat, are undoubtedly goal-directed as judged by our criteria of appropriateness, persistence, and searching. However, analyses of many such activities have shown that they are not innate in the sense of being independent of prior experience. Certain forms of prior experiences seem to be essential to the development of all directed activities. As examples of the experimental approach to the study of the development of apparently innate goal-directed activities, we shall consider (1) hoarding in rats, (2) elicitation of directed acts, and (3) shifts in dietary preferences.

## HOARDING IN RATS

*Description of hoarding behavior.* If a rat is deprived of food for a day or two and is then given access to food placed at a short distance from its cage, it will, under appropriate conditions, transport some of the food to the cage. This activity is called *hoarding;* the term is used only as a convenient label and does not imply that the aim of the activity is the accumulation of food for future use. A typical experiment employs a runway about 30 in. long, one end of which contains a bin with pellets of food in it. At the other end of the runway is placed the home-cage of a rat; the door of the cage is left open to allow free entry into the runway. Rats are tested individually for about ½ hr. each day. During the test period the animal can go through the alley to the bin and bring back pellets of food to its cage. If a food-deprived rat is given daily ½-hr. tests, it is likely to show fairly persistent hoarding activity within three or four days. On the first day or two it may bring back no more pellets than it can consume in a short period, but there is likely to be a rapid increase in hoarding on subsequent days. The ratio of time spent eating to time spent hoarding decreases rapidly until the animal spends about 90 per cent of the test time running between the bin and the cage, transporting pellets. A rat may bring back as many as a hundred pellets, each weighing about 4 grams, in a ½-hr. test. Some animals pile up the pellets neatly in one corner, while others scatter them all through the cage. (The transported pellets are normally removed from the cage by the experimenter immediately after the test.) The characteristics, such as the odor and illumination of the runway, cage, and bin are important determiners of whether hoarding will take place (Miller & Viek, 1944). A rat that does not hoard, a "nonhoarder," may remain in the cage or go to the end of the runway and eat in the bin. Bindra (1948a) has shown that, by rearranging certain characteristics of the runway, it is possible to turn the nonhoarders into hoarders. However, given a particular situation, it is unlikely that all the animals will hoard.

Earlier investigators tended to ascribe hoarding activity to the operation of a "hoarding instinct." For example, Morgan, Stellar, & Johnson (1943) and Morgan (1947) held that an unlearned behavior pattern specifically concerned with hoarding (food) is set off by some specific physiological deficit resulting from food deprivation. However, food hoarding without any previous deprivation—and, therefore, without any deficit—was demonstrated by Bindra (1948) and Licklider & Licklider (1950). In the Bindra experiment it was found that nondeprived rats would hoard a food which differed from their normal diet only in that it contained some saccharin and, therefore, was presumably more palatable. Licklider & Licklider, employing an unusual apparatus, obtained hoarding activity in nondeprived young rats. These facts show that dietary deficit is not a necessary condition for the onset of hoarding.

About the same time it was shown (Bindra, 1947) that rats would hoard water pellets when they had been deprived of water. Water pellets are rolls of cotton soaked in water; like pellets of food, they can be carried between the teeth. Water hoarding is strikingly similar, in its onset, decline, and other characteristics, to food hoarding. The transportation of nesting material, as described by Kinder (1927), is an activity that is also similar to the hoarding of food and water. And the pup-retrieving activity of the puerperal female, described in Chapter 2, also resembles hoarding in all essential features. It is obviously unnecessary to complicate the rat's conceptual nervous system with such a variety of instincts—an instinct to hoard food, an instinct to hoard water, an instinct to hoard nesting materials, and an instinct to retrieve pups. An alternative is to postulate the existence of only one general activity concerned with hoarding or transporting materials from a place outside the "home" to inside the "home." *What* the animals transport could then be said to be determined by various internal and external conditions: When rats are deprived of food, they transport food; when they are deprived of water, they transport water; when the environmental temperature is low, they transport nesting material (Kinder, 1927) and food (McCleary & Morgan, 1946); when they are rearing their young, they transport the pups. The main question that is relevant to the present discussion does not concern the conditions that determine what objects are transported; rather it concerns the nature of the activity of transporting itself. Is this activity, which shows all the characteristics of goal-directed behavior, acquired, or is it independent of past experience? If our generalization, which denies the existence of unlearned goal-directed activities, is correct, we should be able to show that the act sequences involved in hoarding are acquired through experience.

*Development of the activity.* To begin with, let us have a closer look at hoarding when it has been well practiced and has become stable. For descriptive purposes, the hoarding activity may be looked upon as consisting of the following discrete acts: leaving the cage (L), walking or running to the bin at the end of the runway (Wb), picking up a pellet between the teeth (P), walking back to the cage (Wc), entering the cage (E), and dropping the pellet inside the cage (D). Let us, for the moment, take for granted the existence of these component acts in the repertoire of the animal. In the act sequence of hoarding these acts follow each other in an integrated way (L Wb P Wc E D L Wb . . . etc.) resulting in the observed behavior. How do these acts become integrated into the goal-directed activity we call hoarding? The answer provided by our generalization is that the acts are integrated by virtue of being reinforced by a common reinforcing event. That is, our generalization requires that the sequence L Wb P Wc E D be followed by a reinforcing event; otherwise the complex act of hoarding would not develop. The rapid onset of hoarding behavior suggests that such terminal reinforcement must occur within the first one or two tests. Marx (1951) has studied the effects of terminal reinforcement in the initial tests on the development of hoarding activity.

In some preliminary observations Marx (1950a) noted that rats which later developed strong hoarding habits tended to be those that had spent several minutes in active feeding after bringing the first two or three pellets to the cage. He then designed an experiment (1951) to test the hypothesis that hoarding is dependent upon the terminal reinforcement which follows the first few pellet returns. Rats were divided into two groups, one experimental and one control, of 20 animals each. During the training phase of this experiment, the animals were food-deprived and given a chance to transport 10 food pellets from the bin to the cage. In the case of the experimental animals, the pellet was taken away from the rat following each pellet return, thus preventing the animal from eating any part of it. Control animals were allowed to feed on the pellets they brought back from the bin. (All control animals actually did feed on the first pellet returned for a median time of about 10 min. Feeding dropped rapidly on the second and third pellets.) Thus the control animals received terminal reinforcement, but the experimental animals did not. After this training trial, all animals were put on *ad libitum* feeding for 23 hr., and were then tested for hoarding for about ½ hr. in the usual manner. Marx found that the mean number of pellets hoarded by the experimental group was 12.4, and by the control group 51.5. The proportion of animals which hoarded on the test trial was also significantly greater in the control than in the experimental group. Only three animals in the experimental group hoarded 5 or more pellets. In each of these cases, the experimental protocol revealed that some terminal reinforcement had taken place through the small pieces of food left in the animal's mouth during the process of removing the pellet. In general, the experimental animals continued to show the component acts (leaving and returning to the cage, manipulating and carrying food pellets, etc.) but failed to show the integration of these acts into the normal hoarding pattern. Marx concluded that terminal reinforcement plays an essential part in the onset of hoarding in the laboratory rat.

However, some later experiments (Marx, 1957; Marx & Brownstein, 1957) have caused Marx to modify the above conclusion to a certain extent. These experiments show that terminal reinforcement of the type provided in Marx's (1951) first experiment is not necessary when rats are tested under certain deprivation conditions. Therefore, now Marx looks upon terminal food reinforcement only as a facilitator of food-hoarding activity rather than as an essential condition for its development. If the terminal-reinforcement interpretation of the development of hoarding activity is correct, it is conceivable that further research will reveal a number of factors that can serve as terminal reinforcers and which, acting alternatively or in combination, lead to the integration of component acts into hoarding activity. For example, it is likely that the re-entry into the safe "home" has some reinforcing effects and that they play a crucial role in the strengthening of the hoarding habit to such an extent that the rat spends more time hoarding than eating.

Once the hoarding activity has started, on each successive daily test the typical animal spends more time transporting pellets and less time eating, reaching a more or less stable hoarding-eating ratio within six or seven days. Such a stable level of hoarding will continue indefinitely in spite of the fact that all the transported pellets are removed from the cage immediately after the test. The animal receives only a deprivation ration of food after each test. Some animals continue to hoard even after they have been restored to *ad libitum* feeding for weeks and have ample food in the cage during the test. Marx (1950) is inclined to interpret such persistence of hoarding activity partly in terms of regular reinforcement from manipulating pellets and feeding. Licklider & Licklider, on the other hand, are inclined to the view that "Once the rat has started hoarding, the motor mechanism becomes partially autonomous—independent to a considerable extent even of the perceptual processes that got it started" (1950, p. 134). Without denying the role of reinforcement, it appears reasonable to consider the fully developed hoarding habit as a partially autonomous one. Whatever the exact nature of this "autonomy," it appears that some such concept as Woodworth's (1918) "mechanisms become drives" or Allport's (1937) "functional autonomy" of activities correctly describes not only the fully developed hoarding habit but also other similar persistent activities. This general problem will be discussed in Chapter 10.

It should be noted that the role ascribed by Marx to terminal reinforcement is only that of integrating the component acts into the directed hoarding activity. The obvious next question concerns the origin of the individual acts involved in hoarding. As Marx (1950) has pointed out, before it is ever exposed to the hoarding situation, the laboratory rat has in its repertoire acts involving the seizure, carrying, and release of food material, as well as acts of leaving and returning to a familiar place. Whereas learning probably does play some part in the development of these responses too, they are certainly more likely to develop in certain species than in others. There are, for example, marked species and strain differences in the ease and frequency with which an animal leaves its "home" and the periods for which it stays away. This characteristic may be referred to as timidity or shyness. Bindra (1948a) has related the individual and strain differences in hoarding in rats to this variable of shyness. Albino rats, which are more shy than rats of the Lashley strain, are more likely to hoard in the closed, "safe" alleys. In such closed alleys, many rats of the Lashley strain do not hoard, but simply go down the alley, sit in the food bin, and eat. However, these very nonhoarders can be made to hoard by making the situation less safe, either by removing the side walls of the alleys or by illuminating the apparatus brightly. This means that the likelihood that a given rat will hoard in a given situation depends upon its shyness, which in turn depends upon its strain; and strains reflect genetic makeup. Thus, though it is incorrect to attribute differences in hoarding to differences in the strength of hoarding instinct, it is quite true that the acts involved in hoarding are more likely to develop in rats of a certain genetic makeup than in rats of other strains.

The above ideas can probably be extended to species differences in hoarding as well. For example, cats and dogs do not normally hoard food or any other materials. Why not? The answer probably lies in the fact that component acts involved in hoarding normally do not exist in the repertoire of carnivores. For one thing, carnivores are not as shy as rodents. It should be interesting to see if cats and dogs (or any other species that normally does not hoard food) can be made to do so by manipulating their early experience so that they develop the component acts required in hoarding, and designing an experimental situation that is as unsafe for them as an alley is for rats. In this connection, it should be noted that when packs of (undomesticated) street dogs live on the occasional morsels or bones thrown at them, they do develop a tendency to pick up the food quickly and run to some familiar spot; they sometimes even bury the food and return to search for some more.

The above considerations show that the strain and species differences in hoarding are not interpretable simply as the outcome of variations in some unitary hoarding instinct. They rather suggest that the differences result from differences in the development of the component acts involved in hoarding. Marx has shown that, given the component acts, they can be integrated into the goal-directed hoarding activity by terminal reinforcement. But the genetic, morphological, and other factors that determine the individual, strain, and species differences in the development of the component acts themselves still remain to be investigated.

## Elicitors of Directed Acts

Related to the question of the innateness of certain instances of goal-directed acts is another issue. This concerns the effectiveness of certain situations or stimulus patterns in eliciting goal-directed activities. Are there any innate connections between certain stimuli and certain directed responses? It is clear that our hypothesis denies the existence of such connections. (However, the possibility of innate connections between certain stimuli and non-directed responses, such as reflexes, is not denied.)

*"Innate releasers."* Perhaps the best way to examine the issue of the innateness of connections between a particular stimulus pattern and a particular directed act is to discuss one aspect of the theory of instinct proposed by Lorenz (1937, 1950), and Tinbergen (1951), and systematically discussed by Thorpe (1956). The central concept in the Lorenz-Tinbergen theory is that of "endogenous movement" or *instinctive act*. They employ this term to designate certain goal-directed and coordinated response sequences, such as sucking and licking movements of infants, the following of moving objects by certain birds, and egg rolling by the gray goose. The fact that Lorenz and Tinbergen consider such instinctive acts to be innate is not relevant to the present issue. Whether the instinctive acts, as defined by Lorenz and Tinbergen, are innate or are acquired through past experience, they already exist in the animal's repertoire. What concerns us here is the fact that Lorenz and Tinbergen believed that some instinctive acts are innately connected to specific stimulus patterns, the stimulus pattern being able to "release" or elicit the act without prior experience. This view is obviously opposed to our hypothesis.

Painstaking and ingenious observations by Lorenz, Tinbergen, and their colleagues have brought forth data which seem to support the idea of innate connections between certain stimuli and goal-directed activities. They claim to have found a number of stimulus patterns which release an instinctive act without prior association with it. For example, according to these authors, the shape of the teat is an innate releaser of sucking and licking acts (Prechtl & Schleidt, 1951), a smooth-outlined hard object near the nest elicits innately the act of egg rolling (Lorenz & Tinbergen, 1938), and the shape of a hawk innately evokes "fear" in fowl while the shape of a goose evokes "interest" (Tinbergen, 1948). Unfortunately, the studies on which these conclusions are based often failed to employ the type of experimental controls that would enable one to draw unequivocal conclusions. Adequately controlled investigations bearing on this issue have only recently begun to appear in the literature.

An experimentally controlled study by Hirsch, Lindley, & Tolman (1955) is relevant here. They tested the Tinbergen hypothesis that certain specific stimulus shapes are innately related to (directed) "fear response" in the fowl. They observed the responses, such as crouching, wing flapping, taking shelter, and the like, of each of 24 naive, laboratory-reared, eight-week-old White Leghorn chickens to hawk-shaped and goose-shaped stimuli. The observations were made in a standard alley, and the two stimuli were moved in an identical manner, speed, and order. Contrary to the results of Tinbergen's study, Hirsch, Lindley, & Tolman found no difference in the responses of the chickens to the two stimulus objects. An almost identical investigation was carried out independently by Rockett (1955) in the White Rock chicken. His results were similar to those of Hirsch, Lindley, & Tolman. He attributes the Tinbergen results to the operation of some uncontrolled variable. However, since Tinbergen's original observations were made on turkeys and mallards, the above discrepancy is also consistent with a species-difference interpretation (Tinbergen, 1957).

Such properly controlled tests of some of the specific innate connections between stimulus patterns and directed acts described in the writings of Lorenz and Tinbergen have only recently been undertaken. It will be some time before we can formulate any final answers concerning the possible existence of innate connections between directed acts and certain specific stimulus patterns.

"Spontaneous fears." For considering the same problem in a mammalian context, one can refer again to the experiment by Hebb (1946), which was described in Chapter 1. In that experiment some chimpanzees were found frequently to show directed avoidance behavior in response to apparently innocuous objects (e.g. cast of snake and anesthetized chimpanzee) which had never been associated with noxious stimulation. Looked at superficially, this result may be considered as evidence for innate connections between certain stimulus patterns and directed withdrawal acts. The usual criterion of innateness employed by psychologists is that the eliciting stimulus should evoke the specific response the *first time* the animal is exposed to it. This criterion is clearly met in the case of Hebb's chimpanzees. However, Hebb questions the validity of this criterion and interprets his results differently.

Hebb (1946a) argues that the fact that the animal shows a particular act on its first exposure to a stimulus pattern does not necessarily mean that the connection between them is independent of prior experience. He points out that even though his chimpanzees had had no specific (painful) experience associated with the test stimuli, the effectiveness of these objects in evoking the avoidance acts does depend on some learning; that is, it is not independent of prior experience. Hebb attributes his results to the novelty or strangeness of these stimulus patterns as compared to the normal, familiar environment of the chimpanzees. The fact that the usual environment of the chimpanzees had become so familiar to them that a prostrate (anesthetized) chimpanzee, or the cast of a snake, appeared novel or strange to them obviously implies that prior experience (in developing familiarity with recurring environmental stimulus patterns) was essential to the appearance of the (avoidance) acts on the first exposure to the (strange) stimulus patterns.

As further support for his thesis, Hebb refers to another study (Hebb & Riesen, 1943) in which chimpanzee infants were found to show "fear" of strange humans. Yet they did not in any way avoid the familiar attendants in the laboratory; the withdrawal was elicited by strangers only (including strange chimpanzees). This directed act of withdrawal could not be attributed to any innate connection between it and certain types of visual stimulus patterns. For, what is strange for one animal is not so for another, and any patterns whatever may be made strange by arranging the prior experiences of the animal. Furthermore, a chimpanzee blindfolded from birth to the age of four months did not show any avoidance on its first perception of a human being. However, after it had become familiar with the sight of the laboratory personnel, exposure to a new face promptly evoked the withdrawal acts.[1] Thus Hebb concludes that, whereas such spontaneous fears do occur on the first exposure of the animals to the particular stimulus patterns, they nevertheless depend upon prior experience. (However, the required prior experience is of a general nature only and does not involve specific associative learning of the type demanded by drive theorists.)

It is clear that connections between certain stimulus patterns and directed acts that may appear to be innate are not necessarily found to be so on closer scrutiny. The learning hypothesis proposed here states that stimulus patterns that evoke directed activities in an animal do so by virtue of the fact that the animal has had certain types of past experience. It is the past experiences of the animal that determine the efficacy of certain stimulus patterns in evoking directed responses. However, it appears that there are marked species differences in the "sensitivity" to various types of stimulus patterns, so that, for a given species, certain stimulus patterns are more likely than others to become associated with the responses that exist in the repertoire of the members of that species. The ethological concept of "innate releasers" mentioned above can be interpreted as referring to the greater sensitivity for certain stimulus patterns of the members of particular zoological groups. Though ethologists have used the term "innate" in this connection, the exact roles of genetic, morphological, and experiential factors in determining such differential sensitivity to stimulus patterns still remain to be investigated. (As examples of the experimental approach to this problem, see Rheingold & Hess, 1957, and Fantz, 1957.)

It should be noted that the above discussion does not deny the possibility of the existence of innate connections (i.e.

[1] Why the novel stimuli evoked avoidance more frequently than other types of responses (e.g. attack and friendly acts) is a question that will be answered below and in Chaps. 6 and 8.

connections that are independent of past experience) between certain stimulus patterns and particular nongoal-directed responses, such as smiling and grasping in the human infant and various other reflexes and chain reflexes.

### SHIFTS IN DIETARY PREFERENCES

When an animal is given the choice of a variety of dietary materials, it typically consumes more of some of these substances and less of the others. Some of the factors that determine such "food preferences" have been extensively studied in recent years. (For a review, *see* Young, 1948, and Morgan & Stellar, 1950.) One factor that determines them is what are sometimes called "specific hungers." Richter (1936) has shown that specific dietary imbalances in the animal can determine food preferences; for example, he has demonstrated a marked preference for salt in rats made salt-deficient by adrenalectomy. *Deficiencies* or *excesses*, or both, of dietary substances such as calcium, phosphorus, sugar, protein, fats, and some vitamins have also been shown to make significant changes in food preferences. In general, though by no means always, the preference changes in a direction that would bring the animal back to its normal, pre-experimental, dietary state. The shifts in preferences brought about by dietary deficiencies and excesses can, of course, be prevented or hastened by making it more or less difficult for the animal to discriminate between the test substances.

Young has emphasized that variation in the intake of the normal diet components is not the only factor that determines changes in food preferences. Young (1944) and Young & Chaplin (1945) have demonstrated that *dietary habit* is an important determiner of food preferences. They have shown, for example, that rats that are used to eating sugar will continue to prefer sugar to casein (protein) even when they are in a state of protein deficiency. Another factor that determines food preferences is the *stimulus characteristics*, other than those necessary for discrimination, of the test substances. Thus, Beebe-Center *et al.* (1948) have shown that, as the concentration of a saccharin solution is increased, it is first preferred to tap water by rats, but that later, at higher concentrations, the preference is reversed. Bare (1949) has shown that a similar shift in preference with increasing concentration occurs when the concentration of a salt solution is varied. He has also demonstrated that in salt-depleted (adrenalectomized) rats the "reversal concentration" (the concentration

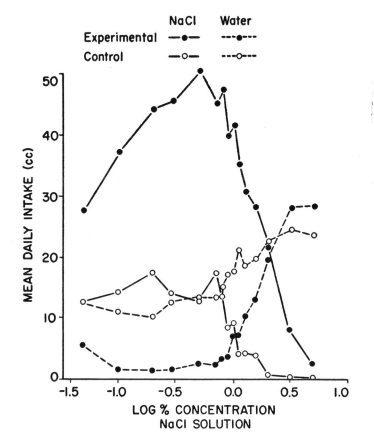

Fig. 2. Salt and Water Intake of Adrenalectomized Rats

Postoperative mean daily intake of sodium chloride solution and tap water for adrenalectomized and normal animals. (*Source:* J. K. Bare, The specific hunger for sodium chloride in normal and adrenalectomized white rats. *J. comp. physiol. Psychol.*, **42**, 249.)

of salt solution at which the reversal in preference from salt solution to water occurs) is higher than in the case of normal animals. The "preference threshold" (the concentration at which an animal begins to prefer salt solution to water) is also lower in the case of salt-depleted animals. Both these results are shown in Fig. 2. These findings suggest that specific hungers may be looked upon as specific dietary imbalances that modulate the normal preference curve for a given substance and a given animal.

The behavior of an animal in a preference situation is evidently goal-directed. Variations in the location of the preferred substance evoke appropriate behavior on the part of the animal, and it shows considerable persistence of the relevant responses. This goal-directed preference behavior can, of course, in some cases be clearly attributed to prior learning. However, the shifts in preference brought about by specific dietary imbalances and by variations in the concentration of the substances are often considered to be "innately" determined. For example, Richter (1939) is inclined to the view that the depletion of a certain substance in the body lowers the taste threshold for that substance and thus enables the animal to select that substance more readily. However, Pfaffman & Bare (1950), Carr (1952), and Harriman & MacLeod (1953) have shown that no differences in the taste threshold for salt exist between normal and salt-depleted animals. Thus, salt deficiency cannot be said to alter the sensitivity of taste receptors.

Meyer (1952) determined the relation between food deprivation and human taste thresholds for sweet, salty, and bitter substances. He found no changes in thresholds for any of the three modalities over a 34-hr. deprivation period. Furthermore, though the preference threshold of salt-depleted animals is lower than that of the normal animal, the preference threshold of both salt-depleted and normal animals is higher than their taste threshold, as determined by gustatory afferent nerve discharges. The lowered threshold interpretation is, therefore, untenable. Even if a lower taste threshold were demonstrated in salt-depleted animals, the question as to why a lower threshold leads to greater intake, rather than less, would still remain unanswered. Thus, Richter's explanation is both incorrect and incomplete.

An alternative to Richter's explanation can be found in the following line of speculation. It is based on Young's (1948) statement that preferences for particular foods rest upon the effects of ingesting those foods. If this is correct, then it can be stated that the food preferences shown by an animal in a given set of circumstances do not appear innately formed in its repertoire, ready to be elicited by the appropriate dietary imbalance, but are acquired in the preference-test situation. They are acquired quite quickly, but nevertheless they are acquired. And they are acquired on the basis of the reinforcing effects that follow immediately upon the ingestion of the given (preferred) substances. If this view is correct, we should expect to find considerable trial and error on the first exposure of the animal to the preference-test situation, and only a gradual strengthening of one set of responses (i.e. one choice) over the others. And, since this differential learning is presumed to occur quickly, a detailed analysis of (only) the initial preference tests should yield a learning curve.

It is well known that, typically, the preferences of animals deprived of specific dietary components change gradually, increasing from one preference test to the next and yielding a gradually increasing function. This type of function is, of course, consistent with a learning interpretation of food preferences, but it is also consistent with the "innate" hypothesis inasmuch as a gradual increase in preference may arise from a gradually increasing deficit of the particular dietary component. Epstein & Stellar (1955) have tried to find out which one of these two interpretations is correct. They found that adrenalectomized rats that were given salt-solution–vs.–water preference tests immediately after adrenalectomy showed a gradual increase in salt preference over the 10 daily 1-hr. tests. However, another group of rats, which were adrenalectomized and then salt-deprived for a few days before being given the preference tests, showed a high level of preference for salt on the very first preference test. Thus, the experience of the

10 preference tests for the animals in the first group did not significantly increase their salt preference over the animals that had no such experience but had a greater salt deficit. On the face of it, this evidence may seem to be opposed to the reinforcement interpretation of dietary preferences proposed above. But, in fact, it is not. For, according to the present view, the learning of preferences occurs within the first preference test and depends on the differential reinforcing effects of the test substances. Thus, a crucial test would come from a study which determines whether or not learning takes place within the first few minutes of a preference test. For example, in the Epstein & Stellar experiment, data on the course of preference of salt solution to water during each of the 12 5-min. periods constituting the first preference test would have provided a basis for accepting or rejecting the reinforcement hypothesis. Such detailed analyses of the initial preference tests have not yet been made.

If one looks upon changes in dietary preferences as the outcome of differential reinforcing effects of the available dietary materials, then the focus of research interest shifts to the source of differential reinforcing effects themselves. Why do different dietary substances differ in their reinforcing capacities? And, why do the reinforcing effects of a given substance for a given animal differ with the dietary state of the animal? Another related question concerns the differences in the reinforcing effects that a given substance has in animals of different species and strains. Experimental studies of these questions have hardly begun (*see* Chap. 5), and much systematic work needs to be done before any answers can be given to them. Research in this area may well reveal some basic biochemical determinants of the efficacy of reinforcers.

CONCLUSION

As Beach (1955) has pointed out, the assurance with which innate acts are attributed to a given species is inversely related to the extent to which its behavior has been analyzed from a developmental point of view. The three sets of studies discussed above all point to the need for detailed developmental analysis of the activities that are frequently labeled as "instinctive." Readers interested in the general problem of the analysis of goal-directed species-specific activities are referred to the following articles: Beach (1951, 1955), Beach & Jaynes (1954), Bindra (1957), Hebb (1953, 1954), and Lehrman (1953). Suffice it to say here that a review of the recent literature provides no reason to modify our general hypothesis, which denies that any goal-directed acts in mammalian behavior are independent of past experience. However, such a review does suggest that there are marked species and strain differences in the conditions or characteristics of the organism that determine the development of various goal-directed activities. Such conditions include the availability of component acts, sensitivity to certain stimulus patterns, and degree of reinforcing effects produced by particular dietary substances and other reinforcing objects and events. It is the study of the constitutional and experiential determinants of these characteristics that requires, and is now beginning to receive, a part of the research energy of psychologists.

## DEVELOPMENT OF OTHER MOTIVATIONAL ACTIVITIES

This section deals with the development in the repertoires of animals of motivational activities that were described in Chapter 2. Inasmuch as all those activities, as they occur in the normal adult animal, are clearly goal-directed, one would expect learning to play a crucial role in their development. However, to say that experience determines what goal-directed activities develop in the repertoire of an animal is not to say much. One needs to know the specific experiences that determine the development of each of the various motivational activities in any given species or strain of animals. This problem has been neglected by most motivation psychologists. They have been concerned primarily, if not exclusively, with the factors that determine the increases and decreases in the occurrence of motivational activities. In order to correct this one-sided emphasis, in this section an attempt will be made to bring together what little evidence is available on the specific experiential factors that determine the development of particular motivational activities in the repertoires of animals. It should be noted that the type of constitutional and experiential factors that are important in the development of these activities are no different from those that determine other activities, such as perceiving, maze learning, and problem solving.

## DEVELOPMENT OF GENERAL ACTIVITY AND EXPLORATION

As was pointed out in the first chapter, the facts of exploration have generally been considered to pose a problem for drive theorists. Exploratory activity seems not to be easily interpretable as a secondary drive acquired on the basis of association with hunger, thirst, sex, and pain drives. Some workers have, therefore, resorted to postulating another primary drive to account for exploratory activity. This drive has been called "curiosity" by Berlyne (1950), "exploratory drive" by Montgomery (1953a), and "exteroceptive drive" by Harlow (1953, 1953a). These terms refer to the same general class of responses that were described as "investigatory" by Pavlov (1928). Similarly, the facts of general activity have been interpreted by Hill (1956) in terms of an "activity drive." And if one were to continue this procedure of postulating new drives to account for data not easily interpretable in terms of the four primary drives as they are usually listed, one would end by postulating a "problem-solving drive" and a "play drive," and perhaps many more. Most of these interpretations in terms of new drives will, of course, be no more than redundant descriptions.

The general approach adopted in this book suggests another way of dealing with acts of exploration, problem seeking, play, and general activity. One can look upon these various activities as consisting of directed acts which have been built up in the animal's repertoire in exactly the same way as the act sequences involved in any other activity, such as eating, pedal pressing, attacking, and so on. Furthermore, the act sequences that make up exploration, play, and the like, pose the same two questions for psychologists as do all other types of directed activities. How exactly do the directed sequences develop? And, having been acquired, what are the factors that determine the occurrence of these activities? It is the first of these questions that concerns us here. Unfortunately, however, there is hardly any experimental evidence that bears directly on the problem. The following discussion, therefore, is necessarily incomplete and tentative.

It appears likely that before an adult animal is placed in an activity-measuring device it already possesses in its repertoire the responses which contribute to the various indices of general activity. All adult rats, for example, have already acquired and perfected such responses as walking, rearing, grooming, stretching, and sniffing. (However, as yet we know little about the exact way in which these responses are developed in the animal's repertoire.) Although the responses which go to make up the activity score are thus potentially available when the animal is first introduced to the apparatus, their incidence or frequency of occurrence in the activity-measuring situation is not always "spontaneous" or a matter of chance. This point can be clarified with reference to the experiments by Sheffield & Campbell and Seward & Pereboom.

Using a stabilimeter-type device, Sheffield & Campbell (1954) recorded daily for a 5-min. period, which was marked by a sudden environmental change (variations in noise and illumination), the activity of food-deprived rats. For the experimental animals the 5-min. environmental change was always followed immediately by food rations delivered directly into the cages. For the control animals the daily ration was also dropped into the cage, but the delivery of the ration was in no way associated with the period of environmental change. The results of this experiment are shown in Fig. 3. It is seen that the experimental animals showed a progressive rise in activity over the 12-day testing period. The control animals, on the other hand, showed a decline in activity over the same period. These results can be interpreted as suggesting that the increase in the incidence of the responses relevant to this type of activity score can be brought about by positive reinforcement in the form of food. When food is not associated with the responses made during the environmental change, as in the case of the control animals, there is a progressive decrease in activity; this can probably be attributed to increasing adaptation to or familiarity with the recurring situation. The reinforcing effects of food in the experimental animals apparently more than counteract the adaptation ef-

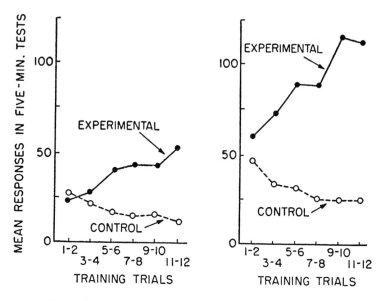

Fig. 3. General Activity as a Function of Feeding Schedule

Acquisition of activity in response to a 5-min. environmental change that regularly precedes daily feeding (experimental group) compared with adaptation to the change when it does not precede feeding (control group). The environmental change for the results on the left was cessation of a masking sound and a shift from darkness to light; the results on the right are with cessation of the sound and a shift from light to darkness. (*Source:* F. D. Sheffield and B. A. Campbell, The role of experience in the "spontaneous" activity of hungry rats. *J. comp. physiol. Psychol.,* **47,** 98.)

fect. These results suggest the possibility that much of what is termed general activity is not "spontaneous" activity in the sense of being independent of the past experiences of the animal. Rather, measures of general activity often represent specific responses whose probability of occurrence is dependent upon the same principles of reinforcement that govern other learned responses. The recent observations of Seward & Pereboom (1955) and Finger, Reid, & Weasner (1957) also point to a major role of learning in the wheel-running response as it operates in the activity-wheel situation. Seward & Pereboom conclude that "it may be fruitful to consider wheel-running not merely an index of vigor but an integrated response subject to principles of learning—not a general activity but a specific act" (1955, p. 142). Seward & Pereboom go on to suggest that the activity involved in the wheel-running itself serves as the positive reinforcer of the wheel-running response. We shall discuss the reinforcement aspect of this problem in Chapter 5.

These studies suggest that, whatever the initial responses of an animal in an activity-measuring situation, and whatever the other factors that determine over-all activity level (*see* Chaps. 8 and 9), the frequency of occurrence of the various classes of responses changes simply with repeated or continued exposure to the situation. It seems likely that some of the changes in the frequency of different classes of acts are brought about by the type of reinforcement mentioned in the above studies. The suggestion of Seward & Pereboom that in some cases activity itself can reinforce the activity-responses has an interesting implication. It implies that, under certain circumstances, left to itself, an organism's responses will become more and more channeled; that is to say, the frequency of certain classes of responses will increase in relation to that of others by virtue of the fact that the kinesthetic impulses arising from certain responses have the capacity to reinforce those responses. This means that, if we place an animal into a situation where it receives no extraneous reinforcement at all, its activity nevertheless will be channeled into specific goal-directed acts. It may be that some of the exploratory and play acts develop in this way.

## DEVELOPMENT OF WITHDRAWAL AND AGGRESSIVE ACTIVITIES

Unfortunately very little is known about the way in which the various directed acts of withdrawal and aggression develop in the repertoire of animals. Only recently have psychologists faced this problem, and here one can do no more than illustrate by a few representative studies the types of research that are now in progress.

*Avoiding pain-stimulation.* Common sense holds the view that the act of withdrawal (e.g. from noxious stimulation) is to be found ready-made, independent of prior experience, in the repertoire of all animals. However, experimental studies seem to indicate that withdrawal, like other directed acts, is acquired through experience. We have already considered the development of withdrawal and approach acts from haphazard responses in both infants and adults. Further evidence against the common-sense view is presented in a recent experiment by Melzack & Scott.

Melzack & Scott (1957) reared a group of 10 dogs from puppyhood to maturity in specially constructed cages. These cages drastically restricted the sensory experiences of the puppies; in particular the animals were screened from all environmental noxious stimulation. There was thus no way in which these "restricted" animals could learn to withdraw from noxious stimulation. At maturity the behavior of this group of animals was compared with that of their 12 normally reared (control) litter-mates. The normal animals had, of course, experienced noxious stimulation from time to time. In tests involving avoidance of a strong electric shock, noseburning, and pin-pricking, Melzack & Scott found striking differences in the speed with which the two groups learned to escape from and then to avoid noxious stimulation. At another place, Melzack (1954) has described some of the behavior of the restricted animals as follows:

> No avoidance responses were observed in the restricted dogs . . . when they were pinched, hit on the head or legs with metal rods, had their skin pierced by a large pin in the abdomen, chest or paws. . . . Each of the . . . control dogs yelped at the first of each of these manipulations, and could not be tested a second time.
>
> The restricted dogs also walked into lighted matches repeatedly. Each poked his nose into the flame, withdrew for a few inches, apparently reflexively, and then walked forward into the match again.

They continued in this manner for five days of testing, walking five or six times daily into each of two matches.

One striking feature of the restricted dogs' behavior when they were out of their cages was the high level of aimless activity. It was observed during test periods that this resulted in their frequently striking their heads against the water pipes that ran along the walls just above the floor. One dog, by actual count, struck his head against these pipes more than 30 times in a single hour. This was never observed once in the normal dogs and its unpredictability as to direction resulted a number of times in the dogs' having a paw or the tail stepped on. There was no sign whatever that the dogs felt pain when this happened, though it would have elicited a howl from a normal dog, and no attempt was made to withdraw from the place where the injury was received.[2]

Melzack (1954) and Melzack & Scott (1957) suggest, essentially, that the directed acts of escape and avoidance are not to be found ready-made in the repertoire of animals, but are acquired as a result of experiences of a certain kind. Though Melzack uses the phrase "withdrew . . . reflexively" in the above description, it does not refer to a directed escape reaction. It refers rather to "spasmodic, reflexive jerks." Melzack & Scott state that the restricted dogs "appeared unaware that they were being stimulated *by something in the environment* . . . [and] . . . made no response whatever apart from localized reflexive twitches . . ." (1957, p. 158). In view of these facts Melzack & Scott ascribe a necessary role to experience in the development of directed withdrawal responses. However, one alternative interpretation of the facts should be kept in mind. It may be that restriction in infancy led to the development of certain response patterns which prevented any possible innate withdrawal reactions to be manifested in response to noxious stimuli. This possibility has not yet been put to test. If Melzack & Scott are correct, the obvious next step is to determine exactly what type of early experiences normally contribute to the acquisition of directed escape and avoidance responses.

*Development of avoidance and aggressive responses in dogs.* Melzack (1954a) has also studied the genesis of avoidance

[2] R. Melzack, The effects of early experience on the emotional responses to pain (Unpublished Ph.D. thesis, McGill University, 1954), pp. 58–60. By permission of the author.

and aggressive acts in the dog. He reared a group of dogs from the time of weaning to maturity in specially constructed cages. The animals in these cages had only a small area to move around in and, though they received normal daylight, were unable to see outside the cages. At maturity, these dogs were taken out of the restricted environment and, after a few weeks of exposure to the normal "free" environment, were tested in standard stimulus situations. Their behavior was compared with that of their litter mates, which had been reared normally. The animals were exposed to seven innocuous but "emotion-provoking" objects, such as a toy car, a live rabbit, and a chimpanzee skull. Three categories of responses were observed: general excitement, avoidance, and aggression. Melzack found that the most frequent response of the restricted dogs was that of general excitement, but for the normally reared animals it was the avoidance response. Aggressive responses were hardly ever shown by either group of animals. Melzack also noted that the "avoidance of the free environment dogs was usually performed by a selective, clearly adaptive movement, while the occasional avoidance response of the restricted dogs involved 'mass activity' and more excitation, with the whole body participating in the response" (1954a, p. 167). About eight months after these observations, all the dogs were tested again with the same stimulus objects. On this second testing, the previously restricted animals were found to show as many avoidance responses as the "free" animals, but the latter now displayed many more aggressive responses as well.

These results show that the development of directed acts of withdrawal and aggression may require prolonged experience in an environment which provides considerable variation in sensory stimulation. The results also suggest that, normally, aggressive acts develop after avoidance acts, presumably because aggressive acts begin to "pay off" (get reinforced) only when the animals are mature and strong.

*"Treacherous attack" in chimpanzees.* Among the common aggressive responses shown by chimpanzees is one that has been described by Hebb (1946) as "treacherous attack." The

chimpanzee first shows friendly responses, such as pressing lips and abdomen against the bars of the cage and extending arms in begging gestures, but when someone (victim) comes within close range, the chimpanzee scratches, bites, or otherwise attacks him. In his study Hebb noted that, while the typical pattern of aggression in the male chimpanzee was quasi-attack (strutting, yelling, etc.) followed by a direct attack, the female chimpanzee's typical mode of aggression was the treacherous attack. Hebb states that the male "faced by an intimidating situation either fights and wins outright, or retreats. The female, on the contrary, when she finds she cannot dominate, is less likely to avoid the situation" (1946, p. 58). Yerkes (1943) considered such sex differences to be innate, and Hebb seems inclined to that view too.

However, without denying some constitutional determination of these differences, one can suggest another explanation. Male chimpanzees are larger than the females; in any random selection of young chimpanzees, the males would, on the average, be larger than the females. Therefore, in competition for food and other common incentives, the acts of direct attack are likely to be reinforced more in the males than in the females, and the act sequences involved in treacherous attack and other nondirect methods of gaining an advantage in a situation will be more highly reinforced in the female. Thus it is possible that, whatever the constitutional predisposition, the typical male and female aggressive responses will be different by virtue of differential reinforcement of the different types of (aggressive) act sequences. This interpretation is supported by the fact that not all male chimpanzees employ direct attack, nor are all females given to treachery. According to this interpretation, exceptionally small males and exceptionally large females reared in the average population would not show the typical aggressive responses of their sex.

*Constitutional factors in withdrawal and aggression.* The above studies pointing to the role of experience in the development of withdrawal and aggressive acts should not be interpreted as denying the influence of constitutional factors in their development. A recent study by Mahut (1955) clearly demonstrates the importance of this factor. Mahut observed the reactions to strange objects of over 200 pure-bred dogs belonging to 10 different breeds. She found the terriers, boxers, and bulls to be remarkably less wary and more aggressive than the other breeds, such as the dachshund and collie. Since she found no evidence of the kind that would account for the observed differences in terms of the early experience of the animals, Mahut attributes them to constitutional factors. Anastasi *et al.* (1955) submitted the scores of 73 pedigreed dogs of six breeds on a number of learning tasks to a multiple factor analysis. They interpreted the correlation matrix in terms of five factors: activity and impulsiveness, docility or responsiveness to a human trainer, manipulation, visual observation, and persistence of positional habit. Anastasi and collaborators are inclined to believe that one or more of these factors may represent breed differences. Insofar as these factors might represent the aggressiveness and withdrawal characteristics of the breeds, the study can be looked upon as pointing to the influence of the constitutional factors in determining the patterns of aggressive and withdrawal responses.

Whatever the nature of such constitutional predisposition, it seems quite clear that differences in postweaning environment cannot fully account for variations in the incidence of aggressive and avoidance activities. There is now growing interest in the role of constitutional (genetic *and* intra-uterine) factors in determining species and strain differences in aggressive and withdrawal behavior. However, the available research goes only so far as to show that certain strains of a species are more likely to engage in, for example, aggressive activities than are other strains, even when all the strains have been identically reared. This suggests that the component responses involved in aggressive acts are more highly developed in certain strains than in others. But the exact genetic and intra-uterine determinants of such differences have not yet been investigated.

*Conclusion.* There are numerous acts involved in the avoidance and aggressive activities of animals. How these acts develop in the animal's repertoire is an important question, but one that cannot be answered satisfactorily at present. In general terms we know that constitutional factors and experience, particularly early experience, are both important in the genesis of all acts. However, as yet we know almost nothing about the exact influence of specific classes of constitutional and experiential factors on the development of specific classes of withdrawal and aggressive acts. Mapping out the details in this area of psychology will require years of systematic research.

The experiments of Hebb (1946a) and Melzack (1954a) both suggest that strange or unexpected stimulation does not necessarily arouse withdrawal and avoidance responses. They have noted that their effective stimuli, which were presumed to be "fear stimuli," actually did not always lead to avoidance behavior; in some animals, they led instead to general excitement, aggressive responses, or even to friendly behavior. In Melzack's study, for example, the restricted animals on their first test showed general excitement on facing the strange stimulus patterns. Similarly, on the second test, a few months later, the free-environment animals displayed many aggressive responses in addition to the avoidance responses. The question raised by such facts is this: What factors determine whether a given strange stimulus pattern will arouse general excitement, avoidance, or aggressive responses in an animal?

A tentative answer to this question may be suggested as follows. A given strange stimulus pattern will evoke general excitement, avoidance, or aggressive responses depending on: (1) the degree of similarity between the new, strange situation and the earlier ones the animal has experienced (*see* Chap. 8 for elaboration of this point), and (2) the prepotence of the withdrawal and aggressive (or other classes of) responses in the animal. Thus, a given unexpected stimulus pattern will evoke general excitement in the infant, or an adult reared in a restricted environment (Melzack, 1954a), in which the directed withdrawal and aggressive acts have not yet developed. General excitement will also be shown by adult animals when they are faced with a situation that bears little similarity to anything the animals have experienced before. However, an adult animal, faced with only a moderately strange situation, will display either withdrawal or aggressive acts depending on which of these two types of acts are prepotent in its repertoire. The prepotent acts will presumably be those that have been, roughly speaking, reinforced more frequently than others. Such an interpretation in terms of the relative prepotence of aggressive and withdrawal acts would reasonably account for the individual differences in responses to the same situation that have been noted in a variety of studies. It also enables us to see why, in a disproportionately large number of strange situations, animals display avoidance rather than aggressive or friendly responses. Avoidance responses are likely to be more easily reinforced than aggressive or friendly responses (*see* Chap. 6), and thus are more likely to develop earlier in the animal's repertoire and attain a degree of prepotence that is seldom achieved by other types of responses.

## DEVELOPMENT OF EATING, DRINKING, AND SEXUAL ACTS

*Eating and drinking.* Little is known about the exact manner in which eating and drinking acts develop in the neonate. Undoubtedly, constitutional and learning factors both are important in determining the particular acts that develop in the various species, but there is hardly any reliable knowledge about the specific types of constitutional and experiential factors required for the development of any given class of eating and drinking acts. Studies of instrumental conditioning in adult animals suggest that almost any response that is reinforced by food (or water) will become a part of the eating (or drinking) pattern. It is likely that the development of the typical eating and drinking acts in the normal neonate involves instrumental conditioning, as suggested by Sears (1943). However, no direct evidence on this point appears available at present.

The role of experience in determining the amount and rate of eating has been the subject of a number of studies. Ghent (1951) has shown that the amount of food ingested in a half-hour period increases progressively for about seven days after rats have been switched from *ad libitum* feeding to one half-hour period of feeding each day. Apparently, the rate of eating in rats is dependent upon the feeding schedule on which the animals are maintained. This proposition is borne out by the results of a more extensive experiment by Baker (1955). He obtained measures of food intake and of time spent in eating during feeding periods of 40 to 120 min. for five groups of rats. Each group was maintained on a different deprivation schedule over a 40-day period. One group was placed on a 12-hr. schedule, the second one on 24-hr., the third on 36-hr., the fourth, the random group, was randomly subjected to all these deprivation schedules, and the fifth group, serving as a control, was fed *ad libitum*. Baker found that, in general, a progressive increase in amount eaten and time spent in eating occurred in all the experimental groups. The increase continued for a period of about 10 days. He interprets his data as showing that the adjustment to a new feeding schedule is a gradual process.

Lawrence & Mason (1955) and Reid & Finger (1955) have confirmed Baker's finding. Lawrence & Mason have in addition shown that, when animals are returned to a schedule of *ad libitum* feeding after a period of deprivation, there is a comparable period of readjustment during which the animals gradually decrease their food intake to an *"ad libitum* level." In another investigation, Lawrence & Mason (1955a) compared the food intake of a periodic group, which had been fed for 3 hr. each day at the same time, with that of an aperiodic group, which had also been fed for 3 hrs. at a time but after deprivations varying from 4 to 48 hr. in irregular succession. After 27 days of this differential treatment, the food intake of the rats in both groups became proportional to the interval of deprivation (for deprivation intervals not exceeding 24 hr.). However, the critical finding for our present problem was that, for a given deprivation interval, the periodic group ate more if tested at the regularly scheduled time of day than if tested at any other time. These studies show that the amount and rate aspects of feeding behavior are dependent, apart from the degree of deprivation, upon the experiences connected with the feeding schedule on which the animals are maintained.

Marx (1952) has shown that the rate of eating acquired during infancy can determine rate of eating at maturity. He deprived some weanling rats for 10 days, restricting them to only two brief feedings per day. During the same period, the control animals were fed *ad libitum*. All the animals were then placed on *ad libitum* feeding for 30 weeks. They were then deprived and tested for rate of eating. The data showed the experimental animals, who had been deprived in infancy, ate significantly faster than the control animals on the first day of testing. This difference disappeared by the end of the seventh day of deprivation, since even the control animals had by now increased their rate of eating. This finding by Marx is interesting in itself and also because it suggests one way of interpreting the results of an experiment on hoarding conducted by Hunt (1941) and Hunt *et al.* (1947). Hunt and his collaborators found (this finding itself has been called into question by McKelvey & Marx, 1951) that rats that had been deprived of food in infancy hoarded more pellets as adults than did adult rats that had not been deprived in infancy. Marx's results suggest that the greater hoarding by rats who suffered infantile deprivation represents one aspect of their general responses with respect to food. Both rates of eating and hoarding in the adult may be determined by some common factor associated with infantile deprivation and the related increased rate of eating (in infancy).

Most animals seem to eat periodically, with fairly uniform intervals between successive feedings. For example, it has been shown by Richter (1927) that rats eat every two to four hours when food is continuously available. While the speed of digestion and other nutritional factors undoubtedly provide the conditions necessary for making the animal eat from time to time, it appears that a feeding cycle, as it ordinarily appears in the normally reared animal, depends also upon the presence of external sensory cues that have become associated with feeding. An experiment by Baker (1953) is relevant here. He recorded the feeding responses of rats in a uniform environment, that is, with no differential sensory cues from the environment. The experimental room was kept uniformly and continuously illuminated, and a thermostat maintained the room temperature at 80° F. Food and water were always available to the animals. Under these conditions, Baker found no evidence for a two-to-four-hour or any other feeding rhythms during the 10-day observation period. Since Richter and others have reported the existence of periodic feeding cycles in the rat, Baker attributes the absence of cycles in his study to the lack of associated environmental sensory cues. It is possible that, had Baker extended his observations beyond 10 days, some sort of feeding cycle would have developed, presumably on the basis of internal sensory cues. The exact way in which the internal factors and environmental sensory cues contribute to the observed behavioral cycles is an important and complex problem, and it will be dealt with more fully in Chapter 10. For the present, we can note that an animal's past experiences with relevant sensory cues contribute to the feeding cycles as they normally appear.

*Sexual responses.* How the directed sexual acts involved in *coitus* develop in the repertoire of male and female animals is a question that cannot be definitely answered at present. It is likely that in the rat some of the component responses, such as the erection of penis, rhythmic movements of the pelvis, and ejaculation in the male, and lordosis and moving the tail to one side in the female, are reflex or chain-reflex in nature. Mounting and licking, which are displayed by the male and sometimes also by the female, are responses which seem to be acquired and well-practiced before the animal reaches sexual maturity; they are also displayed in many nonsexual situations and are, thus, not a unique aspect of coitus. The integration of various reflex and acquired responses into the directed coital acts probably results from the terminal positive reinforcement provided by the stimulation of the sensory receptors in the genital area and by orgasm (when it occurs).

This integration seems to occur quite rapidly in the lower mammals, such as the rat. A male and a receptive female rat are likely to mate on their first exposure to each other, and there is little difference in their first mating and the subsequent matings. However, this does not necessarily mean that the act of copulation is insulated from the effects of past experiences of the animal. This is shown in a study by Kagan & Beach (1953). They were able to alter the coital response of male rats by experimentally varying the rearing conditions. Kagan & Beach compared the performance in a mating situation of males that had been periodically exposed to females during prepuberal development with that of males that had not been given this experience. They found that the former group displayed the ejaculatory reaction less often than the latter group. They attribute this result to the "habits of playful wrestling, pawing, and climbing over a second animal" developed by the males that had been exposed to other females (or males) during development. They suggest that "the habit of reacting playfully toward another animal was so strongly ingrained that it persisted in adulthood and interfered with a competing tendency to copulate when the partner was a receptive female" (1953, p. 208). Hayward (1957) has shown that male rats that have been trained in infancy (21 to 36 days) to avoid a female in heat are "inhibited" in all aspects of sexual behavior in mating tests given when they are adult (120 to 129 days). Thus, in lower mammals, while the coital responses themselves appear to be chain reflex in character and while a minimum of *practice* or learning in the mating situation is required for copulation to occur, the prior experiences of the animals nevertheless seem able to alter performance in the mating situation. Experience seems to determine the directedness seen in approaching a sexual object, but erection, pelvic thrusts, and other responses involved in actual copulation appear to be reflexive and independent of the type of experiences manipulated in the above studies.

In higher mammals, the development of directed coital acts requires considerable experience of a specific type within the mating situation. Nissen's (1953) study on chimpanzees, which we discussed in Chapter 1, is relevant here. He found that, when unsophisticated male and female chimpanzees were exposed to each other from time to time, many periods of contact elapsed without any copulation. Apparently, the integration of the component responses into directed sexual acts requires increasing amounts of practice in the sexual situation itself as one moves from the lower to higher mammals. Evidence also seems to indicate that such learning is more important for the male than for the female. Beach (1947), reviewing the results of his extirpation studies, suggests that the cerebral cortex plays a more important role in the control of the sexual acts of the higher as compared with the lower mammals, and of the male as compared with the female sex throughout the mammalian species, including man. If cortical involvement is some indication of the importance of learning, Beach's generalization would seem to fit well with the results of behavioral studies reported above.

The responses involved in *homosexual activity* are not radically different from coital responses. However, the various component responses are much less likely to become integrated into directed acts in unisexual contacts. For, the reinforcing effects arising from the stimulation of the genital region in the case of homosexual mountings are likely to be much less than those arising from heterosexual contacts. Intromission is impossible when a female mounts another female; it seldom occurs, and then with great difficulty, in male-male mountings. Furthermore, it appears that, at least in lower mammals, homosexual contacts rarely, if ever, lead to orgasm. There is another factor that is also likely to contribute to the observed greater frequency of heterosexual rather than homosexual contacts. As we have seen before (Chap. 2), both males and females display, insofar as is anatomically possible, both the masculine and feminine sexual responses. There seems to be good reason to believe that the adoption of masculine and feminine roles depends, in part, on the relative dominance of the animals involved. Since the male mammals are, on the whole, larger than the females of the same species, the males are more likely to mount females than other males. Similarly, females are more likely to be mounted by males than by other females. Thus, in an unselected sample of males and females of any mammalian species, heterosexual copulations are more likely to occur than homosexual contacts. And, having occurred, the heterosexual acts are likely to be more strongly reinforced than homosexual contacts. Any interference with these normal circumstances would presumably change the proportion of heterosexual to homosexual contacts in any given sample of male and female animals. An experiment by Rasmussen (1955) is relevant here. He electrically shocked male rats whenever they tried to copulate with females. When tested later, many of the experimental males tried to copulate with males in preference to receptive females. While experimental manipulation may thus create a preference for homosexual contacts, normally a consistent preference for such contacts is most unlikely to occur. It is only in the human species that one comes across a consistent preference for homosexual contacts by some males and females. This is an exception among mammals and is probably attributable to the influence of social reinforcers contingent upon conformity to the codes of (homo-) sexual behavior that are prevalent in certain human social groups.

The frequency and techniques of *sexual self-stimulation* show considerable individual differences even in animals of the same species. While there are no experimental studies on the genesis of the directed masturbatory acts, it appears likely that they emerge from the variety of responses concerned with exploration of the body. In the course of exploring, grooming, and scratching parts of its body, an animal's responses concerned with manipulating the genital region are likely to be strongly reinforced, whether or not they result in orgasm. It is conceivable how experiences of this type may lead to the development of directed masturbatory acts. It is interesting to note that, according to Kinsey *et al.* (1953), even the human male and female, who have considerable opportunity of acquiring knowledge of masturbation through books and conversation, acquire masturbatory acts through self-exploration more than by imitation or verbal instruction. Techniques of masturbation will naturally depend on the characteristics of physique of the species, and the accidents of relevant experiences in the individual animal. McBride &

Hebb (1948) report that one of the male porpoises captive in a large tank sexually stimulated itself by placing its penis in the jet of the water intake. Other porpoises employed equally ingenious methods. It appears that both the incidence of directed masturbatory acts and the variety of techniques of masturbation increase with phylogenetic level.

While there are many studies (*see* Chap. 9) of the relation between gonadal hormones and the occurrence of sexual acts, we have as yet little knowledge about the role of gonadal hormones in the development of male and female sexual responses. Beach's (1947) review presents much of the relevant available evidence. Some experimental investigations show that castration before puberty produces a retardation or complete inhibition in the development of sexual acts. However, other observations suggest that prepuberal castration may have little or no effect on the normal development and integration of sexual acts. It should be noted in this connection that male and female chimpanzees are known to display the normal component responses of sexual acts years before puberal changes increase the flow of gonadal hormones. In an experimental investigation Warren & Aronson (1957) have shown that mounting with pelvic thrusts can be seen in adult hamsters who have been castrated and adrenalectomized before puberty. Whatever the details of the relation between gonadal hormones and sexual development, it seems quite clear that a high level of gonadal hormones is not necessary for the development of acts involved in sexual activities of the normal adult. As Kinsey *et al.* (1953) have pointed out, even where early castration does interfere with the development of sexual responses, it is difficult to say whether the observed interference is the direct consequence of lack of gonadal hormones or of changes in the pituitary and other endocrine functions brought about by the deficiency of gonadal hormones.

In ending this section it should be emphasized again that much work remains to be done before one can even begin to state the specific role of different classes of experiential and hormonal factors in the development and integration of sexual acts.

## Development of Maternal Activities

There is little reliable information about the development in the repertoire of animals of the various "maternal" activities. But the few experimental studies that are available do suggest the type of investigations that are likely to be fruitful in delineating the relevant factors and processes.

*Nest building.* When the environmental temperature is sufficiently low and nesting material is available, most rats build nests. There are some who do not. Nest building seems to be an immediate reaction to appropriate stimulus conditions and there is little difference in the building activity of rats who have never built before and those who have. These facts suggest that there is little, if any, learning-in-the-nesting-situation involved in the onset of the building activity, though this still needs to be confirmed.

The influence on nest building of experience that has occurred prior to exposure to the first nesting situation is, however, quite a separate question. A study reported briefly by Riess (1950) bears directly on this question. He reared rats from birth in such a way that they did not have any opportunity of learning to hold and transport objects. Apparently, this was achieved by rearing the animals in special cages where they had no access to transportable materials, such as food and feces. At maturity, when tested for nest building, the animals did not build nests, not even during pregnancy. This study shows that whether a nest is built does depend upon prior learning, though such learning may occur in some nonnest-building context. Lehrman (1956) has suggested that transporting food in a hoarding situation likewise may be dependent upon the habits of carrying materials acquired early in life. This suggestion is consistent with the similarities between hoarding and nest building that were pointed out earlier in this chapter. If this line of speculation is correct, animals who do not build nests should also fail to hoard. We do not know whether this is in fact so.

There are other important questions in connection with the experiential factors which determine nest building, but they have not received much attention so far. One of these questions concerns the factors that determine the choice of the location at which the nest is built. Why, for example, do rats build nests in corners rather than in open places? Another question concerns the relation between temperature and nest building. Does the warmth obtained from the nest in any way reinforce the building activity? Again, does infantile experience of warmth associated with nesting materials in any way determine adult nest building?

*Behavior at parturition.* At parturition, even the primiparous mother cleans the young by licking them, and eats the placenta. However, licking does not occur only at the time of parturition. It occurs regularly in all normally reared rats. They lick all accessible parts of their own, and sometimes each others', bodies. That the licking of the vaginal orifice and the fetuses at parturition are not intrinsically related to parturition, but simply represent the extension of licking habits acquired earlier in life, is shown in an experiment by Birch (1956). He reared one group of female rats from infancy with rubber collars around their necks so as to prevent them from licking their bodies. Another, the control, group of animals wore collars in a way that allowed them normal licking experiences. All the animals were then made pregnant. The collars of both groups were removed just before parturition, and their behavior at parturition was compared. Birch found that the latency of initial licking of the fetuses in the experimental group was abnormally long and, once the licking started, the experimental mothers typically consumed the pups. Only 5 per cent of the fetuses survived the initial postparturitive period, and even these died during the nursing period. As a contrast, 95 per cent of the pups of the control mothers survived weaning. Thus, experience in self-licking obtained prior to parturition seems to be crucial in determining the cleaning behavior of the rat mother.

Other questions now present themselves. Why is there increased vaginal licking during pregnancy and parturition, and why do the normal parturient females not eat their young? In answering these questions, it must be remembered that genital licking is a prepotent activity in all normal rats and is not peculiar to the parturition situation. However, it does increase during pregnancy and parturition. It is known that pregnant rats show a greater preference for salts than do normal rats. This increased preference for salts is likely to increase genital licking, for the discharges from the genital area appear to be rich in salts. Lehrman (1956) has suggested that greater irritability of the genital region during pregnancy would also tend to increase genital licking. The fact that normally the mother does not eat but only licks its young can be attributed to the habit of licking but not biting the soft tissues of its own genital region. As Birch's (1956) study showed, when the mother has had no prior experience in licking, it tends to eat the pups in the same way as it does the placenta.

Thus, the cleaning activity at parturition can be interpreted as the occurrence of the previously acquired licking activities under the special conditions of increased salt preference, genital irritation, and the presence of the fetuses covered by salty membranes.

*Retrieving.* As noted before, the retrieving of the young shown by the puerperal female seems to involve the same component acts of picking up, transporting, and releasing that are found in nest building and hoarding activities. It is likely that the various responses involved are quickly integrated into the unified retrieving pattern *during* the initial retrieving tests, in the same way as they are integrated into the hoarding pattern during the hoarding tests.

It will be recalled that, in the case of hoarding, it was argued that the reinforcing effects of food and entering the home cage were responsible for integrating the component responses into a unified pattern. What then is the source of reinforcement in the case of retrieving? There appears to be no evidence bearing directly on this question. However, one may conjecture that the licking of the salty membranes off the pups turns the pups into reinforcing agents. Experiences connected with nursing may also make pups desired objects. It would be interesting to determine whether puerperal female rats, which have had no experience of licking or nursing their young, will nevertheless develop the retrieving pattern. According to the above conjecture, they would not. The conjecture is supported by the fact that nulliparous, nonpregnant female rats do not, in general, retrieve the young pups offered them (Wiesner & Sheard, 1933).

Wiesner & Sheard (1933) have shown that lactating female rats will not only retrieve rat pups, but also pups of mice, rabbits, and cats. It may be that once the retrieving pattern has been established with rat pups as reinforcers, the pattern can be extended to the pups of other animals. Such generalization and "functional autonomy" of retrieving activity is also suggested by the results of Wiesner & Sheard's study of the prolongation of retrieving activity beyond the normal weaning time. They found that female rats which have littered and normally nursed only once will continue indefinitely to retrieve young pups so long as the pups, as they grow older, are repeatedly replaced by younger pups (from other females).

*Nursing.* The main features of nursing behavior of the rat are the crouching over the young and sitting still. The crouching posture is by no means peculiar to the nursing situation, for both female and male rats frequently sit in this position. However, why the puerperal female rat crouches over the young still remains a puzzle. The earlier idea that the mother crouches over the pups because they stimulate its nipples is contradicted by an experimental investigation. Wiesner & Sheard (1933) destroyed the nipples of female rats by cauterization (this also prevented the appearance of mammary swellings in many cases). Then, during the pregnancy and nursing periods, they tested the animals for the various maternal activities. They found that these animals not only nested and retrieved normally but also crouched over the young like a normal lactating mother. Thus, the adoption of the crouching position over the young cannot be attributed to the stimulation or presence of nipples, nor to the swellings of the mammary glands.

Although the stimulation of nipples is not a necessary condition for the adoption of the crouching position over the young, it may still normally contribute to the maintenance of the position and suckling the pups for long periods of time. This has been suggested by Lehrman (1956). According to him, the first suckling is fortuitous. But once the pups begin to nurse, the reduction in the turgor of the mammary glands serves to reinforce the nursing activity on the part of the mother. Normally, the stimulation of the sensitive nipples during nursing may also contribute to the maintenance of nursing activity. If this interpretation is correct, we should expect to find a gradual increase over the first few nursing days in the proportion of time the mother maintains the nursing position. There is some indication (Wiesner & Sheard, 1933) that this may be so.

In concluding this chapter, perhaps it should be pointed out again that the general argument made here recognizes the existence of constitutionally determined species, strain, and individual differences in the readiness with which various activities develop in the repertoire of different animals. However, learning (or the residual effect of prior experience) is considered to be a necessary factor in the emergence of goal-directed activities from the "innately" given or already acquired component responses of the animal. Of course, the precise constitutional, morphological, and experiential factors that determine the differences in the component responses relevant to various motivational activities remain to be determined. But the results of experimental analyses of motivational activities so far available seem to be consistent with the general point of view adopted here.

# Chapter 5

# An Analysis of Reinforcers

In the preceding chapters we ascribed a pivotal role to reinforcement. The development of all goal-directed activities was attributed to the action of reinforcers. This chapter is concerned with reinforcement itself; it deals with the problem of the essential nature of reinforcing events.

## DEFINITION OF TERMS

A brief discussion of the definition of important terms will help to avoid confusion in approaching this rather complicated problem.

### POSITIVE AND NEGATIVE REINFORCEMENT

There is a certain ambiguity about the term "reinforcement" in its current psychological usage. Skinner, working within a general conditioning framework, means by reinforcement an experimental procedure of presenting a "certain kind of stimulus in a temporal relation with either a stimulus or response" (1938, p. 62). If the tendency of the response to be repeated is strengthened, Skinner calls the presented stimulus a reinforcing stimulus. At the opposite pole, as it were, from this procedural definition of reinforcement is the theoretical one by Hull. Hull (1943) defined "primary reinforcement" as "diminution of a need" or drive reduction. More recently, other drive theorists have moved back toward redefining reinforcement in more empirical terms, with no men-

tion of need reduction. Thus, Dollard & Miller (1950) speak
in terms of events that strengthen the tendency of a response
to be repeated, without any reference to the hypothetical
processes which bring about this strengthening.

In attempting to clear up some of the confusion arising
from the ambiguity and vagueness that surrounds this term,
Meehl (1950) has defined reinforcement as the presentation
of a reinforcer. He thus makes "reinforcer" rather than "reinforcement" the basic concept. This change in emphasis is well
suited to the plan of this chapter. Therefore, it seems desirable
to accept Meehl's definition that *positive reinforcement is the
presentation of a positive reinforcer.* Correspondingly, one
can define *negative reinforcement* as *the presentation of a
negative reinforcer.* As used here, the term "reinforcement"
subsumes both positive and negative reinforcement, and the
term "reinforcer" subsumes both positive and negative reinforcers.

Meehl (1950) has defined a (positive) reinforcer as a stimulus change that increases the strength of a preceding response.
In order to avoid the unnecessary, though plausible, implication that certain "connections" inside the organism are
affected by a reinforcer, Seward (1950) has reworded Meehl's
definition as follows: "When a stimulus change X, following
a response R to a situation S, increases the probability of R to
S, X is called a [positive] *reinforcer* and its presentation is
called a *reinforcement.*" A slight modification of Seward's
definition will make it suitable for the present discussion.

A *positive reinforcer* is defined here *as an event* (*i.e. stimulus change) the occurrence of which increases the over-all or
average habit strength of a given response* (or, simply,
strengthens the response). Correspondingly, *negative reinforcer* is defined as *an event the occurrence of which decreases the over-all habit strength of a given response* (or,
simply, *extinguishes,* or weakens, the response). The term
"habit strength" is used here to refer generally to any of the
commonly employed indices of learning, such as changes in
the probability of occurrence of a response, and in its amplitude, latency, and resistance to extinction (*see* Chap. 6).

Three points should be noted about these definitions. First, unlike Meehl's and Seward's definitions, the present ones do not specify that the event, in order to be an effective positive or negative reinforcer, must occur *after* the response. It is true that reinforcers are most effective when they occur (soon) after the response, and no clear-cut evidence for the existence of "backward" reinforcing effects has so far been found. However, the possibility of reinforcing effects of events occurring before the response must be kept open; and, at any rate, there is nothing to be gained by specifying temporal relations in the definition of a reinforcer. For these reasons, temporal relations between the response and the reinforcing events are not mentioned in the above definitions. Second, the term "over-all" in the definitions serves to exclude the relatively transient changes in response brought about by fatigue, drugs, deprivation, and the like. The intention here is to reserve the term reinforcer for such events as those that change the average, long-range habit strength of a response, disregarding the transitory changes brought about by short-term variations in other factors affecting behavior. Third, the proposed definitions do not imply anything about the nature of events or mechanisms that result from the operation of reinforcers. It is not implied that positive reinforcers necessarily reduce needs, or are subjectively pleasant, nor that negative reinforcers necessarily increase drive, or are subjectively unpleasant.

It should be noted that the above definition of a negative reinforcer is quite unorthodox. The currently accepted definition views a negative reinforcer as an event (e.g. loud noise, electric shock) the *removal* of which increases habit strength, as opposed to the positive reinforcer or event (e.g. food, sexual contact) the *presentation* of which increases habit strength. Such a definition of negative reinforcer is based on the common belief that decrease in habit strength (extinction) is obtained by withholding positive reinforcement and not by the presentation of some sort of an "extinguisher." Now that the existence of active "extinguishers" has been demonstrated (*see* below), we need a term to denote the types of events that actively reduce response probability. "Negative reinforcer" appears to be the most logical and convenient term for this purpose. The adoption of this term to signify something different from its currently accepted meaning may lead to some temporary confusion, but this change appears to be necessary and will aid in clarifying certain aspects of the problem of reinforcement. Where necessary, one can employ the term "punishment" to designate what has traditionally been called a negative reinforcer. Thus, we can define *punishment* as *an event the removal of which is positively reinforcing*, and *reward* as *an event the presentation of which is positively reinforcing*.

The meaning of the term "incentive," as commonly employed, overlaps with the meaning of reinforcer, but the two terms do not have exactly the same connotations. Frequently, "incentives," events such as spanking and increasing wages, for example, may be presumed to strengthen or weaken responses, but may in fact not do so. However, a reinforcer, by definition, is an event that has been shown to have reinforcing effects for a given response. Thus, an incentive is an event that is thought of as a possible reinforcer for a response, but whose actual effectiveness as a reinforcer has not been determined. One can thus define an *incentive* as *an event that is presumed to be a reinforcer for a given response*. If the presentation of an incentive is presumed to increase response strength, the incentive may be called *positive;* if it is presumed to decrease response strength, the incentive may be called *negative*. Admittedly, this definition of "incentive" is a broad one, but it seems correctly to describe the sense in which the term is currently used.

To facilitate reference, all the above definitions may be summarized as follows:

*Reinforcer:* An event the occurrence of which changes the overall habit strength of a given response. If it increases habit strength it is a *positive reinforcer;* if it diminishes habit strength, it is a *negative reinforcer*.

_Reinforcement:_ The procedure of presenting a reinforcer in close
temporal contiguity with a given response. It is positive or
negative depending on the type of reinforcer employed.

_Reinforcing effects:_ The effect of reinforcement on habit strength.
A _positive reinforcing effect_ refers to an increase in habit
strength, and a _negative reinforcing effect_ to a decrease in
habit strength (extinction).

_Reward and punishment:_ When a positive reinforcing effect depends upon the presentation of an event, the event is a
_reward;_ when a positive reinforcing effect depends upon the
removal of an event, the event is a _punishment._

_Incentive:_ An event that is presumed to be a reinforcer for a given
response, but which has not yet been shown to be a reinforcer of the response. It is _positive_ or _negative_ depending
upon whether it is presumed to increase or decrease habit
strength.

## PRIMARY AND SECONDARY REINFORCERS

The customary distinction between primary and secondary
reinforcers will be followed in the present discussion. A reinforcer (positive or negative) is said to be _primary_ if its reinforcing (positive or negative) capacity is not dependent upon
prior association with any specific event, and _secondary_ if the
capacity is acquired through association with some other
(primary or secondary) reinforcer.

We can now begin considering the nature of reinforcers.
For reasons that will become apparent, this problem has usually been formulated as "Why do positive reinforcers increase
habit strength?" rather than as "Why do negative reinforcers
lead to extinction of the response?" Most of the following
discussion, therefore, revolves around positive reinforcers
rather than negative reinforcers.

## WHY DO REINFORCERS REINFORCE?

Generally speaking, it is true that we tend to do things that
lead to pleasure and avoid doing things that lead to pain. This
observation has been the basis of much theorizing by philoso-
phers and psychologists. An account of the origin and development of the various opinions and controversies is to be

found in a comprehensive review by Postman (1947). Bain (1868) and Spencer (1872) held the view that positive reinforcers strengthen responses because they are pleasurable and negative reinforcers extinguish them because they are painful. While they did speculate about the physiological mechanisms by which pleasure strengthens and pain extinguishes responses, they failed to give an independent and objective definition of "pleasure" and "pain." Thorndike (1911) replaced pleasure and pain by satisfaction and discomfort, and attributed strengthening and extinction of responses to "satisfiers" and "annoyers." But, unlike Bain and Spencer, he attempted to define satisfaction and discomfort in objective terms: "By a satisfying state of affairs is meant one which the animal does nothing to avoid, often doing such things as to attain and preserve it. By a discomforting state of affairs is meant one which the animal avoids and abandons" (1911, p. 245). Though more suited to psychological analysis than were the views of Bain and Spencer, Thorndike did not present any testable hypothesis concerning the essential nature of satisfiers and annoyers. It remained for Hull (1943) to propose an explicit hypothesis concerning the source of the reinforcing properties of (positive) reinforcers, and it is his position that is taken as the starting point of this discussion.

DRIVE-REDUCTION HYPOTHESIS

Hull (1943) starts with the premise that optimal conditions of certain commodities and occurrences, such as air, water, food, temperature, and intactness of bodily tissue, are necessary for survival of the organism. When such commodities and occurrences deviate from the optimum, that is, when the "homeostatic" balance is upset, a state of *need* is said to exist in the organism. Hull then considers any event that reduces a need to be a positive reinforcer. For example, eating, drinking, and escape will serve as positive reinforcers for, respectively, hungry, thirsty, and noxious-stimulation-exposed animals. Thus, according to Hull, positive reinforcers increase habit strength because they reduce needs. Inasmuch as it can be subjected to empirical testing procedures, the concept of need reduction is better suited to psychological analysis than the concepts of pleasure or satisfaction.

Hull (1943) considered need to be essentially the "receptor discharge" or afferent impulses arising from homeostatic imbalance in bodily processes necessary for survival. Many of Hull's former colleagues, for example, Miller & Dollard (1941) and Mowrer (1946), prefer the more general term "tension," or "drive," to "need." The term *drive* emphasizes the stimulus, tension, or receptor discharge aspects of need without linking it specifically to functions necessary for survival, such as digestion, respiration, and escaping harm. Thus Dollard & Miller (1950) and Wolpe (1950) consider all strong stimuli, whether internal or external, as drives. Whatever the exact definition of drive employed by the various drive theorists, they all agree that "homeostatic drives" (strong stimuli accompanying states of hunger, thirst, sex, or pain) are the fundamental or primary ones. They also agree with Hull in regarding the reduction in drives as the most potent positive reinforcing condition. Events that increase habit strength and yet do not reduce primary drives are presumed either to reduce "learned or secondary drives" (Mowrer, 1939; Dollard & Miller, 1950) or to be "secondary positive reinforcers" (Hull, 1943).

It should be noted that, in general, drive-reduction theorists do not recognize, at least not explicitly, the existence of any negative reinforcers. Thus, while drive reduction is considered as a positive reinforcer, increase in drive is not taken to be a negative reinforcer. According to drive theorists, extinction of a response takes place when the occurrences of the response are not accompanied by a positive reinforcer. Presence of positive reinforcers leads to increase in the habit strength of a response; absence of positive reinforcers leads to its extinction. Thus, for drive theorists, both increases and decreases in habit strength are related to positive reinforcers (among other factors), and no active negative reinforcers are postulated.

There seems to be abundant evidence to show that events that reduce drives tend also to be positive reinforcers; events that reduce or terminate drive stimuli tend to increase habit strength. Thus, eating food acts as a positive reinforcer for a hungry animal, drinking water for a thirsty animal, coitus for a sex-deprived animal, and escape from, or termination of, stimulation for an animal exposed to noxious stimulation. Furthermore, it appears, though this point is by no means settled, that the degree of drive reduction is directly related to the extent of the positive reinforcing effect of a positive reinforcer. The positive reinforcing effect of food is negligible when the animal is not hungry; termination of strong noxious stimulation, in general, increases habit strength more than does termination of weak noxious stimulation. The psychological literature contains numerous experiments which leave no doubt that drive reduction is a dependable, and often a potent, positive reinforcer.

However, all these investigations do not by any means prove that drive reduction is the essential characteristic that makes an event a positive reinforcer. Whether drive reduction is necessary for obtaining an increase in habit strength is an important question, but one which is far from settled. In general, drive theorists are inclined to believe that drive reduction is the only primary positive reinforcer. However, other investigators have other views concerning the essential nature of positive reinforcers. The situation is complicated by the fact that the evidence which apparently supports the drive-reduction hypothesis is open to other interpretations as well. For example, the type of evidence mentioned above has been used by other psychologists to support their own hypotheses concerning the crucial feature which makes positive reinforcers increase habit strength. We turn now to a consideration of these alternate hypotheses.

## Young's Hedonic-Quality Interpretation

For about three decades now Young has been engaged in experimental studies of what introspectionist psychology called "affective processes." Young has reviewed (1948) his extensive work and has brought out (1949, 1955) its theoretical significance with clarity and force. The point in

Young's writings that concerns us here is his hypothesis that "an organism behaves so as to maximize positive affective arousal (delight, enjoyment) and to minimize negative arousal (distress)" (1955, p. 233). He considers these hedonic or affective processes, ranging in gradations from pleasant to unpleasant, as the primary, if not the essential, features of all reinforcers. Thus, according to Young, positive reinforcers like food, water, and pain termination increase habit strength not because they reduce drives but because animals find them enjoyable. He admits a positive correlation between what animals enjoy and what they need, but does not think that this is a one-to-one relation.

By way of an example of the empirical support marshaled by Young, one can refer to a recent experiment by Young & Shuford (1955). They observed rats in an apparatus consisting of a starting box, a goal box, and a 6-ft. alley connecting the two boxes. The goal box contained sucrose solution. On reaching the goal box each rat was allowed contact with the solution for 1 sec. The passage of rats through the alley was timed. Young & Shuford found that the approach response of well-nourished rats that, at the time of testing, were neither hungry nor thirsty could be positively reinforced by the sucrose solution. The rats' speed of running increased with repeated daily contact with sucrose and decreased when sucrose was replaced by distilled water. Also, the speed of approach varied directly with the concentration of sucrose solution. Young & Shuford argue that in this case the reinforcing effects of sucrose could not be dependent upon drive reduction, since the animals were not deprived in any way. They attribute the obtained increase in habit strength to the affectively pleasant taste of sucrose. Some substances which completely lack nutritional value but are affectively pleasant have also been shown to be positive reinforcers. For example, Beebe-Center et al. (1948) and Sheffield & Roby (1950) have obtained positive reinforcing effects from saccharin, a sweet-tasting (pleasant) substance which passes through the body unaltered and is thus completely nonnourishing. A study of the positive reinforcing effects of morphine is also relevant here. H. D. Beach (1957, 1957a) has shown that injecting morphine into a morphine-addicted rat can have reinforcing effects which do not depend upon the relief of withdrawal symptoms. These reinforcing effects, reflected in a preference for the place associated with the relief, continue for a few hours after the administration of morphine and the consequent (immediate) drive reduction in the form of the relief of withdrawal symptoms. He attributes such reinforcing effects to the "euphoric" state that, according to human drug addicts, outlasts the reduction in withdrawal distress. All these facts support Young's hypothesis. Furthermore, since all dependable drive reducers (e.g. food, water, pain avoidance) are also generally affectively pleasant, the evidence cited in support of the drive-reduction hypothesis can be used equally well to support the hedonic hypothesis of Young.

The hedonic hypothesis is perhaps as "right" as some of the other views concerning the essential feature of reinforcers. Yet, somehow, it has been less productive than other current interpretations. Young employs subjective terminology. It is true that Young defines hedonic qualities with reference to approach and avoidance behavior of animals (1955, p. 194); however, he does not propose any theoretical relation between enjoyment-distress and approach-avoidance or any other objectively observable condition. He does not state any empirically meaningful definitions of enjoyment and distress. Young's hedonic hypothesis thus remains untestable. Drive theorists, on the other hand, are careful to give objective reference to the concept of drive reduction. They say that positive reinforcers increase habit strength because they reduce drives, and one can determine whether they in fact reduce drives by some *other* (independent) operations, such as stomach contractions, level of blood sugar, or activity. It is likely that the problems raised for the drive-reduction hypothesis by the experiments of Young and his colleagues would have had more telling effect on drive theory if Young's theoretical formulation did not suffer from subjective terminology and the lack of objective definitions of its central concepts. The recent work of Sheffield and his collaborators, described below, which does not suffer from these handicaps, has undoubtedly been more effective in its criticism of the drive-reduction interpretation of positive reinforcers.

## CONSUMMATORY-RESPONSE HYPOTHESIS

When eating food, for example, is said to be a positive reinforcer, the reference may be to one or both of two separate events: (1) ingestion itself, or taking food into the mouth, savoring, chewing, and the like, and (2) hunger reduction which takes place after the food has reached the stomach. Drive theorists have stressed drive (hunger) reduction as the main source of reinforcement. Sheffield and his collaborators (1950, 1951, 1954), on the other hand, ascribe the reinforcing effects of eating to the consummatory responses of savoring, chewing, and the like. Consummatory responses are normally a part of eating, drinking, coitus, and avoiding, and it is the elicitation of such consummatory responses rather than their drive-reducing effects which Sheffield and his collaborators consider to be the essential feature of positive reinforcers. For example, according to them, certain stimulus patterns elicit the consummatory ingestion response and "this reinforces [positively] instrumental learning in proportion to the strength of the ingestion response" (1954, p. 353).

The reference experiments for the consummatory-response hypothesis are to be found in a number of studies by Sheffield and his collaborators. In one study, Sheffield & Roby (1950) performed three experiments, each involving a different type of response. In each case the response was instrumental in obtaining access to a nonnourishing sweet saccharin solution. In all cases, the saccharin solution was found to be a potent positive reinforcer for hungry rats. The results of one of these experiments, which required the learning of a T-maze, are presented in Fig. 4. The reinforcing effect of saccharin is evident in all of the three measures (correct choices, time, and rate of ingestion) of habit strength employed. Since saccharin has no food value, the authors felt that these results could not be explained in terms of drive reduction. Sheffield

& Roby ascribed the obtained increase in habit strength to the consummatory responses elicited by the taste of saccharin. However, since they used hungry rats, it is possible that the saccharin solution, because of its volume, reduced drive stimuli (stomach contractions). Therefore, drive reduction may have operated as a positive reinforcer instead of, or as well as, consummatory responses.

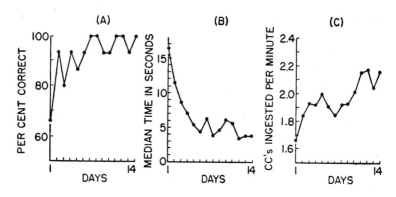

FIG. 4. SACCHARIN SOLUTION AS A POSITIVE REINFORCER

Acquisition in a T-maze with saccharin solution (1.30 grams per liter) as reward. The panels show, respectively: (A) frequency of correct choice; (B) time needed to reach correct side; and (C) rate of ingestion of solution in the goal box. (*Source:* F. D. Sheffield and T. B. Roby, Reward value of a non-nutritive sweet taste. *J. comp. physiol. Psychol.*, 43, 478.)

In a better-controlled experiment, Sheffield, Wulff, & Backer (1951) studied, in male rats, the possible positive reinforcing effects of sexual stimulation without sex-drive reduction through ejaculation. If the consummatory responses involved in sexual stimulation could be shown to increase habit strength in the absence of ejaculation and corresponding drive reduction, it would be an argument in favor of the consummatory-response hypothesis. The instrumental response in this experiment was that of running a 32-in. runway ending in a 4-in. hurdle, which led into the goal box. On the basis of preliminary tests of copulatory activity (without ejaculation), the animals were divided into three groups, experimental and control, matched with respect to copulatory activity, and a third group of noncopulators. After completing each run, the experimental animals found a female in heat in the goal box, the control animals found a male, and half the noncopulators found a male, and the other half, a female. The animals were removed from the goal box after two intromissions or after 2 min. In no case was the animal allowed to copulate to ejaculation. (Normally, the male rat mounts and establishes intromission about a dozen times before the first ejaculation.)

The results are presented in Fig. 5. It can be seen that the instrumental response of running and crossing the hurdle was reinforced more in the case of experimental animals than in the case of the noncopulators and the control animals. The fact that the control-group animals also showed some increase in habit strength is attributed by the experimenters to the fact that these animals often attempted copulations with their male companions. Since certain components of the consummatory responses are the same in male-female and male-male mountings, the latter would be expected to have some reinforcing effects. Thus, the consummatory responses involved in copulation with females in heat and in attempted copulation with males were found to increase habit strength in the absence of any drive reduction in the form of ejaculation.

One can argue that copulatory activity by itself, in the absence of ejaculation, relaxes muscular tension and thus is drive- or tension-reducing. To this possible attack the experimenters' answer is that the effect occurring most closely after the instrumental response (running) is an increase, not a decrease, in tension; even if there is any tension reduction in the absence of ejaculation, it must come after an initial increase in tension. Therefore, the time interval between any such possible tension reduction and the instrumental response of running would be too long for tension reduction to increase habit strength. Sheffield et al. conclude that drive *induction* or the "elicitation of a dependable and prepotent consummatory response is the critical factor in the reinforcement of instru-

mental responses rather than drive-reduction or beneception"
(1951, p. 8).

## DRIVE-REDUCTION vs. CONSUMMATORY-RESPONSE
### INTERPRETATIONS

The experiments of Sheffield and his colleagues, showing
that consummatory responses can apparently serve as positive
reinforcers in the absence of drive reduction, have evoked an
answer from drive theorists. Their answer consists of two

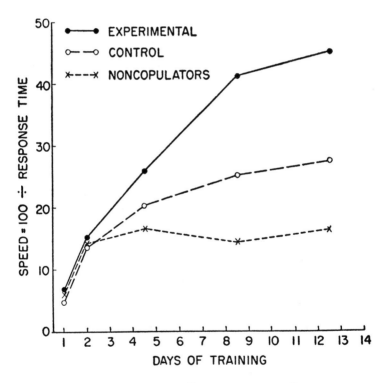

FIG. 5. REINFORCING VALUE OF COPULATION WITHOUT EJACULATION

Experimental animals found a female in the goal box, control animals
found a male, and noncopulators found one or the other but never attempted
to copulate. (*Source:* F. D. Sheffield, J. J. Wulff, and R. Backer, Reward
value of copulation without sex drive reduction. *J. comp. physiol. Psychol.*,
**44,** 5.)

parts. First, in a series of ingenious experiments they have shown that drive reduction can reinforce in the absence of consummatory responses. These experiments, first started by Hull, Livingston, Rouse, & Barker (1951), try to separate the drive-reducing events from consummatory responses. Kohn (1951), Berkun, Kessen, & Miller (1952), Miller & Kessen (1952), Coppock & Chambers (1954), Smith & Duffy (1955), Chambers (1956), and Miller, Sampliner, & Woodrow (1957), have been able to show that nourishment injected directly into the stomach or blood stream, and therefore involving no consummatory responses, can serve as a positive reinforcer.

In the Miller & Kessen (1952) experiment, for example, plastic fistulas were sewn into stomachs of rats. Then the rats were given trials in a T-maze, receiving 14 cc. of enriched milk on one, the "correct," side of the maze and 14 cc. of isotonic saline on the other side. One group received milk or saline through the fistula directly into the stomach, one group drank the milk or saline from a dish, and a third group drank the milk or saline 7 min. 35 sec. after making the choice—7 min. 35 sec. being the time required to complete the injection in the case of the animals in the first group. The main results of the experiment are presented in Fig. 6. It shows that all groups learned to go to the milk side of the T-maze; that is, the correct response was positively reinforced. The fact that the stomach-injection group learned to make the correct choices is interpreted by Miller & Kessen as evidence that hunger-drive reduction, in the absence of consummatory responses, was sufficient to reinforce the instrumental response. It is clear that consummatory responses were not necessary for the obtained reinforcing effects. However, the fact that mouth-fed rats, whether or not they were in the delay group, showed greater increase in habit strength than the injection animals suggests that the consummatory responses normally make at least some contribution to the increase in habit strength brought about by feeding. This is where drive theorists resort to argument.

And this argument constitutes the second part of the attack of drive theorists on the consummatory-response hypothesis.

The greater reinforcing effect of milk received through the mouth is interpreted by Miller & Kessen as resulting from the acquired or secondary positive reinforcing value of consummatory responses. It is argued, in effect, that the primary positive reinforcer is drive reduction; however, owing to the

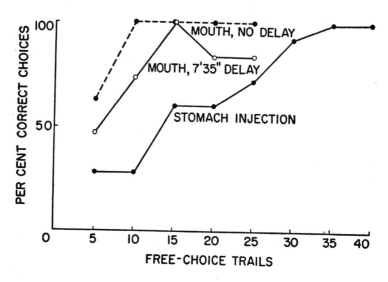

Fig. 6. Positive Reinforcing Effects of Intragastric Injections of Food

Percentage of choices to the correct (milk) side on free-choice trials. After making five successive correct choices on the eleventh to fifteenth trials, one animal in the Mouth, Delay Group reverted to a consistent position habit on the incorrect side. This one animal contributed all the errors made by this group after the first ten trials. (*Source:* N. E. Miller and M. L. Kessen, Reward effects of food via stomach fistula compared with those of food via mouth. *J. comp. physiol. Psychol.,* 45, 560.)

close association between consummatory responses and drive reduction, consummatory responses become secondary reinforcers. Thus, as in their experiment, when milk is taken through the mouth, it increases habit strength by virtue of both drive reduction and the secondary reinforcing value of consummatory responses; the combined effect of these two reinforcers is greater than that of drive reduction alone.

Miller & Kessen go on to argue that the results of the experiments of Sheffield and his colleagues are the outcome of such secondary reinforcing effects.

Sheffield and collaborators counter by pointing out that the operation of secondary reinforcers, as described by drive theorists, cannot account for their results. In their paper describing the experiments with saccharin, Sheffield & Roby (1950) examine and discard the possibility that the positive reinforcing value of sweet saccharin solution is acquired through association with primary drive reduction. They argue as follows:

For one thing, previously experienced sweet tastes (e.g., rat's milk, conversion of starch to sugar in the mouth, etc.) are very unlikely to have been as sweet as the concentrated saccharine solution used. Thus the sweet taste used would be at an unfavorable point on the generalization gradient as an acquired reward stimulus if we make the usual assumption that the generalization gradient falls in either direction from the stimulus intensity reinforced. Moreover, the sweet taste did not lose its reward value throughout the three experiments, with the ingestion of thousands of ccs. of saccharine solution and no doubt millions of instrumental tongue movements. Since the visual, kinesthetic, tactile, and gustatory pattern accompanying this ingestion in all three experiments (drinking from a glass tube protruding from a visible graduated cylinder through quarter-inch wire mesh) received no primary reinforcement, it would be expected that any *acquired* reward value of a sweet taste would have extinguished for this pattern.[1]

Again, in their study (1951) demonstrating the positive reinforcing effects of nondrive-reducing copulatory activity, Sheffield *et al.* point out that the rats in their experiment had never ejaculated, either before or during the experiment. Therefore, no association between copulatory activity and drive reduction could have taken place, and thus no secondary reinforcing value acquired by the consummatory responses. And yet the consummatory responses did serve as positive reinforcers.

It appears that Sheffield and collaborators have successfully defended themselves with these arguments. At least so

[1]F. D. Sheffield and T. B. Roby, Reward value of a non-nutritive sweet taste, *J. comp. physiol. Psychol.*, 43, p. 479.

far as copulation is concerned, consummatory responses do not seem to acquire their reinforcing value through association with drive reduction. Whether or not the reinforcing value of the consummatory responses involved in eating and drinking is also independent of association with drive reduction, only further experimental work can show.

The net result of this controversy between drive theorists and Sheffield and collaborators can be summarized in two tentative propositions. (1) Neither drive reduction nor the elicitation of consummatory responses is a necessary property of positive reinforcers. (2) Either of (a) drive reduction and (b) the elicitation of consummatory responses has the capacity to act as a primary reinforcer. Whether or not these conclusions are explicitly accepted by drive theorists, the experimental results on which they are based are beginning to lead to revisions of the drive-reduction hypothesis. For example, Seward (1956) has attempted to incorporate the consummatory-response hypothesis within a slightly extended drive-reduction interpretation. Such efforts at rapprochement, though intriguing and valuable, need not detain us here. Recently, there have emerged many other sources of data which are relevant to the problem of the nature of reinforcers. For the most part, these studies have tended to show that certain events which are neither consummatory responses nor drive reducers can also serve as primary reinforcers. One must, therefore, consider these studies before attempting any general formulation about the essential nature of reinforcers.

EXTEROCEPTIVE STIMULUS PATTERNS AS POSITIVE
REINFORCERS

The work of Harlow and his colleagues (for a review, see Harlow, 1953) has been referred to before. A number of their studies have been concerned with the positive reinforcing effects of exteroceptive stimulation. The study that is particularly relevant here was carried out by Butler (1953). He trained rhesus monkeys on a color-discrimination problem. Each monkey, sitting in a dimly illuminated box with opaque walls, was faced with two differently colored cards. The "correct" choice (light pressure on the card of a given color) was followed by an opportunity for the animal to look through a window for a 30-sec. period. This "visual exploration" of the part of the laboratory seen through the window was sufficient to reinforce the correct discriminative response. The animals learned the discrimination problem rapidly, as seen in Fig. 7. Furthermore, the animals maintained their performance at a high level of efficiency with visual exploration as the only reinforcer. Butler argues that the reinforcing properties of visual exploration are not derived from "other motivational or drive states." In a similar experiment, Montgomery & Segall (1955) have shown that rats can acquire discrimination habits when the correct choice is followed by an opportunity to explore a large maze. In Jaynes' (1956) imprinting experiment, discussed in Chapter 3, it was found

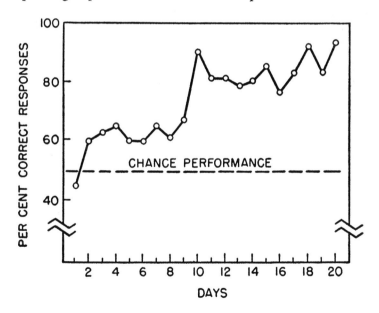

FIG. 7. VISUAL EXPLORATION AS A POSITIVE REINFORCER

Discrimination learning to visual-exploration incentives. (*Source:* R. A. Butler, Discrimination learning by rhesus monkeys to visual-exploration motivation. *J. comp. physiol. Psychol.,* 46, 96.)

that a moving stimulus by itself strengthened the "following response" of chicks. Visual exploration may well turn out to have been the reinforcer for the chicks in that experiment. Auditory stimulation can have similar positive reinforcing effects. Butler (1957a) successfully trained monkeys on a discrimination problem by making a 15-sec. exposure to sounds emitted from a monkey colony contingent upon the making of the correct response.

Exploratory situations of the type employed by Butler and Montgomery & Segall provide a rather complex and uncontrollable form of stimulus patterns. Some recent investigations have sought to study the possible reinforcing effects of more restricted and manageable forms of exteroceptive stimulation. For example, in an experiment by Marx, Henderson, & Roberts (1955), rats were tested in the dark in a modified Skinner box. The bar of the box, when pressed, closed a mercury switch silently, without a click. The top half of the box was separated from the lower half by a diffusion plate and contained one 7.5-w. and one 15-w. bulb. Each animal was given a 30-min. test period daily. On the first few days, bar pressing was not followed by any new stimulation, and the operant (pretest, nonreinforced) level of bar pressing was noted. Then the mercury switch was connected to the bulbs, so that pressing the bar resulted in a mild illumination for a few seconds. The rate of bar pressing on the first test session (bar pressing followed by illumination) was compared with that on the last pretest session. The rate on the test session was significantly higher. Marx et al. attribute the results to the positive reinforcing power of mild light stimulation. After carefully considering it, they discard the possibility that the obtained results were "due to some kind of unrecognized adventitious establishment of secondary reinforcing powers in connection with light stimulation" (1955, p. 75), and suggest the possibility that "stimulus change or novelty" may serve as a positive reinforcer in its own right.

Other experimenters have obtained results similar to those of Marx et al. For example, Kish & Antonitis (1956) discovered that such stimuli as microswitch clicks and relay noises had positive reinforcing properties. In another experiment Kish (1955) found that dim illumination following a bar-contact response reinforced the response in mice. Employing a group which received the illumination at random (not contiguous with the response), he was able to show that the increase in general activity resulting from light stimulation was not responsible for the observed increase in the rate of response. He concludes that illumination per se was the reinforcer. Kling, Horowitz & Delhagen (1956) have confirmed these results with a more stringently controlled test. Their experimental design involved pairs of animals which had been equated with respect to operant rate of responding. Hurwitz (1956) has demonstrated that the rate of bar pressing increases when accompanied by onset of light, but is no different from operant rate when pressing the bar either *turns off* the light or produces no change in illumination. Similar results have been obtained in monkeys by Moon & Lodahl (1956). Thus, light illumination has been shown to have positive reinforcing properties in the absence of any association with drive reduction or consummatory responses. One point to note is that in all these studies it was mild light stimulation (presented in relative darkness) which increased habit strength. Strong illumination, on the other hand, serves as a punishment for rats, and the *removal* of strong light has often been used as a positive reinforcer (e.g. Flynn & Jerome, 1952; Kaplan, 1952). Apparently, at least for rats, only the onset of mild illumination can serve as a positive reinforcer.

Before concluding this section, reference should be made to certain related experiments which also show that increase in sensory stimulation can sometimes have positive reinforcing effects. Harlow, Harlow, & Meyer (1950) found that monkeys could be trained to find the solution to a mechanical puzzle in the absence of reinforcers such as food or water. They attribute the observed increase in the habit strength of the correct response to the reinforcing effects of manipulation per se. In another experiment Harlow & McLearn (1954) have shown that opportunity to manipulate mechanical puzzles can positively reinforce performance on color-discrimination problems. An experiment by Kagan & Berkun (1954) has demonstrated the reinforcing effects of general activity. They found that the response probability of lever pressing in the rat could be increased when the only reinforcement consisted in allowing the animal to run in an activity wheel following each lever pressing. In all these experiments it is not clear to what extent the reinforcing effects depend upon the visual, tactual, and other types of exteroceptive stimulation and to what extent upon proprioceptive stimulation arising from the muscular activity involved in manipulation and running. Whatever the exact source of the observed reinforcing effect, it is undoubtedly accompanied by some increase in sensory stimulation.

If drive is equivalent to sensory stimulation or receptor discharge, then the above findings pose a problem for the drive-reduction interpretation of the nature of positive reinforcers. The experiments with exteroceptive stimulation and activity show that, at least within limits, *increase* in stimulation (drive) has positive reinforcing effects. Both McClelland (1951) and Hebb (1955) have pointed to numerous daily occurrences where responses leading to increase in stimulation and tension are positively reinforced. A ride on the noisy, lurching roller coaster, fascination of the murder story, and exposing oneself to dangerous situations are examples of events that increase tension or drive and, at the same time, appear to serve as positive reinforcers of the instrumental responses leading to them. Whatever the interpretation, it seems clear that, up to a certain point, an increase in sensory stimulation is a positive reinforcer.

## POSITIVE AND NEGATIVE REINFORCING EFFECTS OF INTRACRANIAL STIMULATION

Some years ago, Olds & Milner (1954) published a paper reporting a hitherto unsuspected phenomenon. They discovered that electrical stimulation of numerous places in the brain produced reinforcing effects on the behavior of rats. They implanted bipolar needle electrodes at various points in the subcortical brain of the animals. After recovery from the chronic implantation, each rat was tested in a modified Skinner box. The electrical connections were so arranged that by pressing the bar the animal could deliver 60-cycle alternating current ($\frac{1}{2}$ to 5 v.) through the implanted electrodes, thus stimulating its own brain for as long as the bar was pressed. Olds & Milner found that stimulation in certain places positively reinforced the bar-pressing response, resulting in an extremely high rate, which was sustained over a period of hours. Results from one of their animals are presented in Fig. 8. Disconnecting the electrical stimulator, that is, turning the voltage to zero, led to a prompt and rapid decline in the rate of bar pressing. With some electrode placements, the positive reinforcing effect was probably greater than that observed in any other animal experiment, no matter what the "drive state" or the reinforcer used. However, in other respects, the positive reinforcing effects of brain stimulation were quite similar to those obtained with food and other "natural" reinforcers. These findings have been supported by the independent experiments of Delgado, Roberts, & Miller (1954) and Sidman, Brady, Boren, Conrad & Schulman (1955).

Olds & Milner also discovered the existence of certain places in the subcortical brain the stimulation of which resulted in a decrease in the bar-pressing response, resulting in a rate of responding much below the operant level. That is, the stimulation of certain sites functioned as a negative reinforcer; such stimulation actively extinguished the response which preceded it. It was noted before that drive theorists, and psychologists in general, have hesitated to recognize the existence of negative reinforcers; they tend to attribute all observed decreases in habit strength to *lack of positive reinforcement* or to the positive reinforcement of *other* responses rather than to the operation of any active negative reinforcers. Undoubtedly, lack of positive reinforcement does lead to decrease in habit strength, but this fact does not preclude the possibility of the existence of negative reinforcers as agents actively reducing habit strength. Olds & Milner provide clearcut evidence for the existence of active negative reinforcers corresponding directly to positive reinforcers, and of extinc-

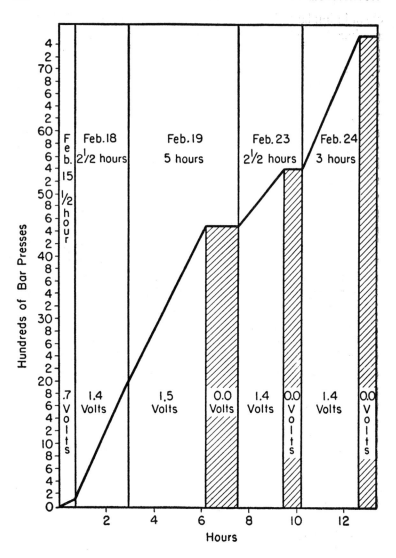

FIG. 8. POSITIVE REINFORCING EFFECTS OF INTRACRANIAL STIMULATION

Smoothed cumulative response curve for rat No. 34. (*Source:* J. Olds and P. Milner, Positive reinforcement produced by electrical stimulation of septal area and other regions of rat brain. *J. comp. physiol. Psychol.*, 47, 424.)

tion directly corresponding to acquisition of a response. However, recognizing the existence of negative reinforcers does not necessarily mean that they are normally as important as positive reinforcers in the control of behavior.

Olds & Milner (1954) employ the term "reinforcing structures" to designate those places in the brain the stimulation of which has positive reinforcing effects. The structures whose stimulation decreased habit strength may be called "negative reinforcing structures." Olds (1956) has attempted to map these areas more accurately than was done in the Olds & Milner study. Using the same experimental setup as before, Olds observed the response rate of rats with electrode implantations at different sites in the brain. He obtained high response rates in rats with electrode placements in rhinencephalic systems II and III. These structures include the septal area, the amygdaloid complex, the anterior hypothalamus, the cingulate cortex, the hippocampus, the posterior hypothalamus, and the anterior thalamus. The stimulation in these areas was therefore considered to be a positive reinforcer. Operant-level rates of bar pressing, that is, showing neither increase nor decrease in habit strength, were observed in cases with electrodes in some parts of the tegmentum, most of the primary sensory system, the caudate nucleus, the thalamic reticular nucleus, and the neocortex and white matter. Evidence of negative reinforcing structures, leading to response rates below the operant level, was found in rats with electrodes in the medial lemniscus, the zona incerta, and parts of the tegmentum behind the medial geniculate. Roughly speaking, the anterior part of the subcortical brain lodged the positive reinforcing structures, while the negative reinforcing structures were located mostly in the posterior part.

It is conceivable that these positive and negative reinforcing structures play some part in all instances where reinforcing effects, positive or negative, are obtained, no matter whether the reinforcers employed are related to drive reduction, consummatory responses, or exteroceptive stimulation. A program of research started by Miller (1957) and his colleagues is designed to throw light on this point. Their detailed experimental investigations are likely to show whether the reinforcing effects obtained by subcortical stimulation are identical in all respects with those obtained with "natural" reinforcers. So far, they have shown that the stimulation of certain parts of the brain acts as a punishment, that is, the stimulation can be used as a basis for establishing a conditioned response and its termination serves as a positive reinforcer. This raises the interesting question of whether punishment and negative reinforcement are identical phenomena. One way of answering this question is to determine whether the stimulation of the negative reinforcing structures found by Olds (1956) also serves as a punishment (i.e., whether the termination of stimulation in those structures has positive reinforcing effects). Another interesting observation by the Miller (1957) group is that the continued stimulation of a particular site in the subcortical brain may first operate as a reward and then, a few seconds later, as punishment. Another of their findings is that, whereas in some cases, as in most of the Olds & Milner (1954) observations, the positive reinforcing effects of intracranial stimulation are not accompanied by the occurrence of eating, drinking, or sexual responses, in other cases stimulation of a positive reinforcing structure may be accompanied by, for example, ejaculation. It is clear that the interrelations between the stimulation of intracranial reinforcing structures and the operation of natural reinforcers are quite complex, but, with the current interest in this area of research, some answers may soon be expected.

## Conclusion

To make the conclusions, and the discussion that follows, more manageable, it is desirable to ignore negative reinforcers from here on. It is likely that the statements made in relation to positive reinforcers apply, with appropriate modifications, to negative reinforcers as well.

If drive reduction is not the unique positive reinforcer (nor drive increment the unique negative reinforcer), the concept of drive ceases to be crucial in a discussion of the nature of reinforcers. In attempting to discover the essential feature of positive reinforcers, one must consider not only the positive reinforcing properties of drive reduction, but should also pay attention to the positive reinforcing effects of consummatory responses, some forms of exteroceptive stimulation, and certain types of intracranial stimulation. The problem of the nature of reinforcers can thus be formulated without any specific reference to the concept of drive or drive reduction.

In view of the similar effects they have on habit strength, it seems reasonable to assume that various types of positive reinforcers share a common mechanism. Let us call such a hypothetical mechanism the *positive reinforcing mechanism* or PRM. How does this mechanism operate? Our discussion so far suggests some of the rules according to which PRM must operate:

1. PRM must so act as to increase the over-all habit strength of those responses that accompany it.

2. PRM must be capable of operating at different levels or intensities, low levels producing small increments in habit strength and high levels producing larger increments in habit strength.

3. PRM must operate at a relatively high level under any one of the following conditions:

   a) certain instances of *decrease in sensory stimulation*, that is, decrease in receptor discharge or drive reduction, arising either proprioceptively (e.g. stomach-fistula experiments) or exteroceptively (e.g. escape training using termination of noxious stimulation as a reinforcer);

   b) certain instances of *increase in sensory stimulation*, that is, increase in receptor discharge or drive increment, arising either proprioceptively (e.g. consummatory-response experiments) or exteroceptively (e.g. light stimulation and visual exploration experiments); and

   c) the stimulation of certain subcortical structures (e.g. the Olds & Milner experiment).

4. PRM must so operate that "neutral" stimuli associated with its operation can acquire (secondary) reinforcing properties.

## PRESENT LINES OF INVESTIGATION

There are currently two promising lines of work concerned with determining the nature of reinforcers. One of these is neurophysiological; the other involves parametric behavioral investigations.

### Neurophysiological Mechanisms

We have defined a positive reinforcer as an event that increases over-all habit strength. Neurophysiologically, increasing habit strength may be thought of as increasing the *strength of a connection* between certain sets of neurons. As Wolpe (1950) has stated, positive reinforcement consists of establishing or strengthening functional neural connections. Thus, within this framework, a positive reinforcer is an event that tends to strengthen connections between the cell assemblies (or neural functional units) corresponding to a response and other, proximal, cell assemblies. Obviously, then, the neurophysiological problem of reinforcing effects concerns the processes that affect the making or strengthening of functional connections between neural units. This means that the PRM belongs to the general class of neurophysiological processes which are involved in the formation or strengthening of all neural connections.

Hebb (1949) has formulated a postulate concerning the manner in which functional neural connections are made: *"When an axon of a cell A is near enough to excite a cell B and repeatedly or persistently takes part in firing it, some growth process or metabolic change takes place in one or both cells such that A's efficiency, as one of the cells firing B, is increased"* (1949, p. 62).

According to this postulate, the strengthening of functional connections between cell assemblies is brought about simply by, roughly speaking, contiguous firing of their component nerve fibers. It follows that each time the cell assemblies representing a particular response fire, their chances of firing again thereby increase; for, according to the postulate, each firing of a cell assembly must to some extent strengthen its connections with other neural units. If this is correct, responses must be strengthened, at least to some slight degree, by the mere fact of their occurrence. Thus, the occurrence of a response, that is, the firing of the cell assemblies corresponding to it, in itself becomes the positive reinforcing mechanism. Within this hypothetical neurophysiological context, the problem then is not one of studying the general nature of the positive reinforcing mechanism; rather, it concerns the high reinforcing potency possessed by reinforcers, events such as eating, drinking, exploring, and terminating noxious stimulation. Why, for instance, is food such a potent reinforcer for a hungry rat? Even if each occurrence of a response is reinforcing in itself, why is an occurrence that is accompanied by a reinforcer much more so?

The high reinforcing efficacy of such reinforcers as some instances of increase or decrease in sensory stimulation, or the electrical stimulation of reinforcing structures, must mean that they somehow *facilitate* the strengthening of connections between relevant cell assemblies, beyond the strengthening that would normally result from the mere fact of firing. How do positive reinforcers increase the probability of the firing of certain cell assemblies? At present, the answer to this question is not known. The problem is now under study. Olds (1955, 1956) and Milner (1957) are two of the investigators actively engaged in pursuing this problem experimentally. Seward (1956a) is approaching the same problem from a theoretical viewpoint.

## PARAMETRIC INVESTIGATIONS

All that has been said so far in this chapter is consistent with the idea that different reinforcers differ in their effectiveness. The reinforcing effects of some reinforcers are greater than those of others. Thus, it is reasonable to regard various reinforcers as lying somewhere on a continuum running from low efficacy to high efficacy. The neurophysiological considerations of the last section suggest that the mere occurrence of a response must positively reinforce that response, but whether in fact this is so is still debatable. But even if the mere occurrence is a positive reinforcer, it is apparently a reinforcer of the lowest efficacy. On the other extreme, we have such high-efficacy reinforcers as, for example, saccharin solution and sexual stimulation for the rat. In between these extremes probably lie reinforcers such as light-onset and exploration. One approach to the problem of the nature of reinforcers seems to be that of parametrically studying the factors that determine the degree of efficacy of various reinforcers. Studies of this type have only recently started appearing in the literature and are too few to be organized in a systematic way. The following discussion is thus meant to be more illustrative than conclusive.

It appears that the efficacy of any reinforcer depends upon the existing state of the organism. The reinforcing effects of food for a hungry animal seem to be greater than those for sated animals. It has been noted (Chap. 4) that the reinforcing effects of a salt solution are likely to be greater for rats with a salt deficit than for normal animals. Butler (1957) has shown that the reinforcing effects of visual exploration increase with increased deprivation of visual stimulation (up to about four hours of deprivation). It is also likely that the reinforcing effects of light-onset vary with the state of visual adaptation of the animal. While it is interesting to study the way in which the reinforcing effects of a given reinforcer depend upon the state of the organism, the organismic state is likely to be a confounding variable when the primary concern is with the relation between the stimulus characteristics of the reinforcer and the degree of its reinforcing effects. The role of the organismic state will be discussed in the next chapter; here the concern is only with the studies that vary the stimulus characteristics of the reinforcers, holding the organismic state constant.

Young & Shuford (1954) studied the reinforcing effects for sated rats of different concentrations and exposure-durations of sucrose solution. For different animals they employed 2, 16, 18, or 54 per cent solution of sucrose, and allowed contact with the solution for 1, 4, or 16 sec. Their results showed that the speed at which the rats approached the sucrose solution was a function of its concentration. If the concentration (i.e. sweetness) of the sucrose solution was increased or decreased, there was a corresponding increase or decrease, respectively, in speed. The change in approach time was also dependent upon the magnitude of the change in concentration. Young & Shuford also found that, in general, the longer the duration (within the limits tested) of the contact with the solution the greater were the reinforcing effects. Similar results have been obtained by Hughes (1957) and Guttman (1953, 1954). In his 1954 study, Guttman compared the reinforcing effects on a bar-pressing response of different concentrations of sucrose and glucose solutions. His results are presented in Fig. 9. He found that, for any given concentration, sucrose was a more potent reinforcer than glucose. Guttman was interested in relating the relative reinforcing effects of the two substances to their relative sweetness, as judged by human subjects. He showed that, within certain limits, the concentrations of sucrose and glucose that yielded equal response rates were the same as would be judged equal in sweetness by man. Young & Asdourian (1957) found the positive reinforcing value of a 1 per cent salt solution to be equal to that of 0.35 per cent sucrose solution. The results of these experiments are consistent with Guttman's statement that the degree of reinforcing effects of a reinforcer are closely related (though not necessarily monotonically) to the receptor activity it generates.

Parametric studies of reinforcing effects obtained by diminishing or terminating noxious stimulation (i.e. by *reducing* receptor activity) have been made by Campbell (1955, 1956). In the earlier investigation, Campbell determined the relative reinforcing effects of different amounts (0, 80, or 100 per cent) of reduction in the intensity of a noxious "white noise." The reinforcing effect was defined in terms of the proportion of time spent by rats on the side of the cage on which they received the lower of two noise intensities. The efficacy of noise reduction as a reinforcer was found to be dependent upon the amount of noise reduction: The reinforcing effects

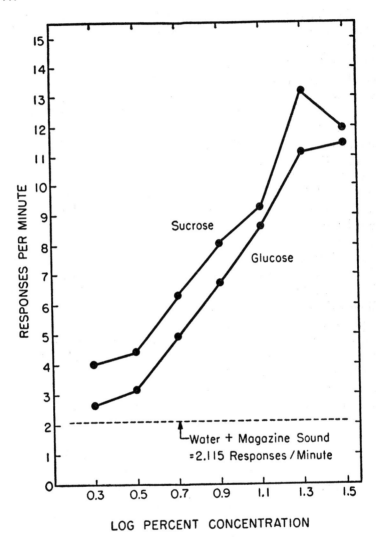

Fig. 9. Comparison of the Positive Reinforcing Effects of
Sucrose and Glucose

Rate of bar pressing as a function of concentration of reinforcing agent
for all 8 Ss. (*Source:* N. Guttman, Equal-reinforcement values for sucrose
and glucose solutions compared with equal-sweetness values. *J. comp.
physiol. Psychol.,* **47,** 359.)

of 80 per cent reduction in noise were intermediate between those of 0 per cent and 100 per cent noise reduction.

Campbell has introduced the concept of *reinforcement threshold* to refer, in this case, to the minimum reduction in noise energy required to produce just noticeable learning—that is, showing a 75 per cent preference for the lower-noise side. He found the reinforcement threshold to be .05 w. when the initial noise level was 95 db. However, at the initial noise intensity of 115 db, the reinforcement threshold was 4.15 w. Thus, the reinforcement threshold seems to increase rapidly with increase in the initial noise level. Campbell (1956) has confirmed these findings with another type of noxious stimulation. He has shown that stronger electric shocks required larger amounts of intensity reduction for producing just noticeable reinforcing effects. Campbell's method of determining reinforcement thresholds seems to be an ingenious one. It provides a simple way of comparing the reinforcing efficacy of different reinforcers. It can be easily extended to the study of rewards, such as sucrose solution and mild light stimulation, and should be useful in all parametric investigations of reinforcing effects.

In concluding this chapter, it is tempting to reflect upon the type of parametric investigations that are likely to reveal the source of all reinforcing effects. One promising line of research seems to be that of linking quantitatively the reinforcing effects of a reinforcer to the amount and type of receptor (and afferent) activity generated by that reinforcer. Another line of attack that may also prove fruitful is that of extensive parametric investigations of events (such as light-onset and contact with salt solution) that serve as rewards at certain (low) intensities or concentrations but become punishments at certain other (high) intensities. Still another fruitful approach may be to investigate the details of the relations existing between early experience and the states (dietary deficit, fatigue, etc.) of the organism on the one hand and the reinforcing effects of particular reinforcers on the other.

# Chapter 6

# Factors Determining
# Habit Strength

Chapter 1 formulated the problem of motivation in terms of two general questions. The first question is concerned with the development of various classes of activities in the repertoire of animals, and the second with the factors that affect the occurrence of these activities. Chapters 2 to 5 were concerned with the first question; we now turn to the second. In doing so, it is assumed that a number of different classes of activities, such as eating, drinking, withdrawing, attacking, and copulating, already exist in the animal's repertoire, and we are now concerned with variables that determine the occurrence of these classes of activities. Of course, the occurrence of any activity under certain circumstances will change that activity to some degree, but here the interest lies only in the factors leading up to the occurrence of any given activity and not in the consequences of its occurrence.

In discussing the occurrence of a given class of activity, one should pay attention to a variety of features of that activity. If the activity in question occurs at all, one should ask whether there are any variations in the form of the activity as described by such measures as errors, latency, appropriateness, and persistence. Thus, if one is interested in the factors that affect the occurrence of eating, he must pay attention not only to the variables that determine whether the animal eats at all, but also to the factors that regulate the amount eaten, rate of eating, intervals between successive periods of eating, and so on.

At the present stage of knowledge there is nothing to be gained by attempting to make any formal classification of the factors which affect the occurrence of various activities that exist in the repertoires of animals. Therefore, one can roughly categorize the factors with reference to the currently active areas of research. These categories overlap to a certain degree, but this is unavoidable at present: (1) habit strength, (2) sensory cues, (3) arousal, and (4) blood chemistry. These factors also, of course, play a part in the development of activities. However, here the concern is only with the role of these factors in the occurrence of activities, assuming that the animal already has them in its repertoire. This chapter deals with the factor of habit strength.

## THE FACTOR OF HABIT STRENGTH

The over-all probability that a given response will occur when a particular stimulus is presented may be small or large. Hull (1943) introduced the concept of *habit strength* to refer to the closeness of such stimulus-response relations. He looked upon habit strength as referring to the strength of relation between "afferent and efferent neural impulses." It may be visualized as the strength of connection between the neurons that correspond to the response and the neurons that represent the stimulus. The stronger this hypothetical connection, the greater the empirical habit strength.

Hull listed four empirical variables as the "indices" of habit strength. The first index, of course, was the *probability of occurrence* of the given ("correct") response on the presentation of the appropriate stimulus conditions. The other three were *amplitude, latency,* and *resistance to extinction* of the response. Increasing probability of occurrence, increasing amplitude, increasing resistance to extinction, and decreasing latency are generally considered to be signs of increasing habit strength. It is clear that Hull implied a high correlation between these measures and looked upon all of them as manifesting a unitary learning process. But the fact is that it is known (*see* Osgood, 1953; Kobrick, 1956) that the intercorrelations between these various measures are not always high, and they generate quite different estimates of habit strength. This means that, when the intention is to be precise or to make comparisons between investigations, one should specify the measure employed rather than talk vaguely about habit strength. Thus, the concept of habit strength, like that of goal direction, can be considered as a global concept referring to any one or more of a number of different measures. The use of the common label "habit strength" is justified on the ground that the different measures can all describe one and the same response, and on the presumption that they may be determined by overlapping neural mechanisms. For a discussion like the present one, it is convenient to talk generally in terms of habit strength, switching to the more refined measures of response probability, amplitude, latency, and resistance to extinction where necessary.

For the present purpose, two general questions may be asked about habit strength: (1) What factors determine increases and decreases in the habit strength of various classes of activities? (2) What is the relation between the habit strength of any given activity and its occurrence? It is not possible to say much about the second question at this stage. It should be noted that the very definition of habit strength adopted here states that the greater the habit strength of an activity the greater will be the probability of its occurrence. The only meaningful problem in this connection is that of the interaction between habit strength and other factors (such as blood chemistry and sensory stimulation) that also affect the occurrence of given activities. Thus, although our second question is meaningless at this stage of our discussion, it will become an important issue in later chapters, where we examine this interaction.

The first question above, which is concerned with the generation and dissipation of habit strength of different classes of activities, can, of course, be meaningfully discussed now. This question has traditionally been linked almost exclusively with the area of psychology labeled "learning," but it is of sufficient relevance to motivational phenomena to warrant its consideration here. However, it is not necessary for us to discuss all the theoretical issues concerning the learning process. We shall concern ourselves with only those issues which are likely to be of particular relevance in understanding motivational activities.

Since a reinforcer has been defined (Chap. 5) as an event that changes the habit strength of a response, it is meaningless to ask whether or not reinforcement is necessarily accompanied by a change in habit strength. The reinforcing effects of a reinforcer are known only through changes in habit strength. However, it is still possible to ask legitimate questions about the details of the way in which reinforcers affect habit strength. Such details will be discussed in the following sections, with reference to the problems of increasing, maintaining, and decreasing habit strength.

## INCREASING HABIT STRENGTH

As we noted in the last chapter, positive reinforcing events, that is, reinforcers that increase habit strength, are of two kinds. Some positive reinforcing events (rewards) involve the presentation of an object or the addition of some new form of stimulation. The other type of positive reinforcing event (punishment) involves the removal of an object or the termination of an existing form of stimulation. Variations in habit strength as a function of a number of parameters of both reward and punishment are discussed below.

### NUMBER OF POSITIVE REINFORCEMENTS

An exact theoretical relation between the number of positive reinforcements and habit strength was stated by Hull (1943). According to him, increments in habit strength from successive positive reinforcements summate in such a way that combined habit strength becomes a simple positive growth function of the number of positive reinforcements. This implies that the increment in habit strength yielded by each reinforcement becomes progressively smaller. There is as yet

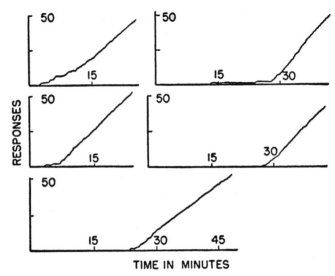

**TIME IN MINUTES**

Fig. 10. Typical Acquisition Curves in the Skinner Box

Original conditioning: all responses were reinforced. (*Source:* B. F. Skinner, *The behavior of organisms: an experimental analysis* [N.Y.: Appleton-Century-Crofts, Inc., 1938], p. 68. Copyright, 1938, D. Appleton-Century Co., Inc. Reprinted by permission of Appleton-Century-Crofts, Inc.)

no empirical support for the idea that Hull's negatively accelerated growth function, or any of the other suggested functions, represents the "true" relation between number of reinforcements and habit strength.[1]

There is also at present little evidence bearing on the question of whether the increase in habit strength brought about by the termination of a punishment follows, in general, the same course as that brought about by the presentation of a reward. There appear to be no studies which compare the effects of the two types of reinforcers in a situation where all the other variables (the instrumental response, the reinforcement schedule, etc.) are kept constant.

[1] Osgood (1953) has discussed the factors that determine the shape of the learning curve, factors such as complexity of the response being reinforced and stage of learning.

In the absence of adequate comparative studies, one must content oneself with examining an example of the course of the build-up of habit strength for each of the two types of positive reinforcers.

Fig. 10 shows some of the curves (cumulative responses) for individual rats obtained by Skinner (1938) in a situation where all occurrences of the instrumental response were followed by a reward. The instrumental response was lever pressing in a Skinner box, the animals were hungry, and the delivery of a small pellet of food constituted the reinforcement. (The animals had undergone some preliminary training prior to making the responses shown in the figure.) It is seen that, after the first two or three reinforcements of the instrumental response, there is a rapid increase in the rate of response. It is difficult to find a comparable example which employs the removal of punishment as a positive reinforcer. For, while the data from reward situations are described in terms of the rate of response, the performance in punishment situations can normally be described only in terms of the latency of escape or avoidance. This is so because, unlike the Skinner-box situation, for example, each response in a punishment situation normally depends upon the presentation by the experimenter of the appropriate conditioned or warning stimulus. However, by employing a novel procedure, Sidman (1953) has been able to obtain meaningful rate data for an avoidance response acquired with termination of punishment as the reinforcer. In one of his studies, Sidman (1955) gave a brief electric shock to rats at regular intervals of 5 sec. unless the animal pressed a lever. Each lever-pressing response put off the shock for 20 sec. The animals learned quickly (see Fig. 11) to avoid the shock by repeatedly pressing the lever. The rate of this instrumental response increased abruptly after the animals had successfully terminated a few shocks. While all the experimental conditions in the Skinner and Sidman studies are by no means identical, there is a remarkable resemblance in the course of the increase in habit strength (rate of response) brought about by the two types of positive reinforcers.

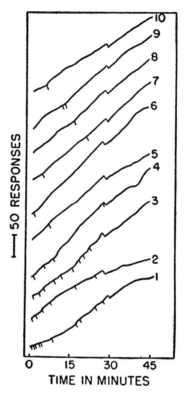

FIG. 11. CURVES OF RATE OF RESPONSE IN AN AVOIDANCE SITUATION

Cumulative lever-pressing curves for one rat during alternate avoidance conditioning and extinction. Extinction periods are offset to the right. The diagonal marks indicate shocks. Numbers indicate the temporal sequence of each conditioning-extinction cycle. (*Source:* M. Sidman, On the persistence of avoidance behavior. *J. abnorm. soc. Psychol.*, **50**, 218.)

A similar comparison has been made by Campbell[2] between his own data obtained in a punishment-terminating situation and those of Williams (1938) obtained with reward. In both cases rats served as subjects, and bar pressing was the instrumental response; it was reinforced by food in the Williams study and by the termination of an electric shock in

[2] In a personal communication to the author, from Dr. Sam L. Campbell, Creedmoor Institute for Psychobiologic Studies, Queens Village 27, N.Y.

Campbell's. Both studies were concerned with finding the relation between the number of reinforcements and resistance to extinction. Each of a number of groups of rats was given a different number of reinforcements and was then tested for responses to an extinction criterion. The results of the two experiments were remarkably similar. In both cases resistance to extinction was found to increase with the number of prior reinforcements. Both sets of data could be fitted to a negative growth function, showing that roughly the first hundred reinforcements were responsible for a major portion of the increase in resistance to extinction.

These comparisons suggest the possibility that increase in the habit strength of any given reinforced response is brought about by processes which operate in the same way whether the reinforcer is a reward or the termination of a punishment.

## Effect of Each Reinforcement

The positive reinforcing effects produced by each occurrence of the reinforcer depend upon a number of circumstances. The more important of them are discussed here.

*Nature of the reinforcer.* Some reinforcers appear to be more potent than others. It has already been noted in Chapter 5 that the positive reinforcing effects of mild light stimulation are quite small, while those of some instances of intracranial stimulation are greater than the effects obtained by the use of any other reinforcers. However, controlled studies, with groups equated with respect to the instrumental response employed, the number of reinforced repetitions, and other relevant variables (*see* below), are needed before any general statements about the relative potency of different types of reinforcers can be made with confidence. A study by Hutt (1954) provides some relevant data. He studied the reinforcing effects on a lever-pressing response of variations in the taste aspect of the quality of a food. By adding saccharin or citric acid to a basic food mixture, he was able to vary taste but to hold constant the color, odor, texture, and nutritive value of the reinforcers. Groups of rats were trained by an identical procedure. Some of his results dealing with effects of the nature of the reinforcer are presented in Fig. 12. It is seen that habit strength, as measured by rate of response, is a function of the quality (taste) of the reinforcer. Reinforc-

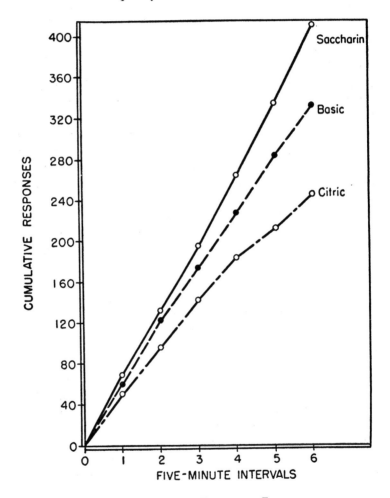

FIG. 12. POSITIVE REINFORCING EFFECTS AS A FUNCTION OF THE NATURE OF THE REINFORCER

Mean cumulative periodic reinforcement curves for day 5. (*Source:* P. J. Hutt, The rate of bar pressing as a function of quality and quantity of food reward. *J. comp. physiol. Psychol.,* 47, 237.)

ing effects of saccharin food are greater than, and those of citric food less than, the effects of equivalent amounts of the basic ration. Similarly, Guttman (1953) and Hughes (1957) have shown that, within limits, the reinforcing effects of sucrose solution increase with the concentration of sucrose in the solution. However, it is not clear whether the concentration in these cases is a "quality" or a "quantity" factor.

*State of the organism.* The state of the organism (e.g. its health, nature and degree of deprivation, etc.) may determine the extent of the reinforcing effects of a given reinforcer. However, whether this is in fact so is not easy to decide. Consider, for example, the positive reinforcing effects of food ingestion. To common sense it appears obvious that the reinforcing effects of food ingestion will be greater in the case of a hungry animal than in the case of one which is sated. But it is difficult to prove this presumption. If one arranges to obtain evidence by employing food ingestion as a reinforcer of an instrumental response, he is likely to find that, while the hungry animal eats the food, the sated one does not. Thus, the instrumental response is followed by reinforcement in the case of the hungry animal, but not in the case of the sated one. Since the reinforcement received is not equivalent in the two cases, the greater reinforcing effects in the case of the hungry animal cannot be attributed to food deprivation per se.

This analysis applies to an experiment by Beach & Jordan (1956). Using male rats, they reinforced the instrumental response of traversing a runway. The reinforcer was copulatory activity with a receptive female placed in the goal box at the end of the runway. The running time decreased rapidly (to a few seconds) in the course of about 15 trials. Then the animals were castrated. Tests following recovery from the operation showed a marked increase in running time. Subsequently, however, daily injections of androgen reinstated the low running times. On the face of it, this experiment may be taken as evidence that the reinforcing effects of copulation depend upon the (hormonal) state of the organism. However, one cannot be certain of this. For, as Beach

& Jordan point out, castration not only increased running time but also decreased coital responses, and both these effects were reversed with androgen injections. Following castration, the animals were sexually less active and, therefore, did not engage in the reinforcing copulatory activity as much as they did before castration. Thus, the changes in running speed may have resulted from changes in the obtained reinforcement or from changes in the state of the animals, or from both these factors. Beach & Jordan point out significantly that ". . . the restoration of preoperative running speeds coincided with the revival of sexual ability, and not with the administration of any fixed amount of testosterone propionate" (1956, pp. 109–10).

Hull (1943) hypothesized that increase in habit strength is independent of "drive level" (e.g. degree of deprivation) at the time of training. A number of investigators have been interested in determining if this is in fact so. It has been quite difficult to devise an experimental design that would allow for the control of numerous relevant variables. However, to a certain extent this difficulty has been overcome in some studies. For example, in a well-designed study Lewis & Cotton (1957) determined the effects on running time of training under three conditions, 1, 6, and 22 hr. of food deprivation. Having found that the rats in the 22-hr. deprivation group ran faster to the goal box, they interpreted their data as showing that the degree of deprivation during training is directly related to increments in habit strength. However, Lewis & Cotton did not report data on the amount of food actually eaten in the goal box by the variously deprived groups. Unless one knows that the various groups ingested equal amounts of food, it cannot be concluded that the degree of deprivation was the crucial variable in determining the differential running speeds.

Obviously, the question at issue can be settled only if equivalent reinforcements are actually received by groups of animals which differ in their bodily states. The fistula-feeding and intracranial-stimulation techniques discussed in Chapter 5 offer possible means for making crucial tests. For example, by reinforcing an instrumental response with fistula feeding in two groups of animals which differ only in degree of deprivation, it should be possible to determine if the reinforcing effects of identical reinforcements are different in the two groups. The studies of the effects of salt deprivation on dietary preferences (Chap. 4) do suggest that the reinforcing effects of a reinforcer are dependent upon the state of the organism, but the applicability of those results to the typical (maze or Skinner-box) learning situations may be questioned. Thus, though it appears plausible that the degree of reinforcing effects of a given reinforcer is dependent upon some aspects of the state of the organism, it is not at present possible to make such a statement with confidence, at least so far as the positive reinforcing effects of the presentation of rewards are concerned.

The same question can also be raised in connection with the positive reinforcing effects produced by the removal of a punishment. We can ask, for example, whether the reinforcing effects of electric-shock termination in an escape or avoidance situation depend upon some aspects of the state of the organism. An answer to this question is provided in an experiment by Wynne & Solomon (1955). The purpose of their experiment was to determine the role of visceral reactions (which have often been considered as indices of "anxiety" and "drive") in the acquisition of escape and avoidance reactions. They used surgery and pharmacological agents to block the activity of the peripheral autonomic nervous system, thereby reducing visceral reactions considerably. Then they compared the performance in an escape and avoidance learning situation of two groups of dogs, one of which—the experimental group—had been prepared in the above manner. The two groups could be said to differ with respect to their visceral ("anxiety" or "drive") state; however, all the animals received identical (electric shocks and) shock terminations as reinforcement for the instrumental response of walking from one side to the other of a shuttle box. Since the sensory processes were not interfered with, there is no reason to believe that the shock was more intense for one group than for the other. The experimenters found that the acquisition of both escape and avoidance responses was retarded in the case of the experimental animals. Also, during extinction trials they extinguished faster than the control animals. However, the control animals were no different from another group of experimental animals which had the surgical and pharmacological block introduced after it had acquired the avoidance response. This study shows clearly that the increase in the habit strength of a response that is reinforced by the termination of a punishment does depend on at least one aspect (visceral reactions) of the state of the organism during the acquisition trials.

*Amount of reinforcement.* Do the reinforcing effects of a reinforcer depend upon the amount in which it is employed? If the exact nature of the reinforcing mechanism were known, this question would become meaningless, because then the extent of the reinforcing effects and the degree to which the reinforcing mechanism operates would be synonymous expressions. However, because we are ignorant of the nature of the reinforcing mechanism, it is quite meaningful to ask about the exact relation between the amount of a reinforcer and the extent of its reinforcing effects.

So far as the reinforcing effects arising from the presentation of rewards are concerned, the available evidence does not permit any simple answer. Some studies show that the reinforcing effects of a given reinforcer are a function of the amount of reinforcement. For example, Crespi (1942) found that hungry rats' speed of running was a function of the amount of food they received in the goal box. This result has been corroborated by Metzger, Cotton, & Lewis (1957). Similarly, in the Hutt (1954) study mentioned before, it was found that increase in the habit strength of the lever-pressing response was dependent, not only upon the quality (taste) of the reinforcer, but also upon its quantity. But other researchers find amount of the reinforcer to be unrelated to the extent of its reinforcing effects. Kling (1956) studied the effect on running speed of amount of water drunk and the duration of contact with the drinking tube in thirsty rats. He found no simple relation between the two independent variables and running speed. However, rate of ingestion and speed of running were found to be related. He concludes that rate of ingestion, and not the amount, is one of the factors influencing the efficacy of reinforcers in situations of this kind. Another example of negative results is provided by Hopkins (1955). He fed different amounts of food to rats in a white goal box. As expected, the white box acquired secondary reinforcing properties; however, the reinforcing effect of the box (secondary reinforcer) was found not to be a function of the quantity of food (primary reinforcement) with which the box had been associated. Still other investigators (e.g. Lawson, 1957) find that the amount of reinforcement affects the acquisition of habit strength only when the subjects have had experience of different amounts in association with different stimuli.

The studies reported above do not point to any clear-cut conclusions. At least three factors may have contributed to this lack of agreement. First, there is some ambiguity about the exact meaning of "amount." Some investigators define amount in terms of quantity, others in terms of strength or intensity. Thus, Dufort & Kimble (1956) use the term "amount" to refer to the strength of saccharin solution. Second, as Kling (1956) has pointed out, the factor of duration of contact with the reinforcer has often been confounded with that of amount. Third, the instrumental response, the particular measure of habit strength employed, the efficacy of the reinforcer, details of feeding schedules, and other relevant parametric values are seldom the same for any two studies. Further research is needed to clarify these various interrelations.

In the context of positive reinforcing effects produced by terminating a punishment, the term "amount" may refer to one of two variables. It may refer to the duration for which the animal is exposed to a particular noxious stimulation, or it may refer to the intensity of the noxious stimulation. While the duration of noxious stimulation can be controlled by the experimenter in the classical conditioning situation, it cannot be controlled in escape and avoidance training. In the latter types of training, the stimulation is terminated when the animal makes the appropriate instrumental response. The intensity of noxious stimulation can, of course, be varied by the experimenter in both the classical and the escape and avoidance situations.

Examples of investigations in this area are the studies of Kimble (1955) and Brush (1957). Kimble compared the reinforcing effects on a wheel-running avoidance response of the termination of four intensities of electric shock. He found that, during training, response latency was inversely related to shock intensity; however, during extinction there was no difference in the response latencies of the different groups of rats. Brush employed a shuttle-box avoidance-training situation and five intensities of electric shock, one for each of five groups of dogs. He compared the groups on a number of indices of habit strength, including trial number of the first avoidance, latency of the first avoidance, asymptotic avoidance latency, and number of trials to extinction. Of all the indices used, only asymptotic latency was significantly related to shock intensity. The relation was a U-shaped one, latency being minimal for the intermediate intensities of shock. This type of relation between intensity of noxious stimulation and acquisition of habit strength was first suggested by Yerkes & Dodson (1908). These investigations show that the "amount" of punishment terminated affects the acquisition of an avoidance response.

*Delay of reinforcement.* Are the reinforcing effects of a reinforcer a function of the time interval elapsing between the instrumental response and the occurrence of the reinforcer? In general it appears that the greater the interval between the response and the reinforcement the less the reinforcing effects. Grice (1948) trained rats on a black-white discrimination task with food as the reinforcer. A number of groups of rats were trained with delays of reinforcement of 0, 0.5, 1.2, 2.0, 5.0, or 10.0 sec. Three of the 10-sec. delay animals did not learn at all. The results for the other groups are shown in Fig. 13. It is clear that the reinforcing effects of the reinforcement decrease rapidly as the interval between it and the instrumental response is increased. Some other investigators (e.g. Perkins, 1947) have reported similar, though not equally steep, curves of this relation. Whether it is the delay

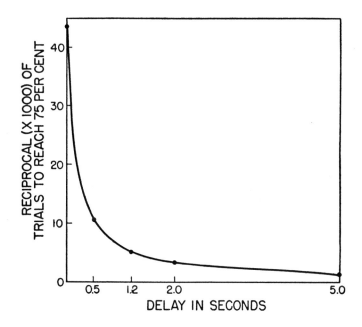

FIG. 13. RATE OF ACQUISITION AS A FUNCTION OF DELAY
OF REINFORCEMENT

The reciprocal x 1000 of the number of trials to reach the level of 75 per cent correct choices is plotted against the time of delay. Experimental values are represented by black dots and the smooth curve is fitted to these data. (*Source:* G. R. Grice, The relation of secondary reinforcement to delayed reward in visual discrimination learning. *J. exp. Psychol.,* **38,** 9.)

of reinforcement per se or some factor associated with it that is responsible for the obtained gradient is still an open question. Grice (1948), following Hull (1943) and Spence (1947), feels that the gradient results from some adventitious secondary reinforcing effects. According to Grice, owing to its close association with the reward, reinforcing properties are acquired by the stimulus trace of the conditioned stimulus. He further assumes that the stimulus trace fades quickly (in about 10 sec.). Then he considers the secondary reinforcing effects to be a function of the strength of the trace and not of time per se. It is difficult to put this hypothesis to test, for there appears to be no easy way of separating the secondary reinforcing effects of a stimulus from its role as the conditioned stimulus.

Delay of reinforcement also determines the degree of reinforcing effects obtained when the reinforcer is the termination of noxious stimulation. Church & Solomon (1956) studied the influence of the interval between instrumental response and the termination of punishment on avoidance learning in dogs. The intervals used were 0, 0.5, 2.5, 5.0, and 10.0 sec. They found that the animals in the four experimental groups required more trials to reach the training criterion than the control (0 delay) group. The escape latencies of the experimental groups were also larger and more variable, and their resistance to extinction was less than that of the control group. Though there is no clear-cut gradient evident in their results, Church & Solomon's study does show that the reinforcing effects of the termination of a punishment decrease if the termination is not synchronous with the response.

The preceding pages have dealt with some of the important factors that determine the increase in habit strength of any given activity. We turn next to a brief consideration of the factors that determine the maintenance of the habit strength of a response that has already been acquired.

## MAINTENANCE OF HABIT STRENGTH

Once the habit strength of a response has reached a certain asymptotic level, it can be maintained at that level without much difficulty. Generally speaking, fewer reinforcements are needed to maintain a certain level of habit strength than are needed to reach that level in the first place. Both "intermittent" and "delayed" reinforcement schedules have been employed in these experiments.

## Intermittent Reinforcement

When <u>only some occurrences</u> of an instrumental response <u>are reinforced we generally speak of the procedure as that of</u> <u>*intermittent reinforcement*,</u> Skinner (1938) has recognized two types of intermittent reinforcement: ratio reinforcement and interval reinforcement. In the *ratio reinforcement* situation the ratio, say, 5:1, of responses to reinforcements is fixed by the experimenter; *interval reinforcement* is said to operate when the experimenter reinforces on a time schedule, say, every one minute, leaving unreinforced all responses that occur during the intervals between reinforcements.

Skinner has shown that, so long as reinforcement schedule does not approach the schedule which would produce extinction of the response, extremely high rates of response emerge under ratio reinforcement schedules. Fig. 14 shows rates of response obtained from rats in a Skinner box under some fixed ratios of reinforcement. It is clear that the rates of response generated under these fixed-ratio schedules are far greater than those obtained when the ratio is 1:1, that is, when every response is reinforced (*see* Fig. 10). Of course, intermittent reinforcement generates such high rates of response only when the response has previously acquired a certain level of habit strength under regular (1:1) reinforcement. Thus, not only proportionally fewer reinforcements are needed to maintain an instrumental response than to acquire it, but the maintenance of the response on a low reinforcement schedule yields much higher rates of response.

In a comparable investigation, Kaplan (1956) has studied the maintenance of an instrumental escape response under a fixed-ratio reinforcement schedule. The response, lever pressing, terminated a noxious strong light for 1 min. on every 5th, 10th, 15th, or 30th response. Kaplan found that the rate of escape responding increased as the fixed-ratio schedule was progressively moved in steps from 1:1 to 30:1. His cumulative response curves in general resemble those obtained by Skinner with fixed-ratio reward reinforcements. However, though the rate of response increased, Kaplan found the latency of the first escape response (in a given session) also to increase with increased reinforcement ratios. That is, the rats became slower in *starting* to press the lever, but once they started their rate of response was higher than the rate under 1:1 schedule. The exact significance of this finding is not clear. However, it is interesting to note that Skinner has

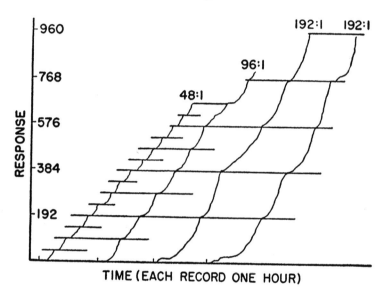

TIME (EACH RECORD ONE HOUR)

Fig. 14. Rate of Response as a Function of the Ratio of Responses to Reinforcements

Reinforcements at several fixed ratios; the ratios are marked. Note the smooth acceleration between reinforcements (at horizontal line). (*Source:* B. F. Skinner, *The behavior of organisms: an experimental analysis* [N.Y.: Appleton-Century-Crofts, Inc., 1938], p. 288. Copyright, 1938, D. Appleton-Century Co., Inc. Reprinted by permission of Appleton-Century-Crofts, Inc.)

reported similar "breaks" or periods of no responding immediately after a reinforcement (*see* Fig. 14) in fixed-ratio reward situations. And Guttman (1953), Hurwitz (1956), and Stewart & Hurwitz (1958) have noticed that, with low-efficacy positive reinforcers, rats typically respond in bursts of high rate with long breaks in between the bursts.

The effects on the maintenance of an instrumental response appear to be somewhat different when the reinforcement schedule involves fixed intervals rather than fixed ratios. Kaplan (1952), employing a setup similar to the one used in the above study, arranged the reinforcement schedule in such a way that a lever press terminated the noxious light, not after a certain number of presses, but 0.2, 0.5, 1.0, 2.0, 3.0, 4.0, or 5.0 min. after the preceding reinforcement. He found that, as the interval between the successive reinforcements was increased, there was a sharp decline in the rate of response. However, the average number of responses emitted per interval increased progressively with increase in the reinforcement interval. In a comparable experiment, Wilson (1954) investigated the relation between the same variables in a reward situation. He also found the rate of response to decrease rapidly as the interval between successive reinforcements was increased from 10 sec. to 6 min. However, the resistance to extinction showed an increase up to the reinforcement interval of 1 min. and then showed a gradual decline up to the 6-min. interval. Thus, in both these studies, as the interval between successive reinforcements increased, the rate of response decreased, but there was an increase in the number of responses emitted and, what is probably the same thing, in resistance to extinction. It will be recalled that in the fixed-ratio situation both the rate of response and resistance to extinction increase with increasing ratios. The significance of this difference between the effects of fixed-ratio and fixed-interval reinforcement schedules is not clear. Nevertheless it is obvious that in both cases the ratio of the *number* of responses emitted per reinforcement is greater than 1:1. Thus, a 1:1 ratio is not required for maintaining a response, though it is usually necessary for acquiring it.

In the case of avoidance responses, a high rate of response can be maintained with only occasional reinforcement. Sidman (1955) found that after an avoidance response had been established through regular reinforcement a cat gave 1502 responses in 3.5 hr. without receiving a single shock-termination as reinforcement. Solomon, Kamin, & Wynne (1953) have also found that avoidance responses in dogs, once established, are extremely persistent and can be maintained with a minimum of reinforcement. It should be noted than in an avoidance situation when the animal makes the appropriate response, the noxious stimulus is *not* presented. Intuitively speaking, if the animal continues to make the avoidance response, it will never know whether its failure to respond would result in noxious stimulation. However, depending upon the experimental conditions, animals sooner or later do fail to respond, receive noxious stimulation, and then continue to respond with renewed vigor. Perhaps it is their extreme persistence (and resistance to extinction), even in the absence of actual contact with noxious stimulation, that makes avoidance responses so prepotent in the repertoires of most animals. In Chapter 4 it was noted that withdrawal responses are the ones that are most frequently shown by animals when they are presented with an unfamiliar situation. This result may be the outcome of the ease with which avoidance responses can be maintained in the absence of reinforcement through punishment termination. Other types of activities (aggressive, friendly, etc.) are more difficult to maintain because in their case the source of the positive reinforcement is usually the occurrence of a reward, and they are readily extinguished in the absence of rewards.

## Delayed Reinforcement

Not only can the habit strength of a response be maintained by intermittent reinforcement, but it can also be maintained under schedules of delayed reinforcement. Working with pigeons, Ferster (1953) obtained a baseline for rate of response (pecking at a key) under conditions of interval reinforcement. Then he introduced short delays of reinforcement, that is, the bird received the reinforcement a certain time after it had made that instrumental response which would normally have been reinforced under the interval-reinforcement schedule. Starting with short delays and gradually increasing them, Ferster was able to sustain normal (baseline) rates of response under delays of up to 60 sec. However, if the delay of 60 sec. was introduced suddenly, without gradually moving up to it, the pigeons showed a decline in rate of response.

The results of all these studies on intermittent and delayed reinforcement show clearly that the conditions required for maintaining the habit strength of an activity at a given level are not so stringent as those required to reach that level in the first place. The ratio of responses to reinforcements can be much higher during maintenance than during acquisition. The changes in rate and resistance to extinction brought about by the various reinforcement schedules are not understood at present. However, they suggest that the principles governing the maintenance of a response may be quite different from those that obtain during its acquisition.

## DECREASING HABIT STRENGTH: EXTINCTION

This discussion of extinction is concerned with the main findings pertaining to factors that bring about decrements in habit strength. Those interested in theoretical interpretations of extinction are referred to discussions by Osgood (1953, pp. 336–59), Dinsmoor (1954, 1955) and Razran (1956), and to other works on learning theory.

The important factors that produce decrements in habit strength may be categorized as follows: number of negative reinforcements, number of unreinforced repetitions, and factors connected with acquisition and maintenance schedules.

### NEGATIVE REINFORCEMENTS

The Olds & Milner (1954) study, discussed in Chapter 5, suggests the existence of active negative reinforcers, corresponding to positive reinforcers. They were able to show that the repeated *presentation* of electrical stimulation of certain areas of the subcortical brain decreased habit strength in much the same way as the repeated presentation of a positive reinforcer increases habit strength. This means that we must recognize that extinction of a response can be brought about by the presentation of a (negative) reinforcing agent. As noted before, drive theorists in general regard extinction to result only from the repetition of a response in the absence of (positive) reinforcement. It is true that, at present, only one type of event can be considered as a true negative reinforcer. This is the electrical stimulation of certain areas of the brain, as described by Olds & Milner (1954) and Olds (1956). The exact way in which such negative reinforcers decrease habit strength has not yet been worked out. However, some of the factors that determine the effects of negative reinforcers are not likely to be different from those that determine the effects of positive reinforcers. Thus, we can expect the factors such as number of (negative) reinforced repetitions, state of the organism, and amount and delay of reinforcement will determine the degree of negative reinforcing effects on habit strength.

It should be noted that negative reinforcement, as defined here, is not synonymous with punishment (i.e. the presentation of a noxious stimulation). Punishment refers to events the removal of which increases habit strength, while a negative reinforcer is an event the presentation of which decreases habit strength. Thus, in order to be able to say that negative reinforcers are identical with punishments one would have to show that (1) the removal of a negative reinforcer has positive reinforcing effects, and (2) the presentation of punishment has negative reinforcing effects. So far as the first of these requirements is concerned, it has already been noted in Chapter 5 that there is as yet no evidence that the removal of a negative reinforcer necessarily has positive reinforcing effects. In connection with the second requirement, it is true that when a response is consistently followed by noxious stimulation, its probability of occurrence is likely to decrease. But, as Dinsmoor (1954, 1955) has argued, the observed decrease in the habit strength of a punished response does not arise from the presentation of noxious stimulation per se. Rather, it arises from the positive reinforcing effects of its termination, as in avoidance training. Dinsmoor has pointed out that the varied responses that precede a punished response are positively reinforced by virtue of the fact that they delay the onset of noxious stimulation. These varied responses gradually acquire enough habit strength to replace the punished response. Thus, the decrease in the habit strength of a punished response results from positive reinforcement of *other* responses, whereas the negative reinforcers, as visualized here, act directly to reduce habit strength.

## UNREINFORCED REPETITIONS

Undoubtedly, the most commonly employed method of decreasing habit strength is that of repetition without positive reinforcement. If the occurrence of a response previously instrumental in producing a positive reinforcement is no longer followed by the reinforcement, its habit strength will diminish rapidly. A period of rest after such an extinction session usually results in "spontaneous recovery" of the response; however, if the animal is exposed to a series of extinction-rest sessions, spontaneous recovery gradually decreases to zero and complete extinction of the response may be said to have taken place. Unreinforced repetitions lead to extinction quite dependably in the case of responses which have been acquired and maintained by positive reinforcement arising from the presentation of a reward. The same is true in the case of escape responses, where the source of positive reinforcement is the termination of a punishment. Studies of Gwinn (1951) and Edmonson & Amsel (1954) demonstrate that, in rats trained to escape an electric shock, the escape response is quickly extinguished when the shock is no longer administered to the animals.

However, in the case of avoidance responses unreinforced repetitions do not lead to extinction so predictably. As noted before, in the case of avoidance learning, the animal can "find out" that its failure to make the avoidance response will not result in noxious stimulation only if it fails to make the avoidance response. The animal may stop making the response because of fatigue, or it may be prevented from making the response by some experimental arrangement. In a shuttle-box avoidance-jumping experiment, Solomon, Kamin, & Wynne (1953) found that even the introduction of a glass barrier between the two sides of the shuttle box led to extinction of the jumping response only in a small proportion of dogs. The glass barrier prevented the animals from jumping and thus gave them a chance to discover that not-jumping no longer meant receiving an electric shock. These investigators also tried another extinction procedure. They punished the animal *for* jumping; that is, when, on the presentation of the signal, the animal jumped over to the other (formerly the safe, no-shock) side, it received an electric shock there too. Even under these conditions the proportion of dogs that showed extinction of the jumping response was small (about 20 per cent), no greater than the glass-barrier procedure. A combined procedure, employing both the barrier and shock *for* jumping, proved to be quite effective, but even this was not effective in all cases. This study, and that of Sidman (1955) referred to before, demonstrate the extreme resistance to extinction of avoidance responses, and the fact that the unreinforced repetitions of a response do not necessarily lead to extinction.[3]

We turn now to a consideration of some of the important parameters that determine the exact effect of unreinforced repetitions on decrements in habit strength.

*Work involved in each response.* Mowrer & Jones (1943) have shown that the ease of extinction of a response is a function of the effort required in making the response. By employing levers of different weight-loadings in a Skinner-box type of situation, they found that the greater the weight of the lever the fewer the unreinforced repetitions required to extinguish the lever-pressing response. Solomon (1948) has confirmed this relation in an experiment in which the effortfulness of a jumping response was controlled by varying the distance between the jumping stand and the landing platform. He found that the rats that had to jump 16 in. reached the extinction criterion in considerably fewer trials than the animals that were required to jump only 8 in. This implies that, other things being equal, responses involving a large part of

[3] *See* Mowrer & Lamoreaux (1942), Schoenfeld (1950), Solomon, Kamin, & Wynne (1953), Solomon & Wynne (1954), Solomon & Brush (1956), and Kamin (1956, 1957, 1957a) for possible interpretations of the above findings.

musculature will be easier to extinguish than responses such as tics and mannerisms, which are almost effortless.

*Operation of secondary reinforcers.* During extinction trials, though the response is not accompanied by the original reinforcer, it may nevertheless be accompanied by stimuli that have acquired some secondary reinforcing properties by virtue of their close association with the positive reinforcer employed during training. It seems plausible that the presence of such secondary reinforcers during the apparently unreinforced extinction trials will increase resistance to extinction. Bugelski (1938) and Skinner (1938) have shown that this is actually so. Miles' (1956) more recent study will serve to illustrate the point. He trained rats to press the lever in a Skinner box with food as the reinforcer. Pressing the lever, during this acquisition stage of the experiment, turned on a light, resulted in the click of the food-delivery mechanism, and caused the delivery of a food pellet. Because of their association with food delivery, the click and light presumably acquired secondary reinforcing properties. During extinction trials, only one of two groups of animals received light-click stimulation; of course, neither group received any food. Miles found that the group that received light-click stimulation during the extinction trials showed greater resistance to extinction.

Such secondary reinforcing effects can also increase resistance to extinction of a response which was originally reinforced by the termination of a punishment. Thus, Finch & Culler (1935) paired the sound of a buzzer with a shock while conditioning leg withdrawal to a tone in dogs. The response was then extinguished under two conditions, in the presence and in the absence of the buzzer. They found the resistance to extinction to be much greater when the buzzer was sounded during the extinction trials. It is clear that the termination of the buzzer, in addition to shock termination, provided some secondary reinforcing effect. Mowrer & Lamoreaux (1942) found that an avoidance response is acquired more rapidly when there is no delay between its occurrence and the termination of the conditioned stimulus than when the conditioned stimulus is continued for a few seconds after the avoidance response has been made. Kamin (1957, 1957a) has systematically studied this relation and has found a gradient of delay of secondary reinforcement (by delaying the termination of the conditioned stimulus by varying intervals) in avoidance learning. These findings suggest that the resistance to extinction of an avoidance response would also be a monotonic increasing function of the extent to which the stimuli associated with shock are present during the extinction trials. Systematic investigations of this relation remain to be done.

Thus, the ease with which a response can be extinguished depends on the extent to which the extinction procedure is free of secondary reinforcing effects. It is likely that many activities in the repertoires of animals are maintained through the operation of such secondary reinforcers.

*Strength of competing responses.* According to Guthrie (1935), and Wendt (1936), the extinction of a given response means only that another response has become prepotent in the given situation. In the present context, this means that unreinforced repetitions of a response do not in any sense diminish the habit strength of the response; rather they provide the conditions for increase in habit strength of other, competing responses. The competing responses emerge from the general activity that the animal typically displays in the situation. According to this view, the extinction of an escape response, for example, occurs because competing responses, such as sitting, sniffing, grooming, and exploring, begin to occur more frequently in the experimental situation. While this line of argument may not account for all the known facts of extinction, there is little doubt that the strength of competing responses is a major factor in determining the resistance to extinction of a given response. It has been shown that a given response extinguishes more readily when conditions are so arranged as to facilitate the emergence of competing responses than when conditions are not so arranged. Hall (1955) trained rats to escape from an electric shock by climbing over a hurdle. Then she tried to extinguish the escape response by employing a number of different procedures. One of these procedures involved introducing another rat into the apparatus during the extinction trials. This was designed to elicit responses which would be antagonistic to the escape response. Hall found that this extinction procedure was significantly more effective than all the other procedures, including those that made use only of unreinforced repetitions. Brady (1955) has shown that the ease of extinction of a conditioned "fear" response in rats is affected by the reinforcement schedules employed in maintaining a competing response. The competing response employed was lever pressing to obtain water. The fear response to be extinguished was "decrement in rate of lever pressing" brought about by a clicking signal that had previously been paired with shock. After this fear response had been acquired, the lever-pressing response was maintained on a variety of ratio and interval schedules of reinforcement (water). Brady found that the fear (decrement in rate of pressing) response to the clicking signal extinguished faster in the case of animals on ratio schedules than in the case of those on regular or interval schedules. Since the rate of response is higher under ratio reinforcement, the fear response had greater competition in this case than in the case of regular or interval schedules. This shows that, by manipulating the variables that affect a competing response, it is possible to affect the resistance to extinction of a given response.

These results suggest that developing competing responses is an effective method of facilitating extinction of a given response. Guthrie (1935) and Shoben (1949) have recommended this "counter-conditioning" method as a psychotherapeutic device for eradicating undesirable habits of response.

*State of the organism.* There is some evidence that, holding constant the condition of the organism at the time of acquisition of a response, the resistance to extinction of the response is a function of the state of the organism at the time of extinction trials. The evidence comes from two types of studies, deprivation experiments and drug experiments. An experiment by Lewis & Cotton (1957) is an example of the first type of study. They investigated the effects of 1, 6, and 22 hr. of food deprivation on the extinction of a running (to food) response in rats. They found that 1-hr. deprivation during extinction resulted in slower running than either 6 or 22 hr. of deprivation. Some of the early drug studies have been discussed by Hilgard & Marquis (1940, p. 119 f.). They point out that in general the administration of the drugs of a depressant nature (e.g. sodium bromide) accelerates the rate of extinction, while the administration of excitant drugs (e.g. benzedrine) decreases the rate of extinction (i.e. increases resistance to extinction).

## Pre-extinction Characteristics of the Response

In addition to the types of factors mentioned above, the course of extinction of a given response is determined by the characteristics of the response before the extinction procedure is initiated. For example, the latency and rate of the response prior to extinction can be expected to be related to resistance to extinction. This relation does exist, but it is not as clear-cut as may be expected. Thus, Kobrick (1956) has found that resistance to extinction is not significantly correlated with either the latency or the speed measures of habit strength. He also investigated the relation between number of reinforcements given during acquisition and number of trials required for extinction. He found no consistent trend in the resistance to extinction of eight groups which, during acquisition, had received from 4 to 50 reinforcements. However, the latencies and speeds were found to vary consistently with the number of reinforcements during acquisition. These findings suggest that the type of mechanisms underlying the extinction of a response are not completely identical with those that operate during its acquisition.

That the state of the organism during the acquisition of a response affects the resistance to extinction of the response has been shown in the Lewis & Cotton (1957) experiment mentioned above. They found that, in the early extinction trials, the rats that had been trained under 22-hr. deprivation ran faster than those that had acquired the response under 6 or 1 hr. of deprivation. Resistance to extinction, as measured by the number of responses to an extinction criterion, was also found to be greater for the 22-hr.-deprivation group. In another type of study, Murphy & Miller (1955) administered daily injections of adreno-corticotrophic hormone to normal rats during the training of an avoidance response. These animals did not differ from control animals in the speed of acquisition of the response, but subsequently they showed greater resistance to extinction. The exact significance of this study is not clear, for the details of the relation between the various aspects of the state of the organism during the acquision of a response and the subsequent resistance to extinction of the response have not yet been studied systematically. It is possible that the state of the organism affects the extinction of responses acquired with a reward as reinforcer differently from those that have been reinforced by punishment termination.

A finding that is contrary to the idea of any simple relation between the initial habit strength (as measured by latency or rate) and the resistance to extinction of a response concerns the type of reinforcement schedule on which the response has been maintained. In general, studies have shown that a response has greater resistance to extinction when it has been maintained on some form of intermittent reinforcement than when it has been regularly reinforced. In their review of relevant studies, Jenkins & Stanley (1950) enumerated over a dozen experiments, employing a variety of responses, which show that resistance to extinction is greater under intermittent than under regular reinforcement. It has also been shown by Crum, Brown, & Bitterman (1951), Peterson (1956), and Scott & Wike (1956) that training under conditions of delayed reinforcement also makes for greater resistance to extinction. While the greater resistance to extinction of responses maintained on intermittent or delayed reinforcement has implications for a theoretical interpretation of extinction, the fact itself is of considerable importance. It suggests a possible reason for the extreme resistance to extinction of many motivational activities which, in the natural habitat of most animals, must often go unreinforced.

This chapter has considered, without getting involved in "learning theory," some of the variables that are important in the acquisition, maintenance, and extinction of responses. By definition, variations in habit strength of a response are directly related to the probability of its occurrence. However, there are other factors that also significantly determine the occurrence of responses that exist in the repertoires of animals. In the following chapters we shall see that the variable of habit strength interacts significantly with situational, chemical, and other variables that, together with habit strength, determine the occurrence of various classes of responses.

# Chapter 7

# The Role of Sensory Cues

Of the numerous activities of varying habit strength that exist in the repertoire of an animal only some occur at any given time. Many factors determine the occurrence of particular responses. One of these is sensory stimulation, originating externally or from within the organism. Sensory stimulation determines the occurrence of responses in two ways. First, it provides "cues" for differential response, thus eliciting one rather than another response from the animal. Second, sensory stimulation produces variations in the general alertness or "level of arousal" of the animal, and these variations affect its responses in significant ways. This chapter is concerned with the role of sensory cues in determining response; in the next we shall turn to the level-of-arousal or the "nonspecific" function of sensory stimulation.

The occurrence of any activity depends, among other things, upon a variety of external and internal sensory cues. No matter how appropriate the other circumstances, a given activity can occur only within a certain range of variation of the sensory cues that were present when the activity was acquired or first occurred. If the pattern of sensory stimulation changes radically, the activity will change too. For example, if the auditory, olfactory, or any other characteristics of the cage in which a rat is eating food are substantially changed, the animal will stop eating and start exploring. However, minor variations in sensory stimulation modify the occurrence of any given activity only in certain limited ways. The nature of such control of activities by sensory cues is the concern of this chapter. The problem is approached first by considering in general terms the role of sensory cues in guiding behavior and then by asking specific questions about the effects of the variation in cues on given responses.

## GUIDANCE BY SENSORY CUES

For convenience, the studies in this area may be divided into those concerned with exteroceptive sensory cues and those dealing with interoceptive cues. Fundamentally, there is no difference between these two types of cues; both result from activity in sensory receptors and the related neural pathways and areas. Modifying Restle's (1955) definition slightly, a *sensory cue* may be looked upon as any characteristic of a stimulus to which an organism can learn to make a differential response.

### EXTEROCEPTIVE CUES

One of Beach's (1942) studies of sexual responses illustrates the role of exteroceptive sensory cues in initiating and guiding behavior. In one part of his study he worked with sexually experienced male rats, all of whom were vigorous copulators. After observing their sexual performance with receptive female rats, Beach subjected the males to various operations so as to eliminate three types of sensory stimulation. Some of the animals were blinded, some were made anosmic, some were deprived of tactual sensitivity in the skin of the snout and lips, some were blinded and deprived of tactual cues, some were blinded and made anosmic, and one rat was blinded, made anosmic, and deprived of tactual stimulation. On the postoperative copulation tests with receptive females, Beach found that all the experienced males with any one or two of the three types of cues eliminated continued to copulate normally. However, the male in whom all three types of cues were eliminated failed to copulate postoperatively. This investigation suggests that (1) none of the three types of sensory cues is necessary for the occurrence of copulatory behavior in the sexually sophisticated male, and (2) there is a definite limit to the number and kind of sensory cues that can be eliminated without greatly reducing the probability of occurrence of copulation in its normal form.

In an analogous experiment on maternal retrieving in rats, Beach & Jaynes (1956) studied the sensory cues involved in the retrieving of young pups to the nest. Sensory cues were varied either by surgical operations on the mother or by altering the stimulus characteristics (e.g. odor, color, temperature) of the pups. As in the case of sexual behavior, the retrieving activity was found to be governed by a combination of cues from different sense modalities, but no single modality was indispensable. Furthermore, the degree of interference with retrieving activity was directly proportional to the extent to which the normal sensory cues were altered. Unfortunately, as yet little is known about the essential features of the stimulus patterns that normally are sufficient for evoking the various types of species-specific behavior. The work of ethologists has created considerable interest in the study of this problem, and many investigations now appear to be in progress. For example, Fisher & Hale (1956–57) have determined some of the stimulus characteristics that normally elicit sexual and aggressive responses in male chickens. They found that postural position rather than sexual morphology of the stimulus animal (or model) was important in determining the responses of cocks. The crouching position, irrespective of sex, was most effective in eliciting sexual responses and, in general, the crouching position did not elicit aggressive responses. Studies of this type not only contribute to an analysis of the cues that are normally effective in eliciting a given type of response, but are also likely to reveal some of the developmental factors that make the particular cues effective (see Chap. 4).

Another part of the investigation by Beach (1942) mentioned above demonstrates an interaction between habit strength and sensory cues. In the part of the experiment described above, all the animals used were sexually experienced, vigorous copulators. Beach also observed the effects of similar operations on sexually inexperienced male rats. As was noted in Chapter 2, a normal sexually naive male rat usually copulates successfully on its first encounter with a receptive female, and this indeed is what the animals in Beach's naive control group did. However, the naive-operated animals behaved differently. Even the animals deprived of only one sensory modality did not copulate as much as the control animals, and no animal deprived of more than one type of sensory cues copulated or attempted to copulate with a receptive female. It will be recalled that in the case of the sexually experienced animals the removal of even two types of sensory cues did not affect normal copulation. Thus, it appears that when the habit strength of the copulatory response is high, as in the sexually experienced males, fewer sensory cues are required to initiate it and to guide it to completion.

Variations in exteroceptive sensory cues also determine the resistance to extinction of a response. Hall (1955) and Hurwitz & Cutts (1957) have shown that extinction is more rapid under altered stimulus conditions than when the acquisition and extinction situations are the same. These investigations suggest that response probability is partly determined by the extent to which the available sensory cues deviate from those present in the training or acquisition situation.

INTEROCEPTIVE CUES

Since internal events result in sensory stimulation similar to that produced by external events, it is legitimate to ask whether interoceptive sensory cues are comparable to those arising from exteroceptive stimulation. It is well known that sensory stimulation does arise from various visceral organs. It is the problem of the possible role of such stimulation in providing cues that is considered in this section.

*Can interoceptive stimuli serve as cues?* Hull (1933) posed this question and attempted to answer it. He wanted to determine if the sensory stimulation arising from the visceral consequences of food deprivation (hunger) and of water deprivation (thirst) could serve as cues. Holding constant other sensory cues, he tried to determine whether rats would make one of two alternative choices when hungry, and the other choice when thirsty. He made animals hungry and thirsty on alternate days and forced them into taking one or the other of two paths, each leading to a goal box. On hunger days the animals were led into the food goal box, and on thirst days into the water goal box. On test trials, the animals, either hungry or thirsty, were allowed a free choice of path. Hull found that the animals took the "food path" when hungry and "water path" when thirsty, thus showing that visceral stimuli can serve as crucial cues in determining differential response. This finding was corroborated by Leeper (1935).[1]

In Hull's (1933) experiment, as well as in many others, the visceral conditions (hunger or thirst, or both) which provided the sensory cues were also relevant to the type of reinforcers employed during training. This is so because the visceral conditions arising from food and water deprivation determine the effectiveness of food and water as reinforcers (see Chap. 5). Evidence that interoceptive stimuli that are not relevant to the source of the reinforcing effects can also serve as cues has been provided by Amsel and by Levine. In their experiments the reinforcer employed was the termination of a punishment, but the interoceptive cues were provided by hunger and thirst. The interoceptive cues were thus quite irrelevant to the source of the reinforcing effects (i.e. punishment termination). Amsel (1949), employing a T-maze, was able to train rats to escape an electric shock by going into one arm of the maze if they were hungry and into the other arm if they were thirsty. Since the only basis for making a left or a right turn was provided by the visceral consequences of food or water deprivation, it is clear that the interoceptive stimulation provided the necessary cues. In the Levine (1953) experiment rats were trained to push one of two panels to remove a noxious light. On some training days the animals were hungry; on others they were

[1] The particular interpretation that Hull (1933) placed on his results has led to a lively controversy among some learning theorists. The point at issue is whether the results of these "drive discrimination" experiments, as they are called, require a radical revision of Hull's (1943) learning theory. This controversy lies outside the scope of the present discussion. Those interested are referred to papers by Spence & Lippit (1940), Kendler (1949), Amsel (1949), Levine (1953), Woodbury & Wilder (1954), and Deutsch (1956).

thirsty. On hunger days, pushing the right panel resulted in light termination, but on thirst days it was a response to the left panel that terminated the light. Inasmuch as most of the animals learned to press one panel when hungry and the other when thirsty, the use of interoceptive stimulation as cues is demonstrated. As will be seen in the following pages, interoceptive stimuli other than those related to hunger and thirst can also serve as cues in guiding response.

That differential response can be made on the basis of cues arising from different intensities of deprivation, and, thus, presumably, different intensities of interoceptive stimulation, has been shown by Jenkins & Hanratty (1949). They trained rats, with 11½-hr. and 47½-hr. food deprivation, in a T-maze. The correct (rewarded) response was a right turn for the shorter deprivation period and a left turn for the longer deprivation period. They found that the animals learned to make the correct turn for each of the two degrees of deprivation. Bloomberg & Webb (1949) have also shown that differential spatial response can be made on the basis of intensity differences in deprivation.

*Effectiveness of interoceptive cues.* The number of discriminations along stimulus dimensions that can normally be made in the case of vision and audition appears to be much greater than that in the case of sense modalities such as touch (pressure), heat, cold, and pain. Since interoceptive (visceral) sensitivity is almost wholly of the latter type, it is likely that changes in visceral stimuli will not be discriminated as efficiently as are the changes in exteroceptive stimuli, especially the visual and auditory. The localization of visceral stimuli appears also to be less accurate than that of exteroceptive stimuli (Boring, 1915). Therefore, it seems reasonable to expect that the use of visceral stimuli as the basis of sensory cues for directing behavior will be much more limited than that of exteroceptive stimuli. However, within the limits of visceral sensitivity, it can still be asked whether visceral stimuli provide as effective cues in evoking differential response as do exteroceptive stimuli.

Bailey (1955) has attempted to answer this question. He trained rats to press one of two panels to turn off a noxious light. Whether one or the other panel was correct on any given day depended upon the type of cues provided. Some animals were required to make the differential response on the basis of hunger-vs.-thirst cues, and others were required to do so on the basis of the presence or absence of a tone just before the response was to occur. The performance of animals to which only interoceptive (hunger-thirst) cues were available was no different from that of the animals which learned the problem with exteroceptive (tone) cues. More investigations are needed, of course, before one can make any general statements concerning the relative effectiveness of interoceptive and exteroceptive sensory cues. However, Bailey's study does suggest that, so long as interoceptive stimuli are discriminable enough to provide cues, they can be as effective as cues arising from some exteroceptive stimuli.

*Source of interoceptive cues.* There are numerous sources of interoceptive sensory stimulation. When there is evidence that a certain differential response is made on the basis of interoceptive cues, one is led to ask about the exact source of the cue-providing sensory stimulation. For example, in the studies discussed in the last section the animals were able to distinguish between the internal consequences of food deprivation (hunger) and those of water deprivation (thirst). This discrimination could have been made on the basis of the presence vs. absence of hunger, or on the basis of the presence vs. absence of thirst, or on the basis of the presence of hunger vs. the presence of thirst. As Heron (1949) has pointed out, from the results reported we cannot determine whether all three of these factors can individually provide the necessary cues for discrimination. Bailey (1955) has answered this question by demonstrating that rats can discriminate between hunger and food satiation, between thirst and water satiation, and between hunger and thirst. Thus, both hunger and thirst can individually provide sufficient cues for differential response.

The hunger-vs.-thirst discrimination could be made on the basis of sensory stimuli arising from variations in stomach motility and distension, or it could be made on the basis of some other sensory stimuli that are normally associated with hunger and with thirst. Bailey & Porter (1955) have started to investigate the exact source of the hunger and thirst sensory cues. They trained cats to make a differential response on the basis of hunger vs. thirst. The trained cats were then tested under conditions of complete food satiation. In this condition stomach motility and distension would provide the type of stimulation that normally occurs in thirst, because thirst does not normally involve an empty stomach. If the cats had discriminated on the basis of stimuli from the stomach, then, during the test, they should have made more water than food choices. However, they did not do this. The cats were also tested when they were very thirsty *and* hungry, so that the cues from the stomach were like those that normally occur during hunger. Now the cats made significantly more water choices than food choices, which is the opposite of what the stomach-stimuli hypothesis would require. Thus, the hunger-vs.-thirst discrimination does not necessarily depend upon differential stimulation from the stomach itself; that is to say, the hunger-vs.-thirst discrimination can be maintained on the basis of cues other than those arising from stomach motility and distension. Whether this discrimination can also be *acquired* in the absence of stomach cues is a question which remains to be answered. It is quite plausible that, at least in the adult animal, the discrimination can be acquired and maintained on the basis of dryness of mouth and throat, "weakness" or muscular fatigue, variations in activity, and other such factors that are differentially related to food and water deprivation but are not associated with stomach distension or motility.

Of course, not all interoceptive stimuli arise as a consequence of food or water deprivation. Variations in sensory stimulation are provided by vascular changes in the genitalia, and it is likely that these variations, too, can serve as cues for differential response. Similarly, other visceral and skeletal events, such as changes in breathing and heart rate, variations in muscular tension, rapid versus slow breathing, provide stimuli which can serve as cues in directing response. A study by

Conger is relevant to this point. Conger (1951) was able to train rats to make a differential response on the basis of whether they were intoxicated or sober. Apparently, the presence of alcohol in the bloodstream led to bodily events the sensory feedback from which served as cues for differential response. The exact source of these "intoxication cues" is not known. They may arise from changes in body temperature, from relaxation of muscular tonus, from inability to focus eyes properly on an object, from changes in breathing, or from a variety of other visceral and kinesthetic effects of alcohol. While the exact sources of interoceptive cues that normally guide the various classes of response remain to be investigated, it seems reasonable to conclude that the sensory feedback from the visceral and skeletal events is at least as important in providing cues for guiding response as is exteroceptive stimulation.

*Interoceptive stimuli in avoidance training.* An interpretation of avoidance conditioning that has been adopted by Mowrer (1939), Mowrer & Lamoreaux (1946), and Solomon & Wynne (1953) and is currently widely accepted is as follows. The repeated presentation of a noxious stimulation (e.g. an electric shock) soon after the conditioned stimulus (e.g. a buzzer) results, first of all, in the conditioning of certain visceral and skeletal responses to the buzzer. The electric shock is the unconditioned stimulus for evoking a variety of visceral and skeletal responses, including changes in heart rate, breathing cycle, perspiration, stomach motility, and so on. (Collectively, these responses are sometimes referred to as "fear" or "anxiety.") When, in the course of its random movements provoked by the shock, the animal lands on the safe, no-shock side of the apparatus (e.g. a shuttle box), the termination of the shock reinforces the response of jumping from one to the other side of the shuttle box. Then as the training procedure continues, the visceral and skeletal responses elicited by the conditioned stimulus provide the cues for making the jumping response even before the shock comes on. Thus, the interoceptive stimuli originating in the visceral and the skeletal musculature, and not the shock itself, begin to evoke the response, and thus it becomes an avoidance rather than an escape response. It is evident that this interpretation ascribes a crucial role to interoceptive stimuli in the establishment of avoidance responses.

The evidence bearing on the role of interoceptive stimuli in avoidance training is both complicated and interesting. Wynne & Solomon (1955), in the study mentioned in the last chapter, worked on the assumption that any interference with the normal sensory feedback from visceral reactions will alter the course of avoidance learning. They subjected dogs to various surgical and pharmacological procedures designed to block peripheral autonomic function without affecting the rest of the sensory and motor systems. They found that the 13 dogs who had been given the surgical-drug procedures before avoidance training were, in general, retarded in making their first avoidance response as compared with normal animals. However, eventually they all reached the learning criterion of 10 successive avoidance responses. An unusual finding was that in 8 of the 13 animals the response extinguished spontaneously between testing sessions—normal avoidance responses extinguish only with great difficulty.

In the case of the animals which were trained before the surgical-drug procedures, the results were quite different. Their performance did not differ from that of the normal animals, which showed a high resistance to extinction. This study demonstrates that (1) the stimuli arising from the autonomically innervated visceral events can contribute to the acquisition of an avoidance response, and (2) once the avoidance response has been well established, it can be adequately maintained in the absence of this type of sensory feedback. Consistent with these results is the finding of Bersh, Notterman, & Schoenfeld (1956) concerning the course of a cardiac response during avoidance training in human subjects. Their subjects showed an increase in the cardiac response during the early training trials, but later, with continued avoidance responding, the cardiac response tended to disappear. Another corroborative result is the one obtained by Black (1956). He found the occurrence of an avoidance response to be highly correlated with the presence of a cardiac response only during the early training trials; this correlation disappeared during extinction trials.

How is an avoidance response maintained when the animal no longer receives any shock and, therefore, no reinforcement from shock termination? This is a question that has puzzled learning theorists for a long time, especially since the avoidance response, when normally established, is highly persistent and resistant to extinction (*see* Chap. 6). The commonly-held view is that the response is maintained because it continues to be reinforced in some way other than by shock termination. According to Mowrer (1939), the reinforcement comes from reduction in "anxiety" or drive, that is, from the reduction of the strong stimuli arising from visceral events. Each presentation of the conditioned stimulus evokes the conditioned visceral reactions, and each time the animal makes the avoidance response the visceral reactions are reduced (drive or "anxiety" reduction). This drive reduction, according to Mowrer, constitutes the reinforcement which maintains the avoidance response in the absence of shock and shock termination. The exact event that reduces visceral reactions is considered by Mowrer to be the termination of the conditioned stimulus—this termination usually occurs as soon as the animal has made the avoidance response. That this factor of response termination of the conditioned stimulus is important in determining the maintenance of the avoidance response has been shown by Mowrer & Lamoreaux (1942) and Kamin (1956). Kamin (1957, 1957a) has also shown that the greater the delay in terminating the conditioned stimulus after the occurrence of the avoidance response the less likely is the response to be maintained. In spite of this experimental support, the main (i.e. the drive-reduction) point of Mowrer's interpretation is not supported by the experimental results reported in the last paragraph. Those experiments show that the cardiac reactions ("anxiety") have a prominent role only in the initial stages of learning. Once the avoidance response has been established, that is, when Mowrer's interpretation most needs them, the cardiac reactions to the conditioned stimulus are all but absent. Of course, it is still possible that some other visceral cues, not connected with cardiac reactions, may persist and serve to maintain the avoidance response, but this remains to be demonstrated.

Schoenfeld (1950) has proposed an alternative source of reinforcement for the maintenance of avoidance responses. He suggests that various proprioceptive and exteroceptive stimuli which are associated with the successful (shock-terminating) response during training acquire secondary reinforcing properties, and it is these secondary reinforcing stimuli that maintain the avoidance response in the absence of primary reinforcement from shock termination. Whether the stimuli of the type considered important by Schoenfeld can and do serve as secondary reinforcers cannot be stated with certainty. Goodson & Brownstein (1955) shocked rats in a black box and allowed them to escape into a white box. Later, on preference tests, the white box was shown to possess (secondary) reinforcing properties. But Nefzger (1957), in a similar experiment, found no indication that stimuli associated with shock reduction acquire sufficient reinforcing power to effect learning in a simple choice situation. In any event, the difficulty with Schoenfeld's interpretation is that it relies too heavily upon secondary reinforcers. It is hard to see why the proprioceptive and other stimuli retain their secondary reinforcing properties for so long after the primary reinforcement, shock termination, no longer operates. In general, studies (e.g. Cowles, 1937) on secondary reinforcers have shown that their reinforcing properties decline rapidly after they cease to be associated with primary reinforcers. Therefore, it is necessary to explain why the stimuli that Schoenfeld regards as secondary reinforcers continue to retain their reinforcing properties for thousands of nonprimary-reinforced trials. This the Schoenfeld interpretation does not do.

Alternatives to the Mowrer and Schoenfeld interpretations can, of course, be found. For example, instead of saying that the visceral and kinesthetic stimuli are directly or indirectly the source of some form of reinforcement, it can be assumed that the internal (and external) stimuli only provide the necessary cues, without serving a reinforcing function, so far as the maintenance of the avoidance response is concerned. Specifically, such a hypothesis can be stated in the form of three propositions: (1) Once established, the continued maintenance of an avoidance response does not depend upon the operation of any primary or secondary reinforcers. (2) The continued performance depends, among other things (not relevant to this discussion), on the presence or absence of external and internal stimuli which have consistently occurred contiguously with the avoidance response. That is to say, after the training has been completed, the occurrence or nonoccurrence of the response depends upon the extent to which the cues associated with the response are present in the situation. If the suggestion of Dinsmoor (1950) and Zimmerman (1957) that the so-called secondary reinforcers are nothing more than discriminated sensory cues is correct, Schoenfeld's (1950) hypothesis would become almost identical with this proposition. (3) As performance continues beyond the stage where the avoidance response has been fully acquired, a progressively smaller number or proportion of relevant cues is required to maintain the response. That is to say, the relative importance of central factors, as opposed to peripheral sensory stimulation, increases. Thus, in later stages, the disappearance of visceral reactions and their sensory feedback, or of any other cues, would have little effect on the probability of occurrence of the avoidance response. The second proposition above only states the position of Guthrie (1935) with respect to learning in general. However, the first and the third propositions add important qualifications to Guthrie's principle.

*Interoceptive cues in eating, drinking, and sexual responses.* The exact role of internal cues in seeking and ingesting food and water, and in sexual activity, is far from clear. It is well known that bodily changes associated with food and water deprivations and with sexual readiness result in the stimulation of interoceptive sensory fibers. Gastric contractions of an empty stomach, dryness of the mouth and throat, and vascular changes in the genitals are communicated to the central nervous system through the afferent system. Furthermore, at least in the case of the consequences of food deprivation, it has been shown by Cannon & Washburn (1912) and Carlson (1912) that gastric contractions form the basis of the subjective reports of "sensation of hunger." It appears that the subjective reports of "sensations of thirst and sexual excitement" likewise depend upon sensory impulses from, respectively, dry throat and mouth and vascularly distended and otherwise changed genital organs. However, assuming that the subjective reports of sensations of hunger, thirst, and sexual excitement depend upon sensory impulses from certain parts of the body, one still must inquire into the role of such impulses in the occurrence of eating, drinking, and sexual responses.

The available evidence points to at least one definite conclusion. It is that in adult, sophisticated animals sensory impulses from the relevant organs are not essential for eating, drinking, and sexual responses to occur. Tsang (1938) has shown that rats whose stomachs have been removed continue to eat and to display the usual activities associated with eating in a normal way. Similar results are obtained when all the nervous pathways connecting the stomach with the brain are denervated. Rats with a surgical operation of this type have been shown by Bash (1939) to eat normally and to perform as well as normal animals on obstruction tests with food as reward. Bellows' (1939) and Holmes' (1941) experiments on drinking in dogs also suggest that dryness of the mouth and throat is not crucially related to drinking, inasmuch as they found that placing water directly into the stomach, with throat and mouth dry, inhibits drinking. Similarly, in the case of sexual behavior, it has been found that normal sexual responses can occur in the absence of sensory stimulation from the genitals. Ball (1934) has shown this in the female rat after removal of uterus and vagina, Bard (1935) in cats with denervated sexual apparatus. Evidence of this kind has inclined Morgan (1943) to the view that sensory impulses from the relevant organs do not play a necessary part in the occurrence of eating, drinking, and sexual responses. However, it must be remembered that almost all the available evidence comes from sophisticated adult animals. It is quite possible

that the type of interoceptive sensory stimulation under discussion plays a crucial part in the development and the earlier
occurrences of these responses but that once the responses are
well established, they cease to be dependent upon such sensory
stimulation. In the adult animal, these responses may be under
the control of external stimulation (sight and smell of food,
etc.) instead of, or in addition to, the interoceptive cues. Some
of the studies discussed earlier in this chapter are relevant in
this connection. They showed that fewer sensory cues are
needed in guiding a response as the response becomes well-
practiced. In order to be able to propose that sensory stimulation from the relevant organs is not at all necessary for eating,
drinking, and sexual responses, one would have to show that
such stimulation not only is not necessary for the occurrence
of these responses in adult sophisticated animals, but likewise
plays no crucial role in the development and the early occurrences of these responses.

*Disruption of normal cues by drugs.* Surgical or pharma-
cologic interference specifically with receptors and their central connections is not the only means of disrupting the cues
that are normally involved in a response. Certain drugs that
have more general effects on the body also affect the occurrence of responses, and presumably they do so by altering the
pattern of interoceptive cues. Bailey & Miller (1952) trained
hungry cats to obtain food by pushing a hinged shield. Later,
the animals were shocked for the same response, and they
stopped approaching the food. Then some of the animals
were given an injection of sodium amytal and others an injection of saline. After the injections, all the drugged animals
started making the food response again but, in general, the
control animals did not resume attempting to obtain food.
Bailey & Miller tentatively conclude that sodium amytal produces a greater reduction in "fear" than it does in the tendency to approach food. These results can be interpreted as
showing that the drug disrupts the sensory cues involved in
the avoidance response more than it disrupts the sensory cues
involved in approaching food. An experiment by John,
Wenzel, & Tschirgi (1958) shows that the administration of

reserpine also reduces the occurrence of an avoidance response more readily than that of a food-rewarded response. These studies suggest that the interoceptive cues normally involved in a food-approach response are less subject to disruption by such sedative drugs than are the interoceptive cues normally involved in an avoidance response.

## CONCLUSION

Clearly, sensory stimulation of both interoceptive and exteroceptive origins serves an important cue function. These cues form an essential part of the conditions which determine the occurrence of any given response. However, the exact cues involved at different stages in the development of various classes of activities have not yet been systematically investigated. Detailed research in this field will provide the basis for generalizations concerning the nature and manner of operation of such cues. The available evidence does, however, suggest one tentative generalization: With all other relevant conditions held constant, the number or type, or both, of cues required for the occurrence of a given response decreases as the habit strength of the response is increased. That is to say, cues that, in the initial stages of acquisition and practice, may have served an essential function, cease to be necessary for the occurrence of the response when it is well-practiced. In a sense, then, the response becomes independent, or "functionally autonomous" (Allport, 1937), of some of the cues that were necessary to establish it.

### EFFECTS OF VARIATION OF SENSORY STIMULATION

When a response has been acquired in a given situation, its elicitation is by no means restricted to that situation alone. The response is also likely to occur in a number of other situations. That is to say, so long as the other relevant conditions remain the same, the response will also occur in a more or less normal way when the stimulus situation (i.e. the pattern of sensory cues) is not quite the same as the one that prevailed at the time of acquisition of the response. A number of specific questions can be asked about this general problem.

Limits of Effective Stimulation

The problem of the limits of variation of sensory cues within which a response acquired in a specified situation will occur is the one that should be faced first. That there are such limits of variation of sensory cues for the occurrence of a given response is obvious enough. In Beach's (1942) experiment, described earlier in this chapter, it was found that, when all the three sets of sensory cues were eliminated by altering the discriminative capacities of the rat, the copulatory responses of the animal were radically different from those shown by the normal animals. Hebb (1946a) has shown that the normal friendly behavior of some chimpanzees may be replaced by aggressive or withdrawal responses when certain stimulus elements in the experimental situation are altered. Berlyne (1950) and many other investigators have shown that resting animals will start exploring as soon as a novel stimulus object is introduced into the cage. In each of these cases we are dealing with a response that was acquired in a particular situation and is now present in the animal's repertoire, and we note that, if the sensory cues associated with acquisition or with earlier performance are altered beyond some (unknown) limit, there is a radical change in the animal's behavior. While there are many questions that can be asked about the limits of effective sensory cues in various types of activities, perhaps the most fruitful point to discuss is the factors that determine the range of variation of sensory cues within which a given response, already present in the animal's repertoire, will occur. Three main variables seem to determine this: (1) habit strength, (2) acquisition conditions, and (3) nature of stimulus variation.

*Habit strength.* Beach's (1942) analysis of the stimuli that contribute to copulation suggests that habit strength or prior performance determines the range of effective stimuli. He tested the copulatory behavior of the male rat not only in the presence of a receptive female rat but also, separately, in the presence of a nonreceptive female rat, a small male rat, a young female guinea pig, and a young female rabbit. He found that the tendency to attempt copulation with these incentive animals was much greater in males who had previously copulated with a receptive female rat than in males with no prior copulatory experience. A similar result has been reported by Hinde.[2] He found that sexually experienced birds had a greater tendency to attempt copulation with a stationary model bird than did inexperienced birds. Both these studies suggest that the range of variation of stimuli within which a given response occurs is a function of the habit strength of that response. Such a relation between habit strength and degree of "generalization" to other related stimuli was explicitly postulated by Hull (1943). (*See* Fig. 15.) He assumed the degree of generalization to vary with both (1) the difference, along a stated dimension, between the training situation ($S_o$) and the test situation ($S_x$), and (2) the amount of habit strength developed by the end of training. The latter statement implies that the range of effective stimuli for a given response is directly dependent upon the habit strength of the response.

Besides habit strength, it is likely that certain other factors that determine the probability of occurrence of a response also affect the range of sensory cues within which that response will occur. For example, transitory changes in blood chemistry may make a certain response (of a given habit strength) more or less likely to occur. It is likely that, if the change in blood chemistry is such as to increase response probability, it will also increase the range of sensory variation within which that response will occur. Beach (1942) has noted that normal male rats injected with large amounts of androgenic hormone tend to attempt to mate with a wider range of stimulus objects than do males without prior hormone treatment. There appear to be no other experiments directly bearing on this point, but the evidence on the roles of arousal (Chap. 8) and blood chemistry (Chap. 9) strongly suggests that any transitory condition that increases (or decreases) response probability will also increase (or decrease) the range of stimuli effective in evoking the response.

[2] In a personal communication to the author, from Dr. R. A. Hinde, Ornithological Field Station, Department of Zoology, Cambridge University, Cambridge, England.

*Acquisition conditions.* The stimulus conditions present during the acquisition of a response are probably also important in determining the range of variation of stimulation within which the response will occur. It appears likely that if the stimulus cues are varied during the acquisition of a response, then the response will occur in a greater variety of (test) situations than if the stimulus cues remain exactly the same throughout the acquisition period. Indirect support for such a hypothesis comes from a study by Luborsky (1945). He studied the performance on an airplane-silhouette recognition task after two procedures of training. In one case only three silhouettes were used in training and, in the other case, five. Subsequently, on tests with previously unseen silhouettes, he found that recognition was more accurate with the five-silhouette training procedure. These findings are consistent with the view that variation of stimulus cues during training increases the range of stimulations under which the response will be made. Harlow's (1949) concept of "learning sets" and the "breadth of experience" concept of Bruner *et al.* (1955) can probably be looked upon as extensions of this principle in the area of problem solving. Wolfle (1935) has shown that speed of acquisition itself decreases with increased stimulus variation. However, once the response is acquired, it is likely to occur within a wide range of stimulus situations if it was acquired under conditions of varying stimulus cues.

*Nature of stimulus variation.* The range of variation of a situation within which a given response will continue to occur seems to depend also upon the exact nature of the stimulus variation. A situation can be varied along a number of dimensions. Even if the crucial training stimulus in a situation were a simple tone, it could be varied in frequency (pitch) or in amplitude (loudness). Ordinarily, any stimulus situation can be varied along numerous dimensions. Now, it appears that the range of variation of a given situation within which a response will occur depends upon whether the situation is varied along a dimension which the animal can and does discriminate. If the animal does not discriminate between stimuli along a given dimension, then it is likely to give similar responses to variations of the stimulus situation along that dimension. A child who has been trained to call a small four-legged animal "cat," will tend to give the response "cat" to a variety of small four-legged animals until he comes across some negative instances, where a small four-legged animal is not called a cat. Razran (1949) has pointed out that conditions such as decortication and the use of certain drugs which reduce discriminative abilities increase the tendency to give "the same" response.

### RESPONSE VARIATIONS WITHIN THE LIMITS OF EFFECTIVE STIMULATION

If sensory cues are varied within the effective range for a given response, the response usually shows minor variations in some of its characteristics. Thus, it may occur with different latencies or amplitudes, or may show alterations in its rate or extinction characteristics. However, in spite of these changes, the response is identifiable as the same response, and in this respect the present discussion differs from that of the last section. Here we shall deal with the problem of the minor variations in a given response brought about by altering the sensory stimulation within the effective range. This is what is usually referred to as the problem of "stimulus generalization," though, as will be seen, this phrase is somewhat misleading.

*The main findings.* In a typical experiment in this area, a group of subjects is trained to respond in a certain way, $R_o$, to a stimulus, $S_o$. After training to some criterion, the subjects are divided into subgroups, and each subgroup is tested on one of $S_l$, $S_m$, $S_n$, $S_p$, $S_q$, or $S_r$, stimuli that are variations, along a certain dimension, of the original stimulus, $S_o$ (*see* abscissa of Fig. 15). The data represent the changes in response $R_o$ as the test stimuli are varied from $S_l$ to $S_r$. The question most generally asked is whether the habit strengths of the responses $R_l$, $R_m$, $R_n$, $R_o$, $R_p$, $R_q$, $R_r$, etc. bear any systematic relation to each other and to the stimulus variations. Fig. 15 shows the relation postulated by Hull (1943).

An early affirmative answer to the above empirical question was provided by Pavlov (1928; 1st publ. 1910), Bass &

Hull (1934), and Hovland (1937, 1937a). In the Hovland experiments, a conditioned galvanic skin response was established to a tone in human subjects, and then the subjects were tested with tones that varied in frequency or intensity from the original conditioned tone, $S_o$. With both frequency and intensity variations Hovland found on the average that the magnitude of the response diminished as the (physical) differ-

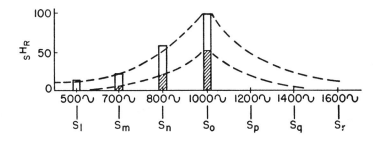

FIG. 15. GENERALIZATION GRADIENTS AS PROPOSED BY HULL

Representation of a bi-directional generalization gradient of the Hull type showing how amount of generalized habit strength (sHr) is assumed to vary with both (a) distance between training stimulus ($S_o$) and test stimuli ($S_1 \ldots S_r$) along the continuum and (b) amount of habit strength developed at the point of conditioning (cross-hatched vs. total extents of vertical bars). (*Source:* C. E. Osgood, *Method and theory in experimental psychology* [N.Y.: Oxford University Press, 1953], p. 352.)

ence between original training tone and the test tones increased. Corresponding extinction gradients are also indicated by some Pavlovian studies, by Bass & Hull, and by Hovland. Though subject to various interpretations, these empirical findings themselves seem no longer to be questioned. However, since only three or four test stimuli were employed in these studies, it is not known how far the decreasing-response gradients extend on either side of the training stimulus. Nor can we make any general statements about the exact shape of these gradients. Razran, after reviewing the available evidence and noting many reversals in the data from individual subjects, inclined to the view that the gradient is "very qualitative and very crude, consisting of only a few steps" (1949, p. 362).

While most, if not all, of the earlier investigators studied salivary or galvanic skin responses, later studies have concerned themselves with instrumental responses. Grice & Saltz (1950) trained rats to respond in a certain way when one of the five circles, 79, 63, 50, 32, and 20 sq. cm. in area, was presented. The animals were then tested for extinction on the other four stimuli. The results showed that the resistance to extinction was highest for the training stimulus, and it decreased progressively as the size difference between the training and the test stimuli increased. Kling (1952) investigated the effects of extinguishing (instead of training) an instrumental response to one stimulus on the habit strength of the response to other, related stimuli. His experimental plan consisted of training rats equally well on two discs of different sizes, extinguishing the response (obtaining food by opening a small door) to one of these stimuli, and then testing the animal on the other stimulus. He found that, in general, the habit strength was greater the farther removed in size the test stimulus was from the extinction stimulus. Thus, gradients representing decreasing habit strength of response with increasing difference between the training or extinction stimulus and the test stimuli seem to exist for instrumental responses, as they do for the classical-conditioning situations. But, as in the classical situation, the gradients are by no means smooth, and they have been established only for a few points on either side of the original training or extinction stimulus.

*Some interpretations of the obtained gradients.* The gradient of habit strength showing decreasing habit strength of responses evoked by stimuli that are progressively further removed from the training stimulus has traditionally been described as the gradient of "stimulus generalization." One view holds that the gradient is the outcome of some sort of an active "generalization process" which, during training, serves to establish bonds not only between the given response and the training stimulus but also (somewhat weaker bonds) between the response and other stimuli that are physically close to the training stimulus. This view, widely held since Pavlov's original writings on this subject, has been criticized by Lashley

& Wade (1946). According to them, the Pavlovian and other early experiments, each of which employed only a single stimulus during training, do not demonstrate true generalization; rather they represent a failure on the part of the animal to recognize, or abstract from the total situation, the crucial stimulus elements or dimensions. Thus, they think that the animal reacts to the test stimuli not because of any generalization of training effects but because the animal does not discriminate the difference between the test and the training stimuli. Lashley & Wade believe that prior discriminative experience with two or more stimuli lying on a stimulus dimension is essential before that dimension qua dimension can have any meaning for the animal. For example, it is only through previous experience in discriminating between tones of different frequencies that the "idea" of a dimension of frequency (or pitch) can be established in an animal. Hence Lashley & Wade are inclined to the view that only when a stimulus dimension has thus become meaningful to an animal can one talk of a true gradient of habit strength; otherwise the responses of the animal to test stimuli only represent failure of discrimination or "sensitization."

This view of Lashley & Wade—that training with single stimuli cannot yield a gradient of habit strength along that dimension—has been commented upon or questioned by Grandine & Harlow (1948), Grice (1948a, 1949, 1951), and Guttman & Kalish (1956). All these investigators report what appear to be true gradients of habit strength along nondiscriminated dimensions (i.e. after training on single stimuli). Grice (1949) concludes that no act of comparison (i.e. "idea" or conceptualization of a dimension) is involved in the differential responses made by the animal to the test stimuli. It appears, however, that a final answer to this question of "primary stimulus generalization" would require an experiment in which animals are reared without any use of a sense modality until the time of experiment. Such a procedure would guarantee that a discriminated dimension has not been established before the animal is subjected to experimentation. But this kind of experiment has not yet been done.

Another interpretation of the obtained gradients of habit strength may be proposed here. This interpretation does not rest on any assumption of conceptualization of relations between the test and training stimuli. Rather, it consists of the simple proposition that *any* change in sensory cues from the training to the test situation affects the response in some way, and the magnitude of the effect is proportional to the degree to which the sensory cues are altered. The change in sensory cues may facilitate the response under investigation, or it may interfere with it in some way.[3] The typical declining gradients of habit strength obtained in the so-called stimulus generalization experiments are thus attributed to the increasing interference with the response brought about by increasing changes in sensory cues. Changes in sensory cues may be brought about either by altering the stimulus situation, as in the typical stimulus generalization experiment, or by changing the sensory capacities of the organism, as in sensory deprivation experiments. But in either event, no distinction is made here between "relevant" and "irrelevant" stimulus cues. That is to say, from the present standpoint, it makes no difference whether some "relevant" or crucial training stimulus (tone, light, disc, etc.) is varied or some "irrelevant" aspect of the total stimulus situation (illumination or texture of the experimental chamber, the introduction or removal of a stimulus component, etc.) is changed. No matter what the source of change in sensory cues, the habit strength of the evoked response will be less than in the case of the original training situation. Another point to be noted is that no implication of discrimination and recognition of the altered stimulus conditions is involved in the present formulation. The interference effect on the response is assumed to be a function of any stimulus change that impinges on the organism's sensorium, that is, any stimulus change that produces a change in the sensory

[3] For this discussion we shall ignore the facilitating effects of changes in sensory cues except to note that even in "stimulus generalization" experiments, the test stimuli sometimes evoke a response of a greater magnitude than that evoked by the training stimulus. This is especially true in the case of stimulus variations along some intensity (rather than quality) dimension (e.g. Miller & Green, 1954).

cues. Thus, the obtained declining gradients of habit strength with increasing change in the test stimuli are not gradients of generalization, but *gradients of interference*. The typical stimulus generalization study thus becomes a special case of the general problem of interfering (and facilitating) effects of changes in sensory cues.

*Some evidence bearing on the proposed interpretation.* In the following paragraphs experimental findings and considerations that support the interpretation advanced here are briefly discussed.

1. Implied in the above interpretation is a distinction between the presence of sensory cues and the discrimination of changes in sensory stimulation. The change in response, according to the present interpretation, is brought about by altered sensory cues; whether the stimulus change underlying the altered sensory cues is discriminated by the animal is quite another question. In everyday life there are many instances where a stimulus change (e.g. change in the hair style of a friend) brings forth an altered response (e.g. exploratory eye movements) while the stimulus change itself is not discriminated until much later, if at all. There are also experiments that show that certain events (i.e. stimulus changes) can affect response without being discriminated or "attended to" as such. For example, in Maier's (1931) study of human problem solving it was shown that the direction of trial and error was significantly altered by providing certain cues, though the cues themselves were seldom recognized by the subjects. And Lazarus & McCleary (1951) have shown that some stimuli (syllables) that cannot be discriminated in themselves can evoke differential reactions (galvanic skin responses) in human subjects. Thus, the discrimination of any given stimuli as such is not necessary for those stimuli to provide cues that affect behavior in particular ways. The present interpretation of the obtained gradients of habit strength need not, and does not, contain any statement about the conditions which determine whether changes in stimuli are discriminated as such, or about the special consequences of such discrimination.

2. Lashley & Wade (1946) have stated that no "irradiation" or generalization effect occurs during training. The change in response is brought about by the fact that the training stimulus is replaced by the test stimulus, and it is at the time of the presentation of the test stimulus that the magnitude and other characteristics of the response are determined. An experiment by Razran (1949) supports this view of Lashley & Wade. Razran trained human subjects to give salivary conditioned responses to four Russian words that were unfamiliar to them. One group was told the English meaning before the generalization tests but after the training, and a second group was given one set of meanings just before the training and another, reverse, set of meanings just before the generalization tests. Then the subjects were tested with the English meanings as the test stimuli. It was found that the salivary response to the test stimuli depended on the meaning given to the Russian words just before the generalization tests and not on the meaning given before training. Razran concludes that "the course and very existence of CR generalization is more likely a function of the subsequent testing for generalization than of the original training of the conditioning" (1949, p. 358). This statement is consistent with the implication of the above interpretation that the response to the test stimuli is determined at the time when the animal is exposed to the altered situation with different sensory cues.

3. The interpretation proposed here states that the change in response is proportional to the extent to which the sensory cues are altered from the training to the testing situation. Direct support for this statement is to be found in an experiment by Fink & Patton (1953). They studied the drinking response in rats in a situation consisting of certain particular visual, auditory, and tactual stimulus components. After training, the animals were divided into a number of groups. Each group was tested in a situation where none, one, two, or all three of the stimulus components had been altered. Fink & Patton observed a decline in water consumption under all conditions where the stimulus characteristics of the situation were altered. Furthermore, they found that response decrement was

directly proportional to the number of stimulus components changed from the training to the testing situation. This suggests that the change in responses to a test stimulus is proportional to the extent to which the available sensory cues deviate from those present in the training situation.

According to the present interpretation, the decrement in habit strength when a response is evoked in the test situation is attributable to the altered sensory cues. There are two ways in which this can happen. First, following Guthrie (1935) and Estes (1950), one can say that the probability of response depends upon the proportion of stimulus elements that are common to the training and the test situations. Since the testing situation in the generalization experiments does not share all the elements of the training situation, the response in the testing situation is attenuated in some way. Second, one can postulate that the changed sensory cues evoke alternative responses (mainly exploratory), and these responses interfere with the occurrence of the response under investigation. These propositions are subject to empirical test.

Sensory Variations Associated with Particular
    Responses

So far we have considered the effects on a given response of variations in sensory cues without being concerned with any other responses that may also be evoked by the new set of sensory cues. Actually, our interpretation of stimulus generalization attributes the decrement in response to interference from other responses evoked by the changed stimulus situation. But in that discussion we left these "other" responses unspecified. There are many psychological investigations in which the particular responses, evoked alternatively or in addition to the one under investigation, are specified and, in some cases, controlled. The particular responses evoked by the changed cues may *interfere* with the response under investigation or they may *facilitate* the response. The term "conflict" is sometimes employed to designate the first of these cases.

*Interfering responses.* Many experiments of Warden (1931) and his collaborators can be considered as studies of the effects of interfering responses on a given learned response. Using rats, they employed what has come to be known as the "obstruction method." Essentially, the animal is trained to go from one compartment to another to obtain some reward. The two compartments are joined by a small passage which has a metal grill floor. After the animal is well practiced at walking over the grill to the reward compartment, the grill is electrified. A few contacts with the grill lead to a sharp decline in the rate of crossing over to the reward compartment. This decline in response rate can be attributed to the "other" responses evoked by the sight of the grilled passage that interfere with the response of going through the passage to the other compartment. Since the primary purpose of the experiments of Warden and his collaborators was a comparison (as shown by response decrement) of different types of rewards during different states of the animal (albino rat), they did not systematically study the exact nature of the interfering responses themselves. Thus, though their studies can be interpreted as studies of interference of one set of responses with another, they are not directly relevant to the present discussion. Detailed investigations of the exact responses that caused the interference would be more to the point.

In his studies of "experimental neurosis," Masserman (1943) employed an air blast or an electric shock to elicit responses that would interfere with the eating response of cats. This general method has been employed in a more analytic investigation by Lichtenstein (1950). He trained hungry, harnessed dogs to eat in a conditioning stock. When each dog had learned to eat the pellets of food as soon as they were delivered from the feeder mechanism, the animal was subjected to a procedure which elicited strong interfering responses. The dog was given a strong electric shock either when the food was delivered or when it began to eat it. Feeding "inhibition" developed quickly in the dogs; in some cases a single shock was sufficient to make the animal not eat in the conditioning stock for several subsequent sessions. Lichtenstein observed and recorded several other responses during the experimental sessions. On the postshock trials he found that, whenever food was delivered into the food box, the animals tended to show tremors, tics, abortive escape responses, and attack on the apparatus, apart from a variety of autonomic responses. Thus, when the delivery of food in the food box is a cue associated with both eating and these interfering responses, there is a marked change in the previously established eating behavior. Another observation of interest was that the interfering responses were not the same in all animals. After considerable initial variability in behavior, some animals settled on barking, others on struggling, others on biting the food box, and still others on tremors and tic-like movements. (It should be borne in mind that, if one chose to focus attention on such "shock responses," one could also study the interfering effects of food, or any other cue that is associated with a different response, on these shock-engendered responses. The definitions of the interfering and interfered-with responses are determined by the aims of the investigator.)

An investigation by Hunt & Brady (1951), the main purpose of which is not relevant here, provides evidence of an interference effect of a more subtle nature. They trained rats in a Skinner box to press a lever to obtain water. A steady rate of response was achieved by a schedule of intermittent reinforcement. Then the animals were given eight "emotional conditioning" trials. Each of these consisted of a 5-min. presentation of a clicking sound the termination of which was accompanied by a mild electric shock. It was found on the later, test, trials with lever pressing that the presentation of the clicking sound significantly depressed the rate of response, as shown in Fig. 16. Unfortunately, Hunt & Brady did not for their purposes need to record the other responses made by the animals during the decrease in lever pressing. They only report frequent defecation during the clicking. While even defecation alone probably interferes with the lever-pressing response, it is likely that the observed response decrement resulted also from other, unobserved, interfering responses such as grooming, sniffing, and "aimless" walking. Amsel & Cole (1953) have also found that the introduction of some of the cues from a shock situation into a drinking situation depresses

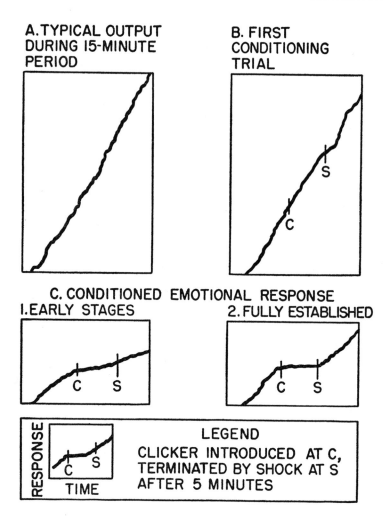

FIG. 16. CONDITIONED EMOTIONAL RESPONSE AS DEFINED BY HUNT
AND BRADY

The conditioned emotional response as it appears typically in the cumulative response curve. (*Source:* H. F. Hunt and J. V. Brady, Some effects of electroconvulsive shock on a conditioned emotional response ["anxiety"]. *J. comp. physiol. Psychol.,* 44, 90.)

the water intake of rats. They suggest a gradient of interference such that "the greater the similarity of the drinking to the shock situation, the greater the drop in level of water-intake" (1953, p. 247). Unfortunately, these investigators also failed to report the particular interfering responses that were evoked by the shock cues in the drinking situation; they simply attribute the interference to "anxiety." This is also true of the earlier studies of Estes & Skinner (1941) and Estes (1944).

In the above studies it was the interfered-with response that was the focus of the investigators' attention. The interfering responses were seldom recorded, and when recorded, as in the Lichtenstein experiment, they were not controlled. Only the stimuli, which were presumed to evoke some interfering responses, were controlled; the responses were not. Investigations in which both the interfering and the interfered-with responses are controlled and recorded have been done following some suggestions by Miller (1944) and Brown (1948). They have explicitly stated and tested in a preliminary way the assumptions on which completely controlled investigations could be carried out. Perhaps the simplest case of this type of study is the one in which the two responses are in simple opposition to each other. Thus, Rigby (1954) trained rats to obtain food by pressing forward on a slide on the presentation of a light, and to avoid an electric shock by pulling the slide backward on the presentation of a buzzer. After these responses were well established, the light and buzzer were presented simultaneously. Rigby found that under these "conflict conditions," that is, when the cues for both the responses were present simultaneously, the animals either sat motionless or became motionless after some initial increase in activity. The animals did not show either one of the two trained responses. The exact behavior shown in situations of this type probably depends upon the habit strength of the opposing responses and of other responses in the animal's repertoire, as well as on other parameters such as degree of deprivation, level of arousal (see Chap. 8), state of blood chemistry, and so on. The exact relation between such variables on the one hand and the occurrence of the interfering, interfered-with, or other alternative responses (sometimes called "displacement" responses) on the other is not known at present. Experimental work in this area has barely begun.

*Facilitating responses.* Though there are numerous studies of responses that interfere with a given response, there are hardly any studies of responses that facilitate the given response. However, a few investigations of facilitation of feeding responses can be interpreted as falling in the latter category. Both Ross & Ross (1949, 1949a) and James (1953) have shown that some dogs eat more in a group situation, in the presence of other dogs, than they do when fed individually alone. Furthermore, animals that had been individually fed and sated were found to start eating again when they were placed in a group-feeding situation. It is likely that the increased eating in a group situation results from the increase in sensory cues (e.g. sight of other animals eating and hearing the eating sounds made by them) associated with eating. In the case of animals that did not show any increase in eating under the group conditions, it is possible that the facilitation brought about by the new or increased sensory cues was counteracted by some interfering responses evoked by other aspects of the group situation. The sight of other animals eating would presumably provide effective sensory cues only if the animals have been reared and fed in groups. However, eating sounds probably become associated with eating even when an animal has been reared alone, for it can hear its own eating sounds. Casual laboratory observation shows that a sated animal reared (since weaning) in isolation will often begin to eat when some hungry animals in an adjoining cage are fed, even though the hungry animals are not visible. Investigations with controlled early experience are needed to throw further light on the mechanism of "social facilitation" of eating behavior.

Another possible approach to the problem of facilitating responses is illustrated by an experiment on the use of response-independent reinforcement in increasing the rate of a given response. Herrnstein & Morse (1957) trained pigeons to press a key at a low rate for a food reward. A procedure of presenting an originally neutral stimulus (yellow light) followed by the food reward was superimposed on the original training schedule. The yellow light was followed by food independently of the animal's response. The investigators found that this response-independent reinforcement led to a marked increase in the rate of ongoing operant response. The obtained increase in response rate may have resulted from an increase in some facilitating (food-oriented) responses brought about by the response-independent reinforcement. Detailed observations of the responses (other than key pressing) of the animal are needed to determine if the facilitation hypothesis is correct.

It is clear that the problem of the effects of the variation in sensory cues on behavior is one of considerable generality. It bears on a number of phenomena, such as stimulus generalization, conflict, and facilitation or "positive transfer," which have traditionally been treated separately, each within a different framework. Further research in this problem area should contribute to the development of a general formulation covering certain aspects of these various phenomena.

# Chapter 8

# Arousal and Behavior

Sensory stimulation determines behavior not only by providing the sensory cues required for guiding behavior, but also by producing changes in the "level of arousal" of the organism. The relation of arousal level to the occurrence of responses that exist in the animal's repertoire is the subject of this chapter. Starting with a general discussion of the concept of arousal, we shall discuss in turn the factors that alter level of arousal and the effects of variations in arousal on the occurrence of responses.

## THE CONCEPT OF AROUSAL

Intuitively, one can recognize various states of the organism. Sometimes the organism is awake, sometimes asleep; sometimes it is excited, sometimes calm; and sometimes it is tense, sometimes relaxed. These descriptions roughly delimit the characteristics of an organism that are described by the term *arousal.* Changes in these characteristics have been considered as variations in degree of "energy mobilization" (Cannon, 1929; Duffy, 1941, 1951), degree of "arousal" (Freeman, 1948), and "activation" (Lindsley, 1951). These terms, as employed by their authors, do not all mean the same thing, but they refer in one way or another to a dimension that represents the "energy" or "excitation" level of an organism. We shall employ the term *level of arousal* to refer to this dimension of behavior. The terms "energy mobilization" and "activation" can then be used to connote, respectively, the auto-nomic-visceral and the cerebral processes related to the behavioral dimensions of arousal. Toward the one extreme end of this dimension stands the excitation aspect of the phe-nomenon of deep sleep or general anesthesia and, at the other, the excitation represented in panic, in a 100-yard dash, or in an epileptic seizure. Our task in this section is to develop an experimentally useful definition of arousal from the preced-ing general statement.

## Logical Status of the Arousal Concept

If one looks upon deep sleep and panic or epileptic seizure as representing the two poles of the arousal dimension, one can begin the search for more exact indices of arousal by in-quiring into the main differences between such low and high arousal states. There appear to be three interrelated differ-ences between these states. First, the involuntary bodily proc-esses that are primarily under the control of the autonomic nervous system function differently in the two states. Thus, blood pressure and heart rate are higher, and sweat glands more active, in states of high arousal than in sleep. Second, the activity in the voluntary musculature, which is primarily under the control of the somatic nervous system, is lower in low arousal than in high arousal states. Muscles are relaxed in sleep, but tense in a state of high arousal. (This does not mean, however, that there is necessarily a greater amount of overt activity in the high arousal states.) Third, the pattern of the firing of nerve cells within the brain is different in the two states. For example, a record of electrical potentials repre-senting activity in the cells of the cerebral cortex during sleep shows a preponderance of "delta waves," which are large in amplitude and slow in speed, but this pattern is replaced by other types of waves in states of higher arousal (see Fig. 17). These differences in autonomic, somatic, and neural functions between the two extreme states suggest that it may be possible to employ measures of these functions to represent all levels of arousal, on a continuous scale, from very low to very high.

However, if one tries to define level of arousal precisely in terms of such measures of physiological activity, one is forced to the conclusion that, for any obtained set of measures, there are not one but several levels of arousal; for the intercorrelations between the various measures are not so high as to war-

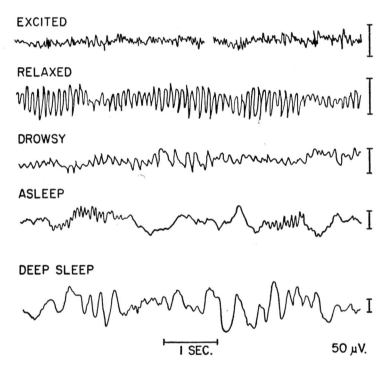

EXCITED

RELAXED

DROWSY

ASLEEP

DEEP SLEEP

1 SEC.                    50 μV.

FIG. 17. VARIATIONS IN ELECTROENCEPHALOGRAPHIC RECORDS AS A FUNCTION OF AROUSAL

Electroencephalographic records during excitement, relaxation, and varying degrees of sleep. In fourth strip from top of illustration, runs of 14-sec. rhythm, superimposed on slow waves, are termed "sleep spindles." Note that excitement is characterized by a rapid frequency and small amplitude and that varying degrees of sleep are marked by increasing irregularity and by appearance of "slow waves." (*Source:* H. Jasper, in Penfield and Erickson, *Epilepsy and cerebral localization* [Springfield, Ill.: Charles C. Thomas, 1941], p. 401. Courtesy Charles C. Thomas, publisher.

rant considering all the measures as reflections of one unitary "arousal process." For example, as will be seen later, muscle tension simultaneously may be high in one part of the body and low in other parts; and heart rate and patterns of cerebral firing may or may not covary with any measure of muscle tension. This means that level of arousal is not a unitary dimension of behavior. Rather, this concept must be looked upon as a crude one, incorporating a number of measures of autonomic, somatic, and neural functions. Some of these physiological measures are closely related to each other; others are not. Thus, the logical status of the concept of level of arousal is the same as that of the concepts of habit strength and goal direction. All these concepts serve as vague labels for a variety of specific and fairly exact measures, and it is these measures, rather than the global concepts themselves, that form the basis of empirical research.

The measures of physiological processes that are usually incorporated under the rubric of arousal, or the "indices" of arousal as they are sometimes called, will be described in the following section. In the discussion to follow, we shall employ the term "arousal" when the intention is to make general statements without any great regard for precision. But when the intention is to be exact, or to make comparisons between investigations, we shall specify the particular physiological measure employed.

### Measures Incorporated in Arousal

Unless otherwise specified, an increase in the measures listed below reflects an increase in the particular function involved, and this is generally taken to mean an increased level of arousal. Similarly a decrease in the measures reflects a decrease in the particular function involved and signifies a decreased level of arousal.

*Indices of autonomic-visceral functions.* Perhaps the most commonly employed indicator of variations in autonomic-visceral functions is the *galvanic skin response* (GSR). Changes in the activity of sweat glands alter electrical resistance, as well as electrical potentials, of the skin. The GSR reflects these changes. All measures of GSR are based on changes in skin conductance or skin potentials.

Changes in *heart rate* can be determined by an electrocardiogram (EKG). The usual measures employed are heart rate per minute or per experimental period, interval between successive heart beats ("heart period"), and the duration for which a given change in heart rate lasts. Variations in *blood pressure* can be determined periodically by means of a sphygmomanometer, which yields measures of systolic and diastolic pressure; the difference between the two is called "pulse pressure." Continuous records of changes in the absolute levels of blood pressure are difficult to obtain. But continuous records of "relative blood pressure" can be obtained; this measure indicates only the deflections of blood pressure above and below an arbitrary zero level. Another type of vascular measure is the one describing *vasomotor* changes. Variations in the constriction and dilation of blood vessels are obtained by determining changes in the volume of a given part of the body (finger, hand, foot, etc.) by means of a plethysmograph.

The pneumograph is a convenient device for obtaining continuous records of *respiration*. Variations in this function are usually described in terms of such measures as breathing-cycle time, inspiration-expiration time, and depth of breathing. The rate of *oxygen consumption* in a resting state is provided by the basal metabolic rate (BMR).

Variations in many other aspects of the autonomic-visceral functions can also be determined and described in terms of some fairly reliable measures. Readers interested in such measures are referred to Wenger (1948), Lindsley (1951), Davis (1957a), Davis & Buchwald (1957), and Davis, Garafolo, & Gault (1957).

*Indices of somatic-skeletal functions.* Variations in *muscle tension* in the various parts of the body are usually determined by means of an electromyograph (EMG), which records muscle action potentials. Increases in the contraction of muscles lead to increased frequency and amplitude of the potentials; muscular relaxation produces opposite effects. Increase in *tremor* is also usually associated with increased muscle tension. Tremor in an extended hand or fingers can be recorded by amplifying the oscillations with appropriate pneumatic or electrical arrangements.

*Indices of activity in the central nervous system.* The events within the central nervous system are described in terms of electrical potentials, which are the normal concomitants of neural activity. Whereas changes in electrical potentials within a single neuron of an intact animal can now be recorded, it is the changes in the over-all activity of large masses of nerve cells that concern us here. The electroencephalograph (EEG) yields records of the activity of the cerebral cortex even though the electrodes are usually placed on the skull. The normal human records, obtained under conditions of relaxation and uniform sensory stimulation, consist of potential oscillations having a frequency of 8 to 12 c.p.s. and amplitude of about 30 $\mu$v. (second strip in Fig. 17). These oscillations are referred to as *alpha rhythm;* and they represent the typical normal human adult record. Any marked sudden change in sensory stimulation, or instruction to attend to or think about something, produces a disruption or "blocking" of alpha waves. The resultant oscillations have a high frequency (20 to 40 c.p.s.) and a low amplitude; the record looks quite flat (first strip in Fig. 17) and is usually referred to as the "activation" pattern. Similar flat records are obtained when the subject is "apprehensive," "anxious," or in any way excited. At the other extreme, during deep sleep, the record (fifth strip in Fig. 17) shows slow frequency (about 3 c.p.s.) waves with extremely high amplitude (80 to 100 $\mu$v.). Drowsiness and light sleep are characterized by a mixture of alpha waves and the large slow waves of deep sleep. The commonest measures derived from the EEG record are "percentage alpha," which is the proportion of a given time that alpha rhythm is the dominant feature of the record, and the frequency and duration of alpha blocking.

*Interrelations between the arousal measures.* Four difficulties must be overcome before the various indices of physiological functions can be reliably interrelated. First, the latencies of the changes in different functions, and within one function in different parts of the body, are not the same. For example, an unexpected stimulus will block the alpha pattern in less than 0.5 sec., whereas the GSR (palmar) to the same stimulus will occur about 1.5 sec. after the EEG change. Latencies of the changes in muscle tension are intermediate between those of alpha blocking and GSR. Similarly, GSR latency increases as the recording electrodes are moved from the head out to the extremities of the body. Second, given a particular function and a particular form of stimulation, the change in the function may be quite different in different parts of the body. The sweat-gland activity in the hands may increase, for instance, without any corresponding increase in such activity in other parts of the body. Similarly, muscle tension may increase in the neck and shoulder region but not in arms or legs. Malmo, Shagass, & Davis (1950) obtained simultaneous EMG records from the forearm and forehead of psychiatric patients during interviews. Their data show that, during various phases of the interview, the pattern of change in muscle potentials from the forehead did not resemble that of the potentials from the forearm. Undoubtedly, in many instances EMG records from different parts of the body may show covariation, but such instances do not argue against the generalization that changes in muscle tension do not necessarily follow the same general pattern throughout the body. Third, all the physiological functions are active continuously, and the change in a function brought about by a given stimulation is dependent upon the level of functioning just prior to the stimulation. Thus, in determining the exact change brought about by any experimental condition, it is necessary to correct the obtained change by some factor that takes into account the prestimulation level. Despite many efforts, no general method of achieving such a transformation has yet been developed. Lacey (1956) has proposed a transformation which apparently overcomes the difficulty in the case of autonomic functions. Fourth, the various physiological functions affect each other in significant ways. For example, changes in muscle contraction in one part of the body lead to changes in blood supply to that part. This, in turn, may produce changes in blood pressure and respiration. What Lacey has called "homeostatic restraint" is also an important factor. A change in an autonomic process often initiates a series of changes that counteract the original change. Thus, the effects of an experimental stimulation are confounded with the effects produced by counteracting ("homeostatic") mechanisms. It should be noted that the above difficulties in interrelating the measures of various functions are relevant primarily when one is interested in comparing *changes* in given measures brought about by a particular stimulus; they are not relevant when the interest is only in the over-all general *levels* of different functions.

Though all the above difficulties have not been overcome, many investigators have attempted to interrelate the various measures that are subsumed under the rubric of arousal. Bancaud, Bloch, & Paillard (1953) found that the presentation of a simple stimulus was followed by changes in both EEG and GSR, but the course of recovery was not the same for the two records. Furthermore, the repeated presentation of the stimulus led readily to an adaptation of the GSR, but the EEG change persisted. Ax (1953) determined 42 intercorrelations between a variety of autonomic and somatic measures. Only a few of these correlations reached statistical significance, and their mean was only .12. Davis & Buchwald (1957) exposed a variety of pictures to human subjects and obtained simultaneous measures of a number of autonomic and somatic changes. Each stimulus picture was exposed for 1 min. and this was followed by a 1-min. rest. Fig. 18 presents the course followed by the various measures over the 2-min. period following the onset of the stimulus. It is clear that the time functions are quite different for the various measures. Some show a monophasic decrease in the particular function, others an increase, and some show a diphasic change. Davis & Buchwald conclude that no single measure can be said to typify the change in all of the several functions. On the other hand, Malmo & Davis (1956) found that the changes in the autonomic (heart rate, blood pressure) measures of a group of subjects, while they were performing a mirror-tracing task,

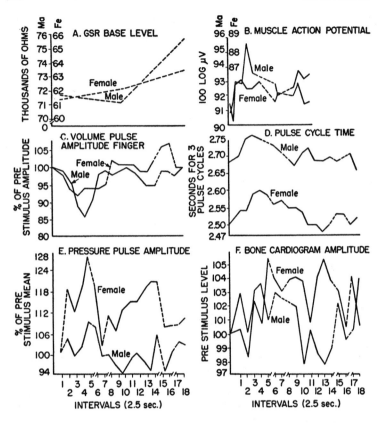

FIG. 18. VARIETY SEEN IN PATTERNS OF AUTONOMIC AND SOMATIC CHANGES
(Continued on page 219)

corresponded closely to each other and to the changes in muscle action potentials.

The above equivocal findings concerning the interrelations between arousal indices suggest that it is too early to decide whether the various measures of autonomic, somatic, and neural functions can be looked upon as representing some unitary "arousal process." Thus, as pointed out before, at present the term arousal can be usefully employed only as an abstract label for a variety of measures of physiological functioning.

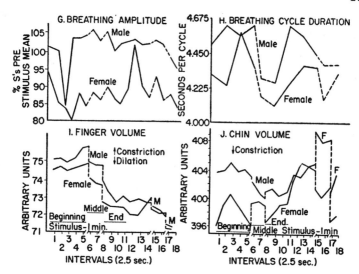

FIG. 18. VARIETY SEEN IN PATTERNS OF AUTONOMIC AND SOMATIC CHANGES

Autonomic and somatic measures as functions of time after the presentation of stimulus pictures. The graphs show means for 18 2.5-sec. intervals selected from the 2-min. records obtained from each of 12 male and 12 female subjects. (*Source:* R. C. Davis and A. M. Buchwald, An exploration of somatic response patterns: stimulus and sex differences. *J. comp. physiol. Psychol.*, 50, 47.)

## PATTERNS OF AUTONOMIC-SOMATIC ACTIVITY

Do the changes in the various autonomic-somatic functions brought about by external stimulation tend to covary in certain ways? This question of the existence of "patterns" of physiological activity has traditionally been linked with that of the basis of "emotional experience." The James-Lange theory of "emotion" (James, 1890; Lange & James, 1922) implied that a distinctive pattern of autonomic-somatic activity exists for each subjective emotional state (i.e. reported experience such as anger, fear, joy, and pride). But Cannon (1927) argued, in effect, that the autonomic-somatic functions could not show as many distinctive patterns of activity as there are reported emotional states. He recognized only two patterns of autonomic activity: one, the "emergency" pattern, characterized by hyperactivity of the sympathetic division of the autonomic nervous system; and the other, the "relaxed" pattern, characterized by hyperactivity of the parasympathetic division.

That Cannon's dichotomy is an oversimplification was pointed out by Gellhorn (1943). Gellhorn's evidence, as well as the evidence discussed in the previous section, shows that the various autonomic (and somatic) functions occur in a variety of combinations which do not follow the sympathetic-parasympathetic division. In a more recent attempt to relate emotional states to various autonomic functions, Ax (1953) exposed human subjects to "emotion producing" situations. He interpreted his recordings as showing two autonomic reaction patterns. One of these ("anger") was characterized by increases in diastolic blood pressure, muscle tension, skin conductance, and a decrease in heart rate; the other ("fear") pattern showed increases in skin conductance and muscle tension accompanied by an increase in respiration rate. However, since the overt responses of Ax's subjects were probably different in the two situations, it cannot be stated with assurance that the two observed constellations of autonomic changes represent true autonomic patterns rather than the consequences of different overt activities.

It is unfortunate that the question of the existence of specific patterns of autonomic-somatic activity has not been separated from the problem of the basis of subjective emotional states. As Davis (1957) has pointed out, because of the vagueness that surrounds the everyday use of such terms as "fear" and "anger," the question of the existence of autonomic-somatic patterns should not be linked with that of subjective states, but should be treated as a separate question in its own right.

In the study of Davis & Buchwald (1957) mentioned above, it was found that, in general, all of the several autonomic-somatic functions do not covary. However, Davis (1957) has examined the data collected by himself and his colleagues in order to determine if some of the functions do nevertheless vary together under certain conditions. An examination of the measures of autonomic-somatic activity obtained under conditions of simple sensory stimulation, mild exercise, and viewing pictures has led Davis to suggest that any new stimulation produces an increase in sweat gland (palmar) and muscular (extensor digit) activity. Other measures, such as pulse rate, finger volume, and respiration rate, vary in different ways with different kinds of stimulation. Davis also noticed some consistency in the patterns of increases and decreases in several measures for each type of stimulating condition. For example, viewing pictures tended to decrease pulse pressure, finger volume, and chin volume, whereas cutaneous stimulation increased these measures. Work in this area of investigating the relations between specific stimuli and the evoked patterns of physiological activity has barely begun, and it is difficult to say whether the patterns described by Ax and Davis are artifacts of their procedures or are in some sense "true" patterns.

## INDIVIDUAL DIFFERENCES

The problem of determining the existence of any general patterns of autonomic-somatic activity is complicated by the fact that there are marked individual differences in both the resting or base level and the reactivity of the various functions.

*Individual differences in base level.* Variation in the base level of any given measure of a physiological function is usually high even within a homogeneous group. Skin resistance measured under identical conditions in normal human adults in a resting state may show a range of 5,000 to considerably above 50,000 ohms. Similarly, the normal range of variation in base pulse rate is 55 to 90, in base systolic blood pressure 90 to 120 mm.Hg, and in oxygen consumption (BMR) 40 to 60 cal./hr./sq.m. The individual variation in muscle tension appears to be equally great. However, generally speaking, each individual tends to be fairly consistent from time to time in his base levels for any given measures.

*Individual differences in reactivity.* If the resting state is disturbed by some form of stimulation, there is a change in the level of activity of the various functions. This degree of change or reactivity, like base level, varies considerably from individual to individual. Even when the differences in the initial levels are corrected for, one finds a wide range of individual differences in reactivity for any given function. Furthermore, the degree of change may differ for various measures within the same individual. For example, an individual may show a marked change in his heart rate but a relatively slight one in palmar conductance and muscle tension; another individual under identical conditions may show the reverse pattern. Fig. 19, from Schnore (1957), illustrates such individual differences. Schnore made simultaneous recordings of nine autonomic-somatic functions. The recordings were made under four different experimental conditions. The figure shows the T-scores (based on deviations from group means) of two subjects for the different functions. It is clear that the different functions are differentially reactive in each subject. Furthermore, a comparison of the two subjects shows marked individual differences in the pattern of reactivity.

Another feature of individual differences is also evident in Schnore's figure. The pattern of reactivity of each subject remains the same under the four different experimental conditions. The presence of such idiosyncratic patterns of response, which remain fairly stable from situation to situation, has been termed *relative response specificity* by Lacey and his collaborators. They define this concept as follows: "For a given set of autonomic [-somatic] functions, individuals tend to respond with a pattern of autonomic [-somatic] activation in which maximal activation will be shown by the same physiological function, whatever the stress" (Lacey, Bateman, & Van Lehn, 1953, p. 8).

Evidence for such response specificity has been found in a number of studies by Malmo, Shagass, & Davis (1950), Lacey (1950), Lacey & Van Lehn (1952), Lacey, Bateman, & Van Lehn (1953), and Davis, Lundervold, & Miller (1957). The investigations show that a variety of changes in stimulation (giving instructions, exposing pictures, requiring performance on tasks, creating "stressful" conditions, etc.) tend to evoke similar patterns of autonomic-somatic activation in each individual. Furthermore, when the patterns are determined at varying levels of over-all physiological activity (e.g. by varying the intensity of stimulation), though there is a change in the level of activity of the various functions, the pattern as

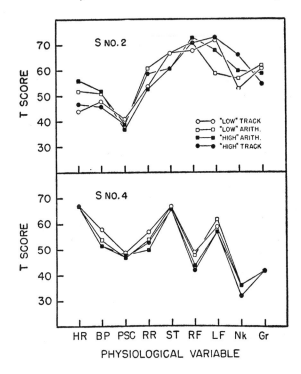

FIG. 19. RELATIVE RESPONSE SPECIFICITY AND IDIOSYNCRATIC PATTERNS OF PHYSIOLOGICAL RESPONSE

Two cases exemplifying different levels of reactivity of the various functions and relative response specificity. The measures are: HR — heart rate; BP — systolic blood pressure; PSC — skin conductance; RR — respiration rate; ST — skin temperature; RF — muscle tension in right forearm; LF — muscle tension in left forearm; Nk — muscle tension in neck; and Gr — grip pressure. The four experimental conditions involved arithmetic and tracking tasks, each of which was performed under conditions of low and high "motivation." (*Source:* M. M. Schnore, Individual differences in patterning and level of physiological activity: a study of arousal [Unpublished Ph.D. thesis, McGill University, 1957].)

shown in the relative standing of the functions, or their hier-archy, remains roughly the same for each individual (as in Fig. 19). Thus, if an individual in a low arousal state shows his highest reactivity in palmar conductance and his lowest in blood pressure, the relative standing of these two measures is likely to be the same under conditions of high arousal as well.

*Group differences in reactivity.* Wenger (1948) compared several groups of Air Force men on about 25 measures of autonomic functions. In one comparison he found that opera-tional fatigue patients significantly differed from aviation stu-dents in 10 measures. These were: salivary output, palmar conductance, systolic blood pressure, diastolic blood pressure, sinus arrhythmia, heart period, sublingual temperature, finger temperature, respiration period, and mean tidal air (depth of breathing). In all but one of these indices the scores of the patients, as compared with those of the students, represented excessive functioning of the sympathetic division of the au-tonomic system. Wenger also found evidence of a hyperactive sympathetic division in a mixed group of patients diagnosed as "psychoneurotics." Whether the sympathetic hyperactivity is a symptom of operational fatigue and neurosis or is a gen-eral characteristic of persons who are prone to develop these ailments cannot be stated definitely. Wenger seems inclined to the view that hyperactivity of the sympathetic division is as-sociated with proneness to operational fatigue but that it is also increased by combat duty.

Malmo & Shagass have compared the pattern of physiologi-cal reactivity of groups of psychiatric patients and normal subjects. Their general plan consisted of obtaining continu-ous records of a number of functions in an experimental ses-sion during which the subjects were exposed to a painful heat stimulation for a few seconds. In one of their studies, Malmo & Shagass (1949) found that psychiatric patients whose pre-dominant symptom was "anxiety" showed much greater mus-cle tension (finger tremor and neck muscle potentials) than did early schizophrenics, a "mixed" group of patients, or nor-mal subjects. In another study (Malmo & Shagass, 1949a), they compared (1) patients with a clinical history of cardiovascular complaints with patients without such complaints, and (2) patients with clinical history of head and neck pains with patients who did not have such symptoms. At the time of testing the majority of the patients did not report these complaints. It was found that heart rate and respiratory variability was greater in patients with cardiovascular complaints than in the group without such complaints, but these groups did not differ in neck muscle tension. The patients with head and neck pains had higher neck muscle tension scores than patients without pains, but these groups did not differ in heart rate or respiratory variability.

The results of another study, by Malmo, Wallerstein, & Shagass (1953), are presented in Fig. 20. It shows that patients with a history of headache complaints, as compared with other groups, show greater muscle tension not only in the neck when the pain stimulation is applied to the forehead, but also in the forearm when the stimulation is applied to the forearm. Furthermore, the increase in tension in both parts of the body is greater for such patients than for other groups whether the painful stimulation is applied to the forehead or to the forearm. These studies suggest that patients with a history of certain types of symptoms, even when the symptoms are not manifest at the time of testing, respond with characteristic patterns of autonomic-somatic activity under conditions of painful stimulation. The characteristic patterns represent over-activity of those functions that are related to the symptoms appearing in clinical history.

In the study involving the exposure of pictures mentioned before, Davis & Buchwald (1957) used both male and female college students as subjects. Their results showed some sex differences in autonomic-somatic reactivity. The male subjects tended to be consistent with each other in giving, to some extent, different patterns of autonomic-somatic activity to different sets of pictures. But the different sets of pictures did not evoke consistent and distinct patterns in the female subjects. Whether these results represent a genuine sex difference in autonomic-somatic reactivity or are simply an artifact of specific experimental conditions (e.g. some of the exposed

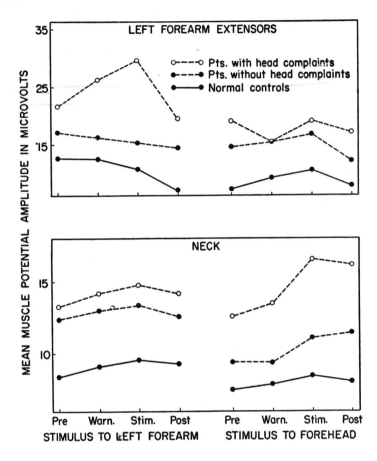

FIG. 20. DIFFERENCES IN THE PHYSIOLOGICAL RESPONSE OF PATIENTS
AND NORMALS

The effect of stimulation site upon differences between headache-prone group and other groups. Note that largest differences between these groups occur in left forearm extensors with stimulus to left forearm, and in neck muscles with stimulus to forehead. Normal control data provide "base line" values. *Pre:* Rest period of 5 minutes, following instructions. *Warning:* at end of rest period brief warning was given that stimulations would soon begin. *Stimulation:* ten stimuli (on arm or forehead) spaced one minute apart. *Post:* Rest period of 3 minutes. (*Source:* R. B. Malmo, H. Wallerstein, and C. Shagass, Headache-proneness and mechanisms of motor conflict in psychiatric patients. *J. Pers.,* 22, 171.)

pictures were of a nude woman but none were of a nude man; both the experimenters were male) still remains to be determined.

*Source of individual differences.* Relatively little is known about the exact role of constitutional (genetic and intra-uterine) and experiential factors in the determination of individual differences in physiological reactivity. One finding that is well established concerns the successful breeding of strains of low-reactivity and high-reactivity rats. When rats are placed in a situation with which they are unfamiliar, they characteristically urinate and defecate during their exploratory activity. On repeated exposure to the same situation, however, elimination diminishes steadily. Moreover, there are marked individual differences in the occurrence of elimination in a strange situation. Hall (1938) has produced high-elimination and low-elimination strains of rats through selective breeding. Hall refers to them as "high-emotionality" and "low-emotionality" strains, and considers this characteristic to be related to "fearfulness" of the animals. However, Willingham (1956), in a factor-analytic study, found six separate "emotionality" factors in mice, and concludes that it is an oversimplification to talk in terms of a general emotionality trait. And Bindra & Thompson (1953) have argued that, because of the vagueness of the terms "emotionality" and "fearfulness," it is advisable to state simply that Hall's breeding experiment shows that it is possible to breed high-elimination and low-elimination strains. This successful selective breeding of an autonomic function suggests that many other components of the various physiological functions subsumed under "arousal" may also be determined in part by constitutional factors. Fuller (1951) has shown that there are marked breed differences in the autonomic reactivity of dogs; it appears reasonable to attribute these differences to constitutional factors. The studies of autonomic responses in children and their mothers now being carried on by Lacey (1956) and his collaborators are likely to reveal the role of constitutional factors in man.

Studies on the effects of early experience on autonomic-somatic reactivity have so far failed to produce unequivocal results. The particular variable that is currently receiving considerable attention is that of "gentling." Gentling consists of holding the animal lightly and stroking its back from neck to tail with a hand or brush. Weininger (1956) compared non-gentled rats with rats that had been gentled for 10 min. a day over a 21-day period immediately following weaning. He found, among other things, that gentled rats defecated less when placed in an unfamiliar open-field situation. However, Mogenson & Ehrlich (1958) found no difference in defecation between gentled and nongentled rats, but they did find that rats that were given electric shocks during infancy defecated less than either the gentled or the control animals. Obviously, further work is required to determine the effects of the gentling-shocking type of experience on autonomic-somatic reactivity. Lacey (1956) and his collaborators are engaged in longitudinal studies of human subjects designed to throw light on the effect of early experience in the development of the idiosyncratic patterns of physiological reactivity discussed in the previous pages.

## FACTORS DETERMINING LEVEL OF AROUSAL

So far our concern has been mainly with the physiological functions that are subsumed under the rubric of "arousal indices." For that discussion it was necessary to be fairly precise about the specific measures of the functions employed in the various investigations. As noted before, level of arousal is a vague concept referring to one or more of the several measures that differentiate between states such as sleep on the one hand and highly excited states on the other. The types of problems to be faced in this and the following sections cannot be precisely discussed at present, and, if they are to be discussed at all, they have to involve a rough definition of arousal in terms of the sleep-excitement continuum or in terms of indices (e.g. GSR, EMG) that appear to be closely associated with that continuum. This section deals with the factors that determine the level of arousal of an organism at any given time; for the reason noted, we shall employ the term "arousal" quite loosely, referring to specific measures of physiological activity only when it is possible to do so.

Let us call the level of arousal of an individual who is relaxed and is resting comfortably in a familiar environment but is not sleeping his *base arousal level*. If such a person is brought into a laboratory as a subject, harnessed into the various devices for measuring physiological activity, and asked to relax, his arousal level will probably be considerably higher than his base level. However, if the subject goes through this experience repeatedly, or for a long enough time, his "laboratory arousal level" is likely gradually to approach, or even to become identical with, the base level. Thus, for present purposes one can consider the arousal level in a familiar laboratory setting as a satisfactory index of base arousal level. Here we are concerned primarily with laboratory investigations of the factors that raise and lower arousal level above and below the base level.

## ENVIRONMENTAL CHANGE: SIMPLE STIMULI

Any sudden or unexpected change in sensory stimulation typically increases the arousal level of a resting relaxed subject. This increase is most clearly and consistently seen in records of EMG and GSR. Davis and his colleagues have systematically studied the effects of simple auditory (e.g. tones, noise) and cutaneous (e.g. heat, prick, pressure) stimuli on a variety of autonomic-somatic functions, including palmar conductance and muscle tension. In one of their experiments Davis, Buchwald, & Frankmann (1955) studied the adaptation of GSR to a 98-db. rough tone of approximately 800 c.p.s. The subjects were given 10 identical exposures of the tone at 1-min. intervals, but were instructed not to respond to the tone in any overt way. The subjects showed a considerable increase in palmar conductance on the first presentation of the stimulus. The response to successive presentations was found to decrease rapidly, so that the increased conductance on the 10th presentation was only 15 per cent of that on the first. Similar rapid adaptation to auditory stimuli has also been reported by Davis (1948) for the increased-muscle-tension response.

In another experiment Davis, Buchwald, & Frankmann (1955) investigated the effects on arousal of different intensities of auditory stimulation. They exposed their subjects to a 1000-c.p.s. tone at intensities of 70, 90 or 120 db. Fig. 21 shows their results for both GSR and muscle tension. It is seen that the responses for the highest intensity are much greater than for the two lower intensities; the authors state that the effects are proportional to the sound pressure. They also found that repetition of each stimulus intensity led to a systematic decrement in the two measures, and this adaptation occurred more rapidly for the low intensity than for the high one. Very high sound intensities (e.g. gun shots) are known to be quite resistant to adaptation (Davis & Van Liere, 1949). Furthermore, adaptation to one intensity did not necessarily decrease response to other (higher or lower) intensities; to a certain extent the adaptation effect was specific to the stimulus intensity applied. This implies that "novelty" or strangeness of the stimulus, as well as its intensity, affects level of arousal.

These results suggest the following generalization: When the subjects are under instructions not to respond in any overt way, the presentation of a simple stimulus increases level of arousal, and the increase is roughly proportional to the intensity of the stimulus. The increase in arousal is also a function of the "novelty" of the stimulation; the first stimulus produces a high response, but repeated presentations lead to adaptation of the response.

### ENVIRONMENTAL CHANGE: COMPLEX STIMULI

Changes in the more complex aspects of a given familiar situation also produce increase in arousal. We have already noted (Chaps. 2 and 4) that the addition of certain new complex stimulus patterns (e.g. masks, stuffed animals, a moving toy snake) into a familiar situation evokes considerable excitement in chimpanzees (Hebb, 1946a) and dogs (Melzack, 1952). (It is likely that changing a familiar situation by re-

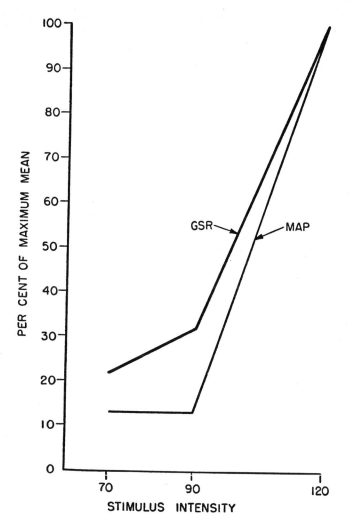

FIG. 21. STIMULUS INTENSITY AND PHYSIOLOGICAL RESPONSE

Muscle-action potential (MAP) responses and galvanic skin responses (GSR) plotted as a function of a 1000-cycle tone. (*Source:* R. C. Davis, A. M. Buchwald, and R. W. Frankmann, Autonomic and muscular responses, and their relation to simple stimuli. *Psychol. Monogr.,* **69,** No. 20, 28.)

moving certain stimulus patterns from it will also increase arousal.) Similar observations in birds have been reported by Tinbergen (1951) and Hinde (1954). Their studies show that certain shapes and objects when added to a familiar situation evoke marked overactivity and excitement. Hinde has made quantitative investigations of the "investigatory-fear" or "mobbing" of the chaffinch, taking the frequency of "chink" call as an index of the response. If we accept this response as an index of arousal or general excitement, Hinde's experiments show that stimulus patterns such as a live or model owl produce much greater increase in arousal than do other stimulus patterns (e.g. a cardboard circle) of equal size. The fact that in all the above studies the animals were considered as making a "fear" response is probably due to the fact that withdrawal and avoidance responses are highly prepotent in the repertoires of adult animals (*see* Chap. 6 and below). However, in this discussion we are not concerned with the specific responses as such, but only with the increased arousal represented in the general excitement and withdrawal responses shown by the animals.

An indication of increased arousal brought about by certain complex stimulus patterns can also be found in reports of some other types of experiments. Tinbergen (1951, p. 29) has reported a study which suggests that the newly hatched chicks of the herring gull become more excited, as judged by the frequency of pecking, on the presentation of a model of a herring gull head which has a red dot on the bill than by a model without a red dot. Jaynes (1956), in the study reported earlier (Chap. 3), found that chicks imprinted more readily on a green cube than on a red cylinder. These differences in imprintability can be looked upon as representing differences in the capacities of various stimulus patterns to increase arousal. Hess (1957) has shown that imprinting is a function of the excitement or activity shown by the animal in the presence of the imprinting object, and we have noted the reinforcing effects of the sensory consequences of activity in Chapter 5. Thus, a variety of studies can be interpreted as showing that changes in complex stimulus patterns lead to an increased level of arousal, and that the degree of increase brought about by different patterns is different.

Observations reported in the above studies also indicate that, if a particular stimulus pattern is repeatedly presented, the increase in arousal on successive trials diminishes steadily. This adaptation effect has been systematically studied by Hinde (1954a) for the mobbing "chink" call of the chaffinch. In one of his studies, with live owls as stimuli, he found that a presentation for 20 min. a day on successive days led to a rapid decline in the increased-arousal response, so that on the 10th day the response was only 10 per cent of the first-day response. Hebb (1946a) and Melzack (1952) have noted similar adaptation effects in chimpanzees and dogs, respectively. The reduction of exploratory activity with repetition of the same stimulus object or situation (Chap. 2) can also be interpreted as representing an adaptation of the increased-arousal response. Thus, repeated presentations of a change in complex stimulus patterns lead to an adaptation effect similar to that seen with repeated presentations of simple stimuli.

Experiments with both simple stimuli and complex stimulus patterns show that the novelty or strangeness of a situation tends to increase the level of arousal of an animal. Also, the adaptation effects noted above can be attributed to decrease in novelty brought about by repeated exposure to the same situation. The obvious next question is: What constitutes novelty? The answer to this question is not known. However, it is known that any stimulus pattern is novel only with respect to, and by virtue of, other stimuli to which the animal has been exposed in the past. Many of the stimulus objects employed by Hebb (1946a) evoked great excitement in chimpanzees because they had never been exposed to objects of that type before. For example, a snake or the cast of a snake is likely to be a novel stimulus for most mammals brought up amidst the rectangular forms of a laboratory. If some animals could be brought up in an environment with snake-like characteristics, they might well show great excitement on first encountering a wooden block but show no increase in arousal on seeing a snake. This point is supported by the fact that certain objects that do not evoke excitement in a newly born animal begin to do so as the animal grows up. For example, Hebb & Riesen (1943) have noted that whereas the infant chimpanzee may show little excitement on seeing different laboratory attendants, by the age of six months the approach of a stranger evokes marked excitement and withdrawal responses. It is clear that before a new attendant can be classified as a "stranger," the chimpanzee must have become familiar with one or more attendants. Similarly, Hinde (1954) observed that a stuffed owl produced little response in yellow buntings who were 14 to 21 days old, but evoked much greater excitement in older birds. And Hinde, Thorpe, & Vince (1956) observed, in an imprinting experiment, that moorhens were more likely to flee rather than follow the test stimulus if they were first exposed to it several days after hatching instead of being exposed to it from the day after hatching. It seems reasonable to conclude that a stimulus pattern becomes novel only after the animal has been familiarized with an environment of which that stimulus pattern is not normally a part.

Another piece of information we have about novelty is that a stimulus pattern as a whole may be reacted to as novel even when all its components are familiar. Thus, for a chimpanzee another chimpanzee in the same cage may be a familiar figure; but, when the latter is anesthetized and is carried prostrate and limp by the experimenter, it evokes a great deal of excitement in the onlooking chimpanzee. A clearer example is the case, reported by Hebb (1946a), in which the sight of one familiar attendant in the customary clothing of another familiar attendant evokes excitement in the chimpanzee. It seems that novelty is determined not only by the stimulus components to which an animal is exposed, but also by the associations which the animal has previously developed with those components.

The above discussion of novelty is necessarily vague. It rests on an implied definition of the novelty of an object as its capacity to produce increase in arousal. The discussion is, therefore, circular, for our purpose here is to show how novelty affects arousal. A definition of novelty completely in terms of the stimulus characteristics of situations and the past experiences of the animals is needed for a precise discussion of the problem. Such a definition has not yet been formulated. However, a tentative generalization about the relation between the features of a complex environmental change and the increase in arousal level brought about by it may be stated as follows: The greater the novelty (and intensity) of a stimulus pattern, as compared with a completely familiar situation, the greater will be the increase in arousal level above the base level. Repetition of the stimulus pattern typically will lead to an adaptation of the increased-arousal reaction.

## REDUCTION IN SENSORY VARIATION

If the repeated presentation of a novel stimulus leads to a progressive decrease in the increased-arousal response, it is reasonable to expect that any condition that reduces the normal variation in environmental stimulation would tend to produce a below-normal arousal level. Environmental stimulation varies considerably from moment to moment whenever the organism is awake, and the base arousal level is partly determined by such constant variation in sensory input. By reducing the normal sensory variation, that is, by exposing a subject to a "monotonous" situation, it should be possible to reduce his arousal level below his base level. Casual observation suggests that this can be done. Persons engaged in a simple repetitive task for a long time, as well as pilots and radar-watchers who are exposed to situations in which "nothing" may happen for hours, often report drowsiness and lapses in attention that can be interpreted as reduced arousal. What is called "hypnotic sleep" is also usually induced by reduction in sensory variation and repetition of simple words and phrases.

Bexton, Heron, & Scott (1954) studied the effects on behavior of decreased variation in the sensory environment. They paid college students to lie on a comfortable bed in a lighted cubicle for 24 hr. a day (except for feeding and toilet activities) for as many days as they could. (No subject continued for more than eight days.) Sensory variation was minimized by making the subjects wear translucent goggles (which prevented pattern vision) and cardboard cuffs on arms, and by making the cubicle partially sound-proof. Apart from observed deterioration of performance on intellectual tasks, and perceptual and emotional disturbances, Bexton, Heron, & Scott noted a tendency in the subjects to spend the first day or two of the experimental session in sleep. In another investigation, Heron (1957) observed that, after two or three days in the above situation, the EEG pattern of the subjects, even when they were awake, was different from their normal waking pattern; the change was in the direction of a normal "drowsy record." Although detailed studies of the effects of such "sensory deprivation" on the various arousal indices have not yet been conducted, the above two investigations indicate that it can lead to decrease in arousal level.

## Task Performance

Another type of environmental stimulation that can alter arousal level is provided by requiring the subject to perform a task. Davis (1937) obtained EMG records during mental multiplication and the learning of nonsense syllables. He found that muscle tension increased while the subjects were working on the tasks, and decreased during rest and on instructions to relax. Similar increases in tension have been reported for a mirror-tracing task by Malmo, Shagass, & Davis (1951) and Smith (1953), and for a size-discrimination task by Bélanger (1957). Increase in arousal can also be brought about by a task which requires no overt muscular movements. Smith, Malmo, & Shagass (1954) and Wallerstein (1954) instructed their subjects, lying comfortably, to listen to sound recordings. The instructions, as well as the recordings, produced a marked increase in muscle tension. In all the above cases the level of arousal began to increase as soon as the instructions for the task were given to the subject and did not return to the base level for some time after the task had been completed.

The details of the effect of tasks on arousal seem to depend upon a number of factors. One of these factors is the *difficulty* of the task, greater arousal being associated with greater difficulty (Davis, 1937). Another factor is the *stage* of per-

formance; in certain types of tasks there is a progressive increase in arousal from the initiation of the task to its end, with
a sudden drop in arousal after completion of the task. Such a
gradient of arousal, following the different stages of the task,
has been reported by Smith (1953), Wallerstein (1954), and
Bartoshuk (1955). Some of the results of Wallerstein's experiment are presented in Fig. 22. The subjects listened to the
same recorded detective story three times. Each time they

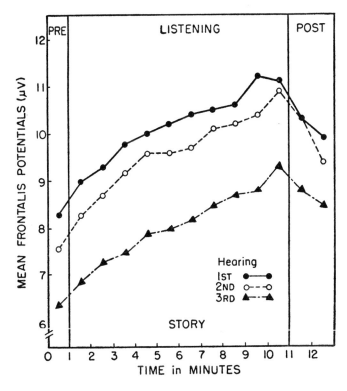

FIG. 22. MUSCLE TENSION DURING THE PERFORMANCE OF AN
"EFFORTLESS" TASK

Effect of listening to a detective story on *frontalis* tension. Approximately
five minutes intervened between each presentation. (*Source:* H. Wallerstein,
An electromyographic study of attentive listening. *Canad. J. Psychol.*, **8**,
231.)

showed a progressive increase in muscle tension until the end of the story. That the increase in arousal was a function of the "interest" evoked by the recording is suggested by the relative position of the three curves, as well as by Wallerstein's observation that listening to a philosophical essay produced gradients that were less steep than those produced by the detective story. A third factor that determines the exact effect of task on the level of arousal is the presence or absence of an *incentive* for performing the task. This has been shown by Surwillo (1956) and Stennett (1957). In the Stennett experiment EMG records were obtained while the subjects performed on a tracking task under three incentive conditions. In the minimum-incentive condition the subject was asked to perform just for "calibration," and, in the maximum-incentive condition, the subject's score determined whether he avoided an electric shock and earned a bonus of a few dollars. Stennett found the steepness of the obtained gradients of muscle tension to vary directly with the degree of incentive.

The above studies show that the level of arousal increases when a human subject prepares for and begins to perform a task. For some of the tasks investigated, there is a progressive increase in arousal from the initiation to the completion of the task; however, it is likely that continued performance on a task that is not too effortful will eventually bring the arousal level back to normal. The task need not require overt muscular activity in order to evoke an increase in arousal.

Noxious Stimulation

Noxious stimulation typically leads to an increase in level of arousal. This observation has been made in a variety of experiments. It is well known that rats defecate and urinate profusely on receiving electric shocks in an escape or avoidance training experiment. Both rats and dogs become highly excited on receiving electric shocks in any type of learning situation. Increase in palmar conductance of human subjects as a result of electric shock administration has been reported by a number of workers (e.g. Diven, 1937). We have already noted the finding of Malmo & Shagass (1949) that painful heat stimulation applied to subjects leads to increased muscle tension, as well as other autonomic-somatic changes. The exact effects on arousal of the repetition of a given type of noxious stimulation, with no opportunity to escape, are not known. Under these conditions, whether the animal adapts to an electric shock probably depends on the intensity of the shock; adaptation is more likely to occur at low intensities. It is possible that, for some intensities of shock, there occurs a cumulative effect, so that the increase in arousal brought about by later shocks is greater than that evoked by the initial ones. However, when an opportunity to escape or avoid the shock is provided, the increased-arousal response decreases with repetition of the shock or the signal for shock.

Of all the different types of events that produce an increase in the level of arousal, noxious stimulation is the most suited for studying the role of conditioned stimuli or signals in evoking increase in arousal. We have already noted in Chapter 7 that events (e.g. a buzzer) that are followed by noxious stimulation come to evoke some autonomic responses ("anxiety") even in the absence of the shock. It was also noted that these conditioned autonomic responses seem to play an important role in the acquisition of avoidance responses. Over the last two decades, a number of investigations have been concerned with the study of what has come to be called "conditioned or experimental anxiety." The typical investigation in this area consists of repeatedly pairing a signal with an electric shock. After the signal comes to evoke the autonomic-somatic ("anxiety") response originally made only to the shock, the response is studied as a function of some selected experimental variable. For example, Diven (1937) established a high GSR to the signal-word "barn" in human subjects. Then he obtained GSR's to a variety of words, some of which (e.g. hay) had rural connotations like the signal-word "barn," while others (e.g. sidewalk) did not. He found that GSR "generalized" more to words with rural connotations than to words without such connotations. Bindra & Cameron (1953) studied the change in a conditioned autonomic reaction (GSR) as a function of the passage of time (rest). Other investigators (e.g. Haggard, 1943) have investigated the effects on conditioned GSR of different ("therapeutic") experiences given to the subjects during an interpolated rest interval. Studies in this area are too numerous to be reviewed here; the above investigations will suffice to indicate the type of research that has been and can be carried out on increase in level of arousal brought about by signals associated with noxious stimulation.

It appears that some kinds of pleasant stimulations, for example those provided by sweet-tasting substances and sexual activity, can also raise level of arousal. However, as yet little reliable information involving specific measures of arousal is available about such determiners of arousal level.

Drugs and Arousal

Certain drugs can also be used to alter arousal level. Phenobarbital and other barbiturates are widely used to produce sleep; others, like sodium pentothal and nitrous oxide, are employed as general anesthetics to produce a state of unconsciousness. More interesting for psychologists are the so-called "hypnotic drugs." Certain dosages of hypnotic drugs, such as sodium amytal, can maintain a subject in a state resembling light sleep for an hour or even for longer periods. Human subjects seem to talk freely when in this state, though later, on becoming fully awake, they may not recall what they said. Such a state of semiconsciousness probably represents the lowest level of arousal before the subject falls into deep sleep. It resembles, and may be identical with, the "sleep of deep hypnosis" that can sometimes be produced by talking to a human subject. The subject is placed in a comfortable position, variation in his sensory input is reduced, and he is repeatedly instructed to relax. If the experimenter continues to talk and give occasional instructions to him, the subject can be maintained in the semi-awake state for a long time; otherwise he is likely to fall asleep.[1]

[1] The subject is often highly suggestible in the state of hypnotic sleep, whether it is brought about by a drug or the monotony procedure. By giving him appropriate suggestions the subject can usually be made to show

That reduction in arousal level, while keeping the subject awake, can be achieved by the administration of sedative or tranquilizing drugs is suggested by a number of clinical studies. For example, Tyhurst & Richman (1955) noted that administration of reserpine tended to "calm down" psychiatric patients. Hollister, Traub, & Beckman (1956) have reported similar changes in the behavior of anxiety patients with the administration of reserpine and chlorpromazine. However, we still lack systematic studies of the effects of such drugs on specific arousal measures. The situation is roughly the same with stimulant drugs, such as benzedrine sulphate; clinical evidence suggests that such drugs increase arousal level, but systematic laboratory investigations have not yet been undertaken.

CONCLUSION

Environmental change, reduction in sensory variation, task performance, noxious stimulation, and the administration of certain drugs are not necessarily mutually exclusive categories. They are five convenient categories of factors that can bring about changes in level of arousal. A moment's reflection will show that some traditional psychological concepts, such as "anxiety situation," "stress," "frustration," and "boredom" are represented in the above four determiners of arousal level. All these concepts are vague, but they seem to refer, in one way or another, to situations that raise or lower the arousal level of an animal. (This description does not fit all instances of "physiological stress"; for, whereas generally such stresses increase arousal, anoxia and fatigue, which are also classed as stress, usually decrease arousal level.) As such, the arousal aspects of the so-called anxiety, stress, and frustration and monotony situations can be subsumed under the five categories of determiners of arousal: presentation of simple or

---

local analgesias, amnesias, hyperamnesias, and so on. However, this feature of increased suggestibility is not peculiar to (low-arousal) hypnotic sleep; it also appears to occur in some states of high arousal, for example, in panic. Stage demonstrations of hypnotic phenomena probably involve such increased suggestibility associated with a high arousal level.

complex stimuli (environmental change), reduction in sensory variation, task performance, noxious stimulation, and drugs.

Inasmuch as anxiety, as usually defined, is characterized by increased autonomic-somatic activity, "anxiety situations" belong to the class of events that increase arousal level. The general label "anxiety situations" subsumes a variety of situations, but most of them belong either to the category of environmental change or to the category of noxious stimulation. "Stress" is one of the vaguest terms in modern psychology. It may be employed to describe a situation in which the subject is exposed to noise or low temperature, in which case it would fall into the category of environmental change. Sometimes "stress" may refer to performance on a difficult task or exposure to noxious stimulation, in which case it can be placed in the corresponding category. "Frustration" refers to situations in which the subject's attempts to reach a goal are somehow obstructed. The obstruction constitutes an environmental change. Other such situations can also be classified into the five categories discussed above. For example, a "conflict" situation is one in which two sets of stimuli, which are cues for different responses, are presented simultaneously. This again constitutes a novel environmental change. Some conflict situations (e.g. the one used by Masserman, 1943; *see* Chap. 7) include some noxious stimulation in addition to cues for competing responses. Similarly, "distraction" situations usually require performance at a task while the subject is exposed to some environmental change. Thus, it seems that many situations which are usually assigned special names of their own are, at least so far as their arousal-increasing properties are concerned, special cases of the categories of factors that raise arousal level. The use of the concept of arousal to classify meaningfully a variety of types of psychological data has been illustrated by Duffy (1957) and Malmo (1957).

## AROUSAL AND THE OCCURRENCE OF RESPONSES

Now, we can turn to the main purpose of this chapter. It concerns the effects of variations in level of arousal on the occurrence of different activities of varying habit strength that exist in an animal's repertoire. As will be seen, there are various difficulties in the way of experimental research in this area; we start, therefore, with the results of a few naturalistic studies.

## NATURALISTIC OBSERVATIONS

Observations of the behavior of soldiers in combat have revealed that they often show marked inefficiency in the discharge of their assigned duties, even when the duties have been well-practiced during training. In addition, these observations suggest that the inefficiency almost always results from marked changes in arousal level brought about by the dangerous (novel, noxious, and fatiguing) combat situation. Occasionally a soldier may become unconscious because of circulatory changes associated with increased arousal. But, usually the soldier is unable to discharge his duties either because he is too excited and panicky, or because he is too exhausted and sleepy. Marshall (1947) has estimated that, of the soldiers on the battlefield who are under orders to fire, less than one-third actually fire their rifles—and then not always in the direction of the enemy. Grinker & Spiegel (1945) have reported that some experienced pilots begin to make errors and become generally inefficient in the face of danger. White (1956; 1st ed. 1948), basing his statements on the observations of Mira (1943), has described the complete disorganization of behavior that sometimes occurs in combat:

As danger mounts, control becomes increasingly difficult. The person's mind begins to be occupied incessantly with the danger. He can no longer inhibit the bodily signs of anxiety: perspiration, tremor, restlessness, fast-beating heart, quickened breathing force themselves upon him. Thought and judgment deteriorate, actions are erratic and poorly controlled, new acts are started before old ones are completed. As he finds it impossible to pull himself together, the person "experiences an extremely unpleasant sensation of losing his mental balance" (Mira). Danger seems to be everywhere. When panic begins to reign, the conscious state resembles a nightmare, "consisting of a peculiar, irregular stream of delirious, distorted mental images, most of which are forgotten when the subject returns to normal." Scarcely aware of what he is doing, the panic-stricken person may rush wildly about, laughing, shouting, crying in rapid succession. These reactions sometimes lasted many days in soldiers exposed to prolonged fire. In some cases a stuporous and comatose state follows the peak of panic.[2]

Similar observations, showing a disorganization of the various activities that exist in the repertoire of an individual, have been made in noncombat civilian disasters. Tyhurst (1951) and his mobile team of investigators made on-the-spot observations of four community disasters, two urban fires, one marine fire, and one flash flood. He reports that only about 15 per cent of the people in the disaster situations remained "cool and collected," and about the same percentage became paralyzed, "hysterical," or otherwise completely disorganized. The majority of the people seemed to function well enough to survive but to do so most inefficiently, showing restriction of attention and "automatic" behavior.[3]

Similar disorganized behavior also occurs under conditions of extremely low arousal level. For example, in states of fatigue and drowsiness, or while slowly going under a general anesthesia, the performance deteriorates even on such well-practiced activities as putting on clothes, reading, and counting.

All the above studies suggest a relation between the level of arousal of an individual and the occurrence of various activities (walking, escaping, firing a rifle, flying an airplane, counting, free-associating, etc.) that exist in his repertoire. It appears that many activities, though well-practiced, occur "less efficiently" when the arousal level is too high or too low. Any given activity seems to occur not as a unified course of action, but as a series of discrete (component) responses which are mixed up with many irrelevant responses. This suggests that an activity can occur normally only within a certain range of level of arousal; above or below this range the activity may or may not occur, and when it does occur it may show marked changes in the manner of its occurrence.

[2] R. W. White, *The abnormal personality* (2d ed., N.Y.: The Ronald Press Co., 1956), pp. 207–08.

[3] A survey of the literature on human behavior in disaster situations has been made by Wallace (1956).

## DIFFICULTIES IN THE WAY OF EXPERIMENTATION

It is not easy to determine the exact effect of variations in level of arousal on the occurrence of a given activity. Several variables have to be controlled and specified. First, one must know the characteristics (latency, rate, etc.) of the activity, as well as the level of arousal at which it normally occurs in a subject (control condition). Second, one must be able to change the level of arousal of the subject and observe the various characteristics of the activity under the changed arousal level (experimental condition). Third, the change in level of arousal of the subject must be brought about without radically altering the environmental stimulation, for gross changes in environmental stimulation may obliterate the cues necessary for the occurrence of the activity (*see* below). Fourth, it is desirable to obtain actual records of arousal level in both the control and experimental conditions. Merely manipulating the factors that are presumed to change arousal level is not sufficient guarantee that the desired change will occur in all subjects. There are marked individual differences in susceptibility to change in arousal level, so that the effects of different conditions (even of the administration of certain drugs) may be quite different in different subjects. Fifth, it is desirable to describe the occurrence of the activity in terms of a number of specific measures rather than as "efficient" and "inefficient" or "organized" and "disorganized." This is important because a change in arousal level may differentially affect different measures of the activity. For example, a changed arousal level may bring about an increase in the rate of the responses involved in an activity but a decrease in the number of correct or effective responses; there are many cases where the latency of an activity decreases but "errors" increase. Sixth, it is necessary to control the factor of habit strength of the activity under investigation. As we shall see, there is reason to believe that the effects of changes in arousal level on an activity depend upon its habit strength.

It is obvious that the naturalistic observations described in the last section cannot be said to have met the above criteria.

Perhaps the only way to conform to these requirements is to study the effects of changed arousal level on the performance of a laboratory task rather than of an activity (e.g. withdrawing, attacking, copulating, or exploring) which cannot be easily quantified and whose developmental history is normally neither known nor controlled. Performance on a laboratory task, such as mirror-tracing, bar pressing, drinking or eating, problem solving, and the like, can be controlled more easily. The experimenter can first make the subject practice the task until a certain performance plateau is achieved. Then the subject's level of arousal can be determined while he is performing the task (control performance). This can be followed by changing the arousal level in some way and asking the subject to perform again (experimental performance). Changes in speed, errors, and other measures of performance from the control to the experimental situation can then be related to the degree and direction of the changes in arousal indices. Unfortunately, so far there are only a few studies that have employed this type of experimental procedure.

## Two Tentative Generalizations

Because of the paucity of studies that meet the above criteria, it is not possible to list any general results with confidence. However, the variety of studies that bear upon this problem do suggest some generalizations. This section is, therefore, organized around two tentative generalizations; a few representative studies are then listed in support of each generalization.

Generalization 1. There is an optimum range of level of arousal within which a given measure of performance will reach its highest (or lowest) value; the greater the deviation in either direction from the optimum arousal level, the greater will be the decrease (or increase) in the performance measure.

Such an inverted U-shaped relation between level of arousal and performance was suggested by Freeman (1940); interest in it has been revived by Schlosberg (1954) and Hebb (1955). Fig. 23 shows hypothetical curves for three different types of tasks. All three curves show the inverted-U relation, but the curve for weight lifting is displaced toward high arousal as compared with the one for drawing, and the curve for type-writing falls between the two. This means that the arousal level required for obtaining the highest score for weight lifting is higher than that for typewriting, and the latter in turn is higher than that for drawing. In each case the subject will be "too excited" above the upper limit of the range and "not warmed up" below the lower limit of the optimal range. The

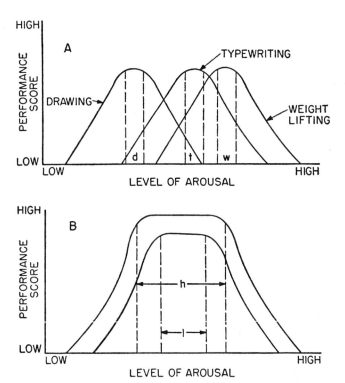

Fig. 23. Relation Between Level of Arousal and Performance

Curves showing hypothetical relations between level of arousal and performance. (A) Ranges (d, t, w) of optimal levels of arousal for performance on three different tasks. (B) Ranges (l, h) of optimal levels of arousal for low and high habit strengths of the same response.

figure also shows that there are upper and lower limits of arousal level beyond which an activity cannot occur at all. For convenience, the general shape of the curves, as well as the optimal ranges ($d$, $t$, and $w$), is shown to be the same for the three tasks; in practice this may or may not be so.

Evidence which directly supports this postulated relation between arousal level and performance comes so far from only a few studies. Freeman (1940), assuming that level of arousal varies in diurnal rhythm, related reaction time to skin conductance level at various times during the day. He found highest speeds of reaction at a moderate level of conductance, with decreasing speeds on either side of the optimal range of conductance. Schlosberg (1954) has reported a similar relation to conductance for both reaction time and hand steadiness; optimal conductance level for hand steadiness was somewhat higher than that for reaction time. In Stennett's (1957) study, mentioned earlier, variations in arousal level (muscle tension and palmar conductance) were obtained by presenting different incentives to his subjects. He found that there was an optimum level of arousal for performance on a tracking task; the lower and higher levels were both associated with lower performance scores.

Following the early work of Luria (1932), there are many studies which indirectly support the generalization stated above. They demonstrate that there is a change in performance when the arousal level markedly deviates from the level which prevailed during the acquisition and earlier performance of the task. However, they are not designed to show that similar changes in performance occur on both sides of an optimal level. For example, we have already seen (Chap. 7) that Hunt & Brady (1951) found the rate of lever-pressing response in rats to decrease when a clicker, which had been previously associated with an electric shock, was turned on. It is likely that in this case the clicker, being a signal for noxious stimulation, increases arousal beyond the optimal level for the lever-pressing response. Similar observations have also been made by Amsel (1950) and Frick (1953). Unfortunately, in all these cases it is not known whether a decrease in arousal level brought about, let us say, by the administration of a sedative drug would also decrease the performance measure; however, it appears likely that this will be the case. A study by Payne, Hauty, & Moore (1957) is relevant here. They trained human subjects on a tracking task. Then they induced fatigue by making the subjects perform for prolonged periods. The ensuing fatigue and monotony (lowered arousal level) resulted in a decrease in performance scores. The subjects were then administered an analeptic drug, which can be assumed to raise arousal level. Payne, Hauty, & Moore found that the performance scores of their subjects increased as a result of the drug administration. They interpret their results in terms of the general relation between arousal level and performance. However, here again the investigators did not study the performance at arousal levels on the other (above-normal) side of the level that existed during control performance.

Thus, the first generalization above does seem to be supported by some studies. However, systematic studies of the postulated relation are still lacking, and we know little about the optimal arousal levels required for different types of tasks and activities.

*Generalization 2.* With increased practice at performing an activity or task (i.e. with increased habit strength of a response), there is an increase in the range of the optimal level of arousal, as well as in the range within which the activity occurs at all.

The hypothetical relation stated in this generalization is shown in part B of Figure 23. It shows a curve for each of two different habit strengths of a given response. It is seen that the range of arousal level within which the performance measure attains its highest value is smaller at low habit strength (*l*) than it is at high habit strength (*h*). (Of course, the performance scores are also higher at high habit strength, but this fact is not relevant to the present discussion.) Furthermore, the total range within which the activity can occur at all is also shown to be greater at high habit strength than at low.

Common-sense observation supports the central idea of the second generalization. When an activity is well-practiced, one is said to be able to perform it "in one's sleep." Again, a great deal of practice is apparently required in training for jobs (e.g. fire fighting, military combat) which must be performed at arousal levels different from those that prevail during training. Certain experimental studies have also yielded some relevant evidence. They show that a small increase in the level of arousal above the level at which a given activity normally occurs may result in a higher performance score. (This means that the arousal level at which an activity normally occurs is not necessarily the optimal level for that activity.) However, the studies in which such an improvement in performance is seen seem to be the ones in which the activity is well-practiced before the increase in arousal is brought about. For example, Siegel & Siegel (1949) determined the effects of an electric shock on a drinking response in rats. The habit strength of the drinking response is high in all normal adult animals. The investigators removed each of the partially hungry and thirsty animals from its cage, shocked it, and then returned it to the cage. Water consumption during the subsequent two hours was found to be greater in the shocked animals than in the control animals, which had received no environmental disturbance. Essentially similar "dynamogenic effects" of shock on eating have been reported by Siegel & Brantley (1951). Similarly, Amsel & Maltzman (1950) trained rats to drink in individual cages during a 10-min. period each day. After the habit strength of this response had reached an asymptote, they electrically shocked the animals before placing them in the drinking situation. They found that shock increased the drinking response. In another experiment, Amsel & Roussel (1952) found that "frustrating" rats (unexpectedly changing one feature of the experimental situation) resulted in an increased speed of running to food. Here again, the running response had been well practiced before the frustrating event (forced delay in starting) was introduced.

The types of studies described above have traditionally been interpreted in terms of the concept of "generalized drive." Conditions such as electric shock, "distraction," "frustration," and "conflict" are assumed to increase drive, and this in turn is regarded as the cause of increased performance scores. The interpretation suggested here relates increased performance scores to increased arousal level, which in turn is assumed to increase under the general conditions described in the section on "factors affecting arousal." It should be noted that, according to the present interpretation, the increase in performance score is likely to occur only when the habit strength of the response is high (Generalization 2), and only when the increase in arousal level is small enough not to pass the upper limit of the optimal range (Generalization 1).

## AN INTERPRETATION OF "DISPLACEMENT PHENOMENA"

The general relation between level of arousal and performance stated in the two generalizations can be applied to the interpretation of the so-called displacement phenomena.

*The phenomenon and its traditional interpretation.* The type of phenomena in connection with which the term "displacement" is used can be illustrated by an example that, whether true or not, is close to the heart of the layman. A man is severely reprimanded by his boss. This makes the man angry, but various social and financial considerations prevent him from talking back to or hitting the boss. Later, the man goes home and acts aggressively toward his wife, who has done no wrong. The term "displacement" is used in such cases because it is assumed that the tendency to be aggressive, initiated by the boss' reprimand, somehow remains active in the individual until he finds a suitable scapegoat. Then the aggressive behavior, originally intended for the boss, is said to be "displaced" on to an irrelevant object such as the wife, a cat, or his desk. This concept of "displaced aggression" has been employed by Dollard *et al.* (1939) and Levy (1941) to account for some phenomena of social behavior.

The concept of displacement is also sometimes used in a slightly different sense. When prevented from engaging in a particular activity, an individual may engage in a completely different activity. For example, a child prevented from eating candy may start to suck his thumb, or a sheep prevented from escaping a noxious stimulation may begin grazing. In such cases the original tendency is said to be displaced, not to another object, but to another activity. Lorenz (1935, 1941; quoted by Tinbergen, 1951) and other ethological writers use the term "displacement activities" to refer to behavior which has been initiated in this way, by the prevention of another activity or by competition between two other response tendencies. Thus, it has been pointed out that when fighting is obstructed in cranes, or copulation in ducks, the birds begin to preen. A parallel to such "displacement preening," as it has been called by Lorenz, has been reported by Tinbergen (1951) in the behavior of the male stickleback. This fish shows a fanning movement during courtship. However, when an unreceptive female arrives, the sexually aroused male "will vent the sexual impulses by bouts of displacement fanning" (1951, p. 192). Lorenz interprets such phenomena in terms of the displacement of the neural "energy" connected to the obstructed activity to another (displacement) activity.

The displacement (e.g. of energy) interpretation of the "displacement phenomena" is unsatisfactory. It is too vague and ad hoc. When an animal is prevented from engaging in an activity for which it is ready, it must show some other activity. Only two possibilities exist. Either its new activity resembles the prevented activity except in that it is directed toward another object, or the new activity is completely different. Now, these occurrences are in no way explained by stating, in the first case, that the original activity itself is displaced to a new object and, in the second, that the tendency to perform the original activity is displaced to a new activity. Statements of this type are only redundant descriptions.

*Another interpretation of displacement phenomena.* A line of speculation proposed by Bindra (1956) suggests another way of approaching the problem presented by displacement phenomena. According to this view such phenomena can be interpreted in terms of three factors: (1) change in arousal level, (2) the relative habit strength of the various activities in the repertoire of the animal, and (3) the sensory cues provided by the stimulus situation.

When an animal is prevented from engaging in an activity which it customarily performs in a given situation ("frustrated"), its level of arousal is likely to increase. It is interesting to note that activities that are categorized as displacement phenomena typically occur when the animal is highly excited. This heightened arousal level usually lasts for some time after the obstruction in the original activity and is, according to the present view, partly responsible for what the animal does subsequently. The activities which are most likely to occur in a state of heightened arousal are those which are prepotent in the animal's repertoire. This point follows from the second generalization discussed in the last section. According to the generalization, only the activities with high habit strength can occur at the extremes of arousal level. Now, it should be noted that the activities described as displacement activities are those that are typically highly prepotent in the animal's repertoire. For example, grazing in sheep and preening in birds are likely to be high habit strength activities. According to the present view, activities which are not prepotent in the animal's repertoire are not likely to occur when the animal is prevented from engaging in some other (the obstructed) activity. The third factor that determines what the animal does is the existing stimulus situation and the responses that are connected to the sensory cues generated by the situation. If, after the obstruction, the animal is placed in the situation in which the animal normally eats, then the animal is likely to eat; if the animal is placed in an "attack situation," it will tend to show aggressive behavior; and if it is placed in a "sexual situation" it will probably copulate. In short, the familiar cues will evoke the customary activity, except insofar as the customary activity is affected by increased arousal. Thus, according to this view, the activity that an animal shows (after being obstructed in some other activity) depends upon what the changed stimulus cues are connected to in that animal. The angry man, of the layman's example, will act aggressively toward his wife only if that is one of the activities that is connected with the wife; if his wife is a cue for relaxing, he may "cry on her shoulder."

Undoubtedly, many problems will arise if a systematic attempt is made to account for all displacement phenomena in terms of the three factors of arousal level, habit strength, and sensory cues. However, this hypothesis does suggest certain new lines of experimental work.

## Mechanism of the Arousal-Performance Relation

Let us now consider the possible neural mechanisms involved in the above relations.

*Some neurophysiological facts.* The primary sensory system, as well as the reticular activating system, is relevant to this discussion. Both these systems are sensory in character, but their functions appear to be quite different. The *primary sensory system* conducts nervous impulses from the various sense organs to the thalamus and from there to the discrete sensory areas of cortex. Conduction in this case is direct, fast, and specific, and thus the inputs into this system can serve as cues or "messages." The *reticular activating system* consists of the reticular formation in the medial brain stem, and parts of hypothalamus, subthalamus, and ventromedial thalamus. Impulses in this system are conducted over devious multisynaptic pathways and are transmitted diffusely to all parts of the cortex. This system receives impulses from all sense modalities and, therefore, is sometimes called the "nonspecific sensory system" as opposed to primary or specific sensory system (*see* Fig. 24).

Thus, every sense-organ stimulation initiates two different types of sensory processes. Some impulses are sent directly to specific cortical areas thereby providing cues for discriminative response (Chap. 7); others are sent through the reticular activating system generally to all parts of the cortex, but these impulses are too diffusely spread to provide cues for specific action. The impulses from the reticular activating system seem rather to serve the function of keeping the cortex active or "toned up." Changes in this diffuse background activity or *activation* of the cortex seem to have profound effects on the way the incoming primary sensory impulses are dealt with.

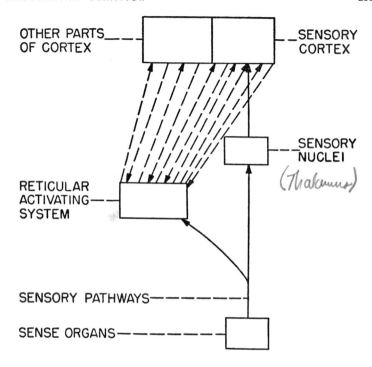

FIG. 24. THE RETICULAR ACTIVATING SYSTEM

Schematic drawing showing the relation of the reticular activating system to sensory input and the cerebral cortex.

Low activation (slow, large waves on EEG) is typically associated with sleep, and high activation (fast, small waves) with excitement. Thus, it appears that the activation of the cortex, which is related to the behavioral changes we have subsumed under "arousal," is determined by the activity of the reticular activating system. It is known that extensive damage to this system produces a permanent comatose state. The nonspecific activation effects of sensory stimulation also seem essential for the maintenance of alert wakefulness.

As may be expected, the two sensory systems do not function independently of each other. Though the nonspecific system affects cortical activity and thus the disposal of specific messages, the arrival of specific messages at the cortex can also affect the events in the reticular activating system. Impulses coming down from the cortex to the reticular system serve to increase activity in that system, which in turn affects cortical activation. (Increase in arousal brought about by the anticipation of an electric shock, or by other symbolic stimuli, probably involves such cortex-initiated stimulation of the reticular activating system.) The activating system is also affected by changes in blood chemistry and is particularly susceptible to anesthetic drugs.

The reticular activating system does not affect the cortex only. It also influences lower centers, and thus the motor outflow to various organs. This motor function of the system is also quite nonspecific as compared with the specific effects which the cortical and hypothalamic motor centers have on the visceral-somatic reactions. The sensory feedback from these reactions, of course, again reaches the cortex in the form of specific cues, or as nonspecific excitation via the reticular activating system.

The above description of the relevant neurophysiological mechanisms is based on the work and writings of Moruzzi & Magoun (1949), Lindsley (1951), and Sharpless (1954).

*Effects on behavior.* It is clear that changes in level of arousal can affect the performance of any given activity in two different ways. The increase or decrease in cortical activation may affect performance by altering the over-all pattern of neural firing, including the firing of phase sequences or neural integrations that correspond to the given activity. On the other hand, the sensory cues arising from the visceral and somatic changes may affect performance by altering the pattern of sensory impulses that normally lead to the firing of relevant phase sequences. Both these possible mechanisms must operate through altering the neural integrations that correspond to the given activity. However, the activation mechanism would do this through its nonspecific effect on a large part of the cerebral cortex, whereas the sensory mechanism would operate more specifically by changing the cues which control the activity. Only one of these mechanisms may be involved in the arousal-performance relation, the two may act conjointly but may have independent effects, or the two may interact in some way. For example, if the administration of an electric shock of moderate intensity increases eating in an animal, the effect may result from (1) change in neural activation brought about by the shock, (2) change in the cues arising from the sensory consequences of visceral and somatic changes that follow the shock, (3) both these changes acting independently of each other, or (4) change in activation, which leads to certain visceral and somatic effects, the sensory impulses from which further change cortical activation, and so on. The obvious problem presented by these alternatives is that of experimentally separating the effects of changes in cerebral activation from those of changes in sensory cues. However, the complex interactions that exist between neural and visceral-somatic events seem to preclude any easy way of isolating the effect of the two mechanisms.

One way to approach this problem is suggested by a method being employed by Mahut.[4] By implanting stimulating electrodes in the reticular activating system she is able to activate the cortex while keeping the stimulation so weak that it does not seem to lead to any gross visceral-somatic effects. If this procedure really precludes the occurrence of visceral-somatic changes, then there is no danger of the cortex receiving altered sensory cues from the visceral-somatic system. Thus, the effects on behavior of reticular-system stimulation could be attributed solely to the activation of the cortex.

[4] In a personal communication to the author, from Dr. Helen Mahut, Montreal Neurological Institute, McGill University, Montreal, Canada.

# Chapter 9

# The Role of
# Blood Chemistry

Besides sensory cues and arousal level, the chemical constitution of the blood also affects behavior in significant ways. Changes in blood chemistry result from the normal metabolic and anabolic processes that characterize all living organisms. These processes lead to variations in the level of oxygen, carbon dioxide, water, sugar, various salts, hormones, and other humoral factors. This chapter is concerned with the effects of such variations in blood chemistry on the occurrence of various motivational activities.

The amount of experimental literature on the relation between blood chemistry and behavior is too vast to be dealt with fully in a book of this kind, and no attempt is made to do so. Rather, only a few representative studies are discussed in relation to each general point. This chapter is also limited in another way. The effects on behavior of drug-induced changes in blood chemistry are not considered. Only the behavioral effects of variations in the levels of those humoral factors that are normally present in the blood stream are discussed here. Of course, the normal components of blood also affect the growth of an organism and the acquisition of various classes of activities. However, our concern here is only with the effect of humoral changes in the occurrence of activities that have already been developed and now exist in the animal's repertoire. We shall first explore the effects of humoral variations on each of the motivational activities discussed in Chapters 2 and 4, and then consider the general mechanisms of blood chemistry–behavior relations.

## CONTROL OF GENERAL ACTIVITY

Variations in both the hormonal and nonhormonal constituents of the blood stream affect general activity.

### Nonhormonal Factors

Prolonged food or water deprivation leads to changes in blood chemistry and thus provides a simple method of studying the behavioral effects of nonhormonal humoral variations. Most of the studies to be discussed here have employed this method.

Siegel & Steinberg (1949) measured the general activity of male rats, groups of which had been food-deprived for varying intervals of time. With deprivation intervals of 0, 12, 24, 36, and 48 hr., they found a progressive increase in activity. The curve of the relation between activity and food deprivation represented a negatively accelerated increasing function. Conversely, Marx (1950b) has shown that activity in rats is markedly reduced by the administration of gossypol, an appetite depressant which delays the passage of food from the stomach to the small intestine. Increases in general activity roughly proportional to degree of deprivation (up to 72 hr.) have also been reported by Finger (1951) for food deprivation and by Finger & Reid (1952) for both food and water deprivation. In both these studies, the investigators noted a sudden decrease in activity, below the normal (sated) level, during the first day following the end of deprivation.

Increase in activity level occurs not only when the animal is completely deprived for a long period of time, but also when it is moved from an *ad libitum* to a restricted feeding schedule. Hall *et al.* (1953) compared the activity level of rats placed on a 23-hr. food deprivation schedule with that of a control group which had free access to food at all times. The activity of the control group showed no remarkable change during the

21 consecutive testing days; however, the experimental animals showed a gradual increase in daily activity, so that activity reached a plateau about the 12th day at a level that was roughly 14 times greater than that of the control animals. Hall (1955a) repeated the above study with water instead of food deprivation. Although the experimental animals were more active than the control animals in this case too, there was no progressive increase in activity corresponding to the one observed in the case of food deprivation. The significance of this difference between the effects of identical schedules of food and water deprivation is not clear.

In interpreting the deprivation-activity relation, Campbell & Sheffield (1953) hold that deprivation does not instigate activity; rather they attribute the rise in general activity of animals to "their greater sensitivity to minimal stimulus changes in the environment" (1953, p. 321). They base this interpretation on their finding that the increase in rat activity brought about by deprivation is quite small as compared with the one brought about by altering the auditory and visual characteristics of the testing situation. Campbell & Sheffield consider such environmental change to be the primary condition for increasing activity; starvation merely serves to lower the threshold of sensitivity to the environmental stimuli.

Hall & Hanford (1954) do not agree with the above interpretation. They reduced environmental stimulation of rats by deafening them, but found that deprivation increased the general activity of deafened animals as much as that of the normal animals. In another experiment, Hall (1956) found that, though change in environmental stimulation did result in increased rat activity, the addition of a food-deprivation state increased it still more. Although these experiments show that deprivation can change activity level, they do not answer the crucial question as to whether deprivation can increase activity independently of environmental stimulation brought about by (presumed) changes in sensory acuity of the animals.

Of course, it can be argued that food and water deprivation lead to bodily changes (e.g. emptiness of stomach, dryness of mouth and throat) the sensory consequences of which provide the change in stimulation, which in turn brings about the increased activity. Therefore, it can still be maintained that it is the change in sensory stimulation per se (whether it is environmental or interoceptive is of no consequence) that is responsible for the increase in general activity seen in deprived animals, as well as in those that are exposed to an environmental change. The important issue is whether the deprivation-activity relation results from changes in sensory stimulation (of any kind: environmental or interoceptive) or from some other consequences of deprivation. It is known that food and water deprivation lead to a decrease in, respectively, level of blood sugar and water content of the blood. There is also reason to believe that such changes in blood chemistry cause the changes in stomach and throat that alter the pattern of interoceptive stimulation. However, it is also possible that changes in blood chemistry directly affect the central nervous system in such a way as to increase general activity. Thus, further research must seek to decide whether changes in blood chemistry affect activity level through alterations in interoceptive sensory stimulation or by directly affecting the relevant mechanisms in the central nervous system, or by both these means. It should be borne in mind that blood chemistry may directly affect activity level in infancy, but, through learning, sensory stimulation (both environmental and interoceptive) may become a more important determiner of activity in adulthood. We have already noted (Chap. 4) that the responses involved in general activity can be positively reinforced in the same way as other responses.

If an animal were deprived of food or water for a long enough time, its activity level would eventually decrease. Prolonged deprivation produces deficiencies of various nutritional factors and these in turn cause the animal to become less active. Morgan & Stellar (1950) have reviewed the literature on the relation between activity level and nutritional deficiencies. They conclude that nutritional conditions that produce a decrement in general activity are those that weaken the animal physically.

HORMONAL FACTORS

The extensive literature on the effects of hormonal variations on general activity has been reviewed by Beach (1948)
and Morgan & Stellar (1950). A perusal of these reviews suggests the following general but tentative conclusions:

1. Extirpation of the thyroid, pancreatic, adrenal, gonadal, or
   pituitary gland decreases the level of general activity. The
   decrease in activity is especially marked in the case of the
   removal of any one of the thyroid, pancreatic, and adrenal
   glands.
2. Replacement therapy, involving administration of the appropriate hormone after the removal of one of the above
   endocrine glands, may or may not reinstate the original activity level. The equivocal nature of the results can probably
   be attributed to variations in the age at which the gland is
   removed, age at which replacement therapy is initiated, dosage of the hormone administered, and other details of the
   experimental procedure.
3. Administration of the hormone of one of these glands to
   normal animals may increase activity level, leave it unaf-
   fected, or may decrease it. Here again, a variety of factors
   probably determines the particular effects obtained. It is
   likely that large dosages decrease activity, but small ones increase it a little.
4. In general, the decrease in activity brought about by the removal of an endocrine gland seems to be attributable to reduced endurance for muscular activity. The reduced endurance may result directly from the hormonal deficiency or
   from the indirect effects of hormonal change (deficiency or
   excess) on the general health of the animal.
5. The cyclic seasonal and estrual changes in activity seen in
   some animals are related to variations in certain hormones,
   especially those of the adrenal, gonadal, and pituitary glands.

Though the extirpation of a particular endocrine gland usually produces a clear-cut change in general activity, it is not
easy to attribute the changed activity level specifically to the
removal from the blood stream of the secretions of that particular gland. It is well known that changes in the level of one
hormone lead to alterations in the secretive activity of other

endocrine glands, so that the observed effect on activity may result from many interacting hormonal changes. This is especially true in the case of the pituitary gland. This endocrine structure secretes many trophic hormones, which directly regulate the activity of other endocrine glands. Another difficulty in discovering the basis of the endocrine-activity relation is similar to the one discussed above in connection with the effects on general activity of the nonhormonal blood factors. It is the problem of deciding whether, or to what extent, the effects of hormonal variations on activity result from the direct or the indirect (sensory feedback) effects of hormones on the central nervous system. We shall return to this general problem later in the chapter.

## HUMORAL CONTROL OF WITHDRAWAL AND AGGRESSIVE ACTIVITIES

In Chapter 4, it was shown that withdrawal (escape and avoidance) and aggressive activities develop in the repertoire of animals by the same process of selective reinforcement that operates in any other form of goal-directed activity. This section is concerned with the effect of humoral variations on withdrawal and aggressive responses.

### WITHDRAWAL ACTIVITIES

Though there are numerous studies of the effects of drugs on escape and avoidance behavior, there are but a few concerning the effects of variations in the normal constituents of the blood stream. Murphy & Miller (1955) investigated the effects of administering adrenocorticotrophic hormone (ACTH), one of the pituitary hormones, on an avoidance response in normal rats. The administration of the hormone, after the shuttle-box-type avoidance response had been acquired, was found not to affect the rate of extinction of the response. But hypophysectomy does have some effect on an avoidance response. Bélanger[1] found that in hypophysectomized rats, though an avoidance response was acquired just as readily as in

---

[1] In a personal communication to the author, from Professor D. Bélanger, University of Montreal, Montreal, Canada.

normal rats, the response extinguished much more quickly. Bélanger's observation that hypophysectomized animals, though capable of responding when shocked, appeared too placid or lazy to continue making the response during extinction sessions suggests that the observed difference in resistance to extinction may have resulted from general weakness brought about by hypophysectomy.

The administration of adrenalin to normal animals causes a sharp decrease in the frequency of a conditioned avoidance response. Kosman & Gerard (1955) established such a response in rats, and then, after administering injections of adrenalin, found a decrement in the frequency of occurrence of the response. They attribute this result to the general weakening effect of adrenalin, which presumably led to a decline in motor capabilities. When these peripheral effects of adrenalin were blocked by an injection of dibenzyline administered shortly before adrenalin, the avoidance responses were not impaired. Since dibenzyline is presumed not to have any central effects, Kosman & Gerard argue that adrenalin affects the occurrence of avoidance activities not through the central nervous system, but by its effects on peripheral organs.

Clearly, many more studies of the relation between blood chemistry and withdrawal responses are needed before any general conclusions can be drawn. The habit strength of the responses at the time that any particular experimental change in blood chemistry is produced is likely to be an important parameter in studies in this area. Such habit strength–blood chemistry interaction is suggested by some of the studies discussed in the last two chapters, as well as by Sidman's (1956) investigations of the effects of drugs on avoidance behavior.

### Aggressive Activities

Observations made on numerous reptiles, birds, and mammals suggest that to a certain extent the incidence of aggressive behavior is determined by hormonal variations (*see* Beach, 1948). The gonadal hormones seem to be particularly important. Castration of animals typically reduces the incidence of fighting, and the administration of androgenic substances, in both males and females, seems to increase fighting. Anderson (1940) observed that female rats became less "timid" during estrus than they were during periods of sexual nonreceptivity. Such a relation between sexual receptivity and timidity was also noted by Yerkes (1943) in chimpanzees. These observations are supported by the finding of Anderson & Anderson (1940) that the administration of estrogen makes castrated female rats less timid.

Animals that live in groups of two or more, or repeatedly come in contact with each other, develop fairly stable dominance-submission relationships with respect to each of the other animals. Presumably, an individual's position in the dominance hierarchy is a function of its aggressiveness and is established as a consequence of earlier fighting and "testing" of relative strengths with the other members of the social group. Such dominance hierarchies are a regular feature of normal primate life. The relation of hormonal variations to dominance-submission relationships has been the subject of a number of well-designed experimental studies, and it is these studies that have revealed some of the important features of the relation between hormones and aggressive behavior.

*Estrogen and dominance.* In general, the administration of androgenic hormones produces similar effects on social dominance in both the male and female. However, the administration of estrogen does not. Birch & Clark (1946) and Clark & Birch (1946) have shown that by increasing estrogen level it is possible to raise the dominance status of the castrate female chimpanzee, but estrogen lowers the status of the male castrate. These differential effects of estrogen have been the subject of an investigation by Birch & Clark (1950). They tested the hypothesis that the differential effects are attributable to the differential effects of estrogen on the genital organs of males and females. Estrogen administration leads to an engorgement of the sex skin in the castrate female chimpanzee (similar to the engorgement seen in a normal estrous female), but does not produce any peripheral genital changes in the male castrate. Birch & Clark were able to separate the effects of changes in estrogen level in the blood stream from those of changes in genital engorgement by simultaneously administering estrogen and progesterone to a female castrate. (Progesterone inhibits genital swelling in the female chimpanzee for brief periods.) The changes in dominance status vis-à-vis another female castrate were determined by observing which one of the two animals obtained a peanut dropped into a cup. Twenty peanuts were dropped each day, and the dominance score of each animal was the number of peanuts it obtained. The results of one such experiment are presented in Fig. 25. It is seen that, though the level of the two hormones in the blood stream was kept constant from day to day, there were marked variations in the dominance status of the female castrate, Nira. These variations can be seen to be highly correlated with the degree of genital engorgement. Thus, the estrogen-induced dominance in the castrate female chimpanzee appears to result not from any

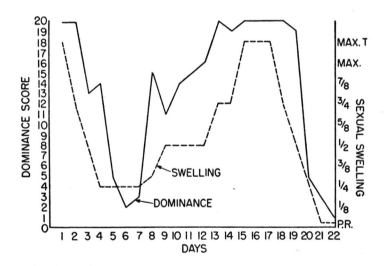

Fig. 25. The Relation Between Dominance and Sexual Swelling in the Female

The relation of Nira's dominance status to her sexual swelling when the daily administration of hormones is kept at a constant level. (*Source:* H. G. Birch and G. Clark, Hormonal modification of social behavior: IV. The mechanism of estrogen-induced dominance in chimpanzees. *J. comp. physiol. Psychol.,* **43,** 188.)

direct effects on the central nervous system, but from the sensory feedback from the peripheral changes in the sex skin. Estrogen does not produce such genital changes in the male; consequently, the male's dominance status is not raised by this hormone.

Apart from the change in dominance status produced through the peripheral changes in the sex skin, the administration of estrogen seems also to have another effect on dominance status. As was noted before, the administration of estrogen to the male castrate lowers its dominance status (Clark & Birch, 1945). Birch & Clark (1950) have also reported a lowering of the status in a normally dominant castrate female when increase in estrogen level is not accompanied by genital engorgement. Thus, it appears that increasing estrogen level, in the absence of peripheral genital changes, tends to decrease aggressiveness in both male and female castrates. Apparently the estrogen-induced peripheral changes in the female castrate raise its aggressiveness so much that the general aggressiveness-reducing effect of estrogen is more than counteracted.

No satisfactory explanation of the effects of estrogen on dominance status is yet available. Two separate questions need to be answered: (1) Why does the sensory feedback from the engorged sex skin increase the incidence of aggressive acts (resulting in a higher dominance status) in the female? (2) Why does estrogen in the absence of genital engorgement reduce aggressiveness in male and female castrates? So far as the first question is concerned, it can be argued that sensory feedback from engorged sensitive sex skin raises the level of arousal of the female. It follows from the discussion in Chapter 8 that, of the various acts existing in an animal's repertoire, the acts that were acquired and are normally performed in a state of high arousal are more likely to occur in a state of high arousal than are acts that were acquired and are normally performed in a state of low arousal. Since aggressive acts are more likely to have been acquired in a state of high arousal than are most other classes of acts, other things remaining the same (*see* below), the female is more likely to show aggressive rather than other types of acts during the period of sex-skin engorgement. According to this line of speculation, the vascular changes in sex skin do not have any specific connection with aggressiveness; rather those changes increase the incidence of aggressive acts by increasing the level of arousal of the animal. It follows that, so long as the test situation provides the cues for aggressive acts, an increase in arousal level brought about by any means (not necessarily through sex-skin engorgement) will also increase the proportion of aggressive acts. Hebb's (1945) observations indicate that noise, "teasing," and other arousal-increasing conditions often precipitate aggressive acts in chimpanzees.

The second question concerns the basis of estrogen-induced reduction in aggressiveness in the male castrate and in the castrated female without engorged sex skin. Birch & Clark (1950) seem inclined to answer this question by attributing a specific central effect to estrogen. Estrogen is assumed to reduce the incidence of aggressive acts by effecting some specific change in the central nervous system. Their position implies the existence of some kind of an "aggressiveness center" on which estrogen can have a specific effect. An alternative tentative interpretation can be formulated in such terms as the following: In both the male and female estrogen may be assumed to have a general sedative effect on the central nervous system, reducing muscle tension, level of activity, and, in general, lowering the animal's level of arousal. If this assumption is correct, the lowered arousal level is likely to decrease the incidence of aggressive acts (*see* above) in both the normal and the castrate male, as well as in the castrate female when engorgement of the sex skin, which normally follows the administration of estrogen, is artificially prevented. In the castrate female, when the engorgement is not prevented, the specific effect of estrogen (in moderate dosage) on the female sex skin would raise the animal's arousal level (counteracting the general arousal-reducing effect of estrogen) and, thus, increase the incidence of aggressive acts. The administration of estrogen to the normal female may also increase its sex-skin engorgement but, because the general level of blood estrogen is likely to be fairly high in the normal female, a further increase in estrogen is not likely to produce much change in its sex-skin engorgement. Thus, in the normal female the effect of estrogen administration may be to reduce aggressiveness because of its general sedative effect. Following this line of speculation, it seems possible to account for the varied effects of estrogen on (castrate and normal) males and females without postulating any specific "aggressiveness center" in the brain.

*Androgen and dominance.* The administration of androgen to low-ranking normal and castrated animals increases the dominance status in both the male and the female (*see* Beach, 1948). This effect of androgen on aggressiveness can be interpreted as resulting also from changes in the level of arousal of the animal. Let us assume that the administration of androgen has a general stimulant effect on the central nervous system, thus increasing muscle tension, level of activity, and arousal level in general. If this is true, then the increase in the incidence of aggressive acts can be attributed to increased arousal level, according to the line of reasoning suggested in connection with the effects of estrogen. It is also likely that a given (moderate) dosage of androgen will increase arousal more in the male than in the female owing to the specific effects of androgen on the male genital organs. The androgen-induced vascular changes in the male genitals is likely to have arousal-increasing effects on the male similar to the effects of sex-skin engorgement in the female. According to this view, androgen administration is likely to advance the dominance status of male castrates more than that of normal or castrated females, but an increase in androgen above the normal level in the noncastrated male would result only in a slight advance in its dominance status.

If the above "arousal interpretation" of the effects on dominance of estrogen and androgen is correct, one would expect that variations in the output of the thyroid hormone will lead to variations in the incidence of aggressive acts, for increase in arousal level seems to be one of the effects of slight increases in thyroid output. There is some reason to believe (*see* Beach, 1948) that variations in the level of thyroid hormone in the blood stream do change the dominance status of animals.

*Other determiners of dominance status.* The above research does not, of course, show that gonadal hormones always produce changes in dominance status; it only indicates that these hormones can produce such changes. Whereas changes in arousal level brought about by the action of estrogen and androgen may operate whenever there is a change in the level of these hormones in the blood stream, it cannot be concluded that the change in arousal level necessarily leads to a change in the incidence of aggressive acts and thereby in dominance status. On the contrary, some other factors also determine the incidence of aggressive acts. Thus, even when gonadal hormone variations do lead to changes in dominance status, the changes must be looked upon as the outcome of a number of interacting factors of which hormonal variation is only one. Indeed, there are many investigations in which gonadal hormone variations were found not to affect the dominance status. Crawford (1940) and Yerkes (1940) noted that only about half of their female chimpanzees in estrus showed an increase in aggressiveness and dominance over their test partners. Clark & Birch (1945) have reported the case of a prepuberally castrated male chimpanzee who was dominant over a normal male of comparable age. And Mirsky (1955) found that the administration of gonadal hormones to certain castrate monkeys did not alter their dominance status in a group consisting entirely of castrate monkeys.

Changes brought about by hormonal variations in the blood stream interact with at least two other factors to produce the observed changes in dominance. One of these factors is the difference in interanimal aggressiveness existing prior to hormone administration. Hormonal variations are less likely to affect the dominance status of one individual with respect to another if the difference in their aggressiveness is large to begin with than if normally the difference in their aggressiveness is small. If the initial difference is large, hormonal variations may not be able to produce a sufficient change in aggressiveness to counteract the existing difference and thereby reverse dominance status. As Mirsky (1955) points out in connection with his negative results on castrate monkeys, initial individual differences in aggressiveness obscure hormonal effects on dominance.

The second factor that affects the outcome of dominance tests is that of habit strength. When dominance-submission relationships between two individuals, or the members of a larger group, are well established, they are less likely to be reversed by hormonal variations than are relationships that are not well established. That is to say, when the habit strength of aggressive or submissive responses in an individual is high in a situation involving another individual or individuals, hormonal variations are less likely to change the dominance status of the individual so long as the membership of the group does not change. The results of many investigations in which variations in gonadal hormones did not produce any noticeable effects in dominance status can be interpreted in terms of the factor of habit strength. For example, in Mirsky's (1955) study the dominance status within each pair of monkeys tested appears to have been quite well established before the gonadal hormones were administered. Not only did hormone administration fail to change the dominance status in this study, but there was also no remarkable change in the incidence of aggressive and subordinate acts. It is clear that, as Crawford (1940) has observed before, the outcome of any test of dominance depends upon the type of response patterns built up during the life of the animal and upon the habit strength of those patterns.

The influence of previously established response tendencies and of other experimental factors in determining dominance status is also seen in other studies. For example, Rosvold, Mirsky, & Pribram (1954) investigated the effects of amygdalectomy on the dominance hierarchy of a group of eight monkeys. Before surgery, the animals were observed for several months in both individual and group cages. Three monkeys who were the most dominant in the group situation were then subjected to bilateral amygdalectomy. As a result, two of the three operated animals fell to the bottom of the hierarchy; the dominance of the third monkey was not lowered at all. Rosvold, Mirsky, & Pribram found no reason to attribute this difference in the effects of amygdalectomy to the size of lesion.

Rather, they noted that, on returning to the colony after surgery in a somewhat weak condition, the two monkeys that were confronted with relatively aggressive cagemates fell in dominance status, but the animal that was faced with a relatively submissive cagemate remained dominant. Thus, they interpret the difference in change in dominance in terms of "the social environment confronting each animal upon return to the group after surgery and to the length of time the pre-operative [dominance] relationships had existed" (1954, p. 178).

It is interesting to note that in rats and other lower mammals, whether the dominance status of an individual is stable or has to be re-established periodically, hormonal variations seem to have consistent and predictable effects on dominance status. On the other hand, in primate groups hormonal variations appear to have quite variable effects on the dominance status of an individual. Obviously, we need systematic investigations of the interactions between previously acquired response tendencies and the effects of hormonal variations[2] at different phylogenetic levels.

### HUMORAL CONTROL OF EATING, DRINKING, AND SEXUAL RESPONSES

As in the case of general activity, the effect of humoral variations on eating, drinking, and sexual activities has been studied either by depriving the animal of substances that are needed for maintaining the normal constitution of the blood stream or by administering appropriate preparations to the animal.

### EATING

Though rate of eating and amount eaten are, within certain limits, a direct function of the degree of food deprivation, the exact relation of eating to the nutritional factors in blood is far from clear. Scott, Scott, & Luckhardt (1938) showed that nor-

---

[2] Of course, the dominance status of animals can be changed by methods other than that of altering the levels of various hormones. For example, Murphy & Miller (1956) have successfully reversed dominance in monkeys by an avoidance conditioning technique, where the submissive member of a pair was used as a conditioned stimulus for an electric shock.

mally blood-sugar level during hunger is not significantly different from the level after satiation. And Siegel & Taub (1952) and Siegel and Dorman (1954) have shown that blood from hungry and sated animals, when injected into others, has no differential effects on the rate of eating of the recipient animals. However, Morgan & Morgan (1940) have pointed out that injections of insulin, which reduce level of blood sugar, tend to increase the rate of eating.

The main obstacle in the way of obtaining consistent results seems to be the variations in the feeding schedules on which the animals are normally maintained and subsequently tested. When animals are switched from an *ad libitum* to a restricted time feeding schedule, changes in their body weight and food and water intake may continue to occur for several days. This has been shown by Ghent (1951) and Reid & Finger (1955). In another relevant study, Lawrence & Mason (1955) found that, for a given deprivation interval, rats ate more if they were given the eating test at the regularly scheduled time of day than if tested at any other time. The amount eaten also appears to be affected by the level of water in the blood stream. Verplanck & Hayes (1953) have shown that the amount eaten by water-deprived animals is only about half as much as that eaten by animals which are not water deprived. It appears that in many studies such factors connected with feeding schedules have tended to obscure the true relation between blood chemistry and eating. Investigations employing identical feeding schedules may well yield results that are more consistent with each other than those obtained so far.

The mechanisms underlying the relation between food deprivation and eating have been investigated and, to a certain extent, clarified in recent years. Morgan & Morgan (1940a) sought to determine whether the increase in rate of eating brought about by injections of insulin is dependent upon increased gastric contractions. They vagotomized the stomachs of rats before administering insulin. The denervated stomachs reacted to insulin normally but, of course, the sensory impulses arising from increased gastric motility could not reach the brain. Nevertheless, they noted an increase in eating rate.

Thus, the sensory feedback from the stomach does not seem to be the essential event in the insulin-induced increase in the rate of eating. Morgan & Morgan are inclined to the view that eating can be facilitated or depressed by the direct action of appropriate chemicals on the central nervous system.

Another investigation of the same problem is that of Smith & Duffy (1955). They maintained rats on a 22-hr. food deprivation schedule and trained them in a Skinner box to press a lever to obtain food. Then they compared the effects on lever pressing of intragastric injections of various substances. Injections of 10 c.c. of normal saline, or of 10 c.c. of a 5 per cent glucose solution, or of varying amounts of inert bulk did not affect the rate of lever pressing. However, a 30 per cent sucrose solution depressed the rate significantly, and the decrement was proportional to the amount injected. On the basis of these and other results, Smith & Duffy tentatively attribute the decrements obtained to the simultaneous operation of two factors, stomach distension and blood-sugar level or some other humoral change. They suggest that neither of these factors in isolation can be effective. In this connection it should be noted that it is not necessary to assume, as Morgan & Morgan (1940a) did, that gastric contractions and direct effect on the central nervous system are the only mechanisms by which humoral factors may affect eating. It is also possible that humoral variations produce changes in muscles and organs other than the stomach, and that the sensory feedback from such nongastric sources affects the occurrence of eating responses. Therefore, the results of the Smith & Duffy experiment can also be interpreted solely in terms of alterations of interoceptive cues, some of which arise from the sensory feedback from the stomach and others from the sensory feedback from those other parts of the body which are also affected by changes in blood chemistry. It is not necessary to resort to an interpretation in terms of direct central effects of changes in the level of blood sugar.

## DRINKING

Siegel (1947) subjected different groups of rats to 6, 12, 24, or 48 hr. of water deprivation and then measured their water intake during a 5-min. drinking period. The curve for amount drunk as a function of hours of deprivation assumed a sigmoid form, with little difference in amount drunk between the 24- and 48-hr. groups. Stellar & Hill (1952) have also reported a negatively accelerated function for the relation between water intake and water deprivation (up to 168 hr.). Richter & Brailey (1929) suggested that water intake is also a function of the surface area of the body. However, Siegel & Stuckey (1947) found no evidence to support a direct relation between skin area and water intake, or between body weight and water intake. According to them, the relation reported by Richter & Brailey is probably a manifestation of the positive relation that exists between food intake and water intake. Bigger animals drink more because they eat more, not because they have larger skin areas. Siegel & Talantis (1950) have shown that when water-deprived rats are also food-deprived before the drinking test they drink less than nonhungry water-deprived rats. Thus, water intake is a function of both water and food deprivation.

Increase in water intake can also be brought about by directly dehydrating bodily tissues. Young, Heyer, & Richey (1952) induced increased water intake in rats by giving them injections of sodium chloride. Salt injections lead to an overall bodily dehydration. Such dehydration takes place quite quickly; correspondingly, Young, Heyer, & Richey found that, on the average, the rats began to drink water within 10 min. of the injection. O'Kelley (1954) has shown that, for a given amount of salt solution, the greater the concentration of the salt solution injected into the body the greater is the water intake during a subsequent (15-min. delay) drinking test.

Dehydration, whether produced by salt injection or by water deprivation, can be quickly relieved by increasing the amount of water available, through the blood stream, to various bodily tissues. The rather accurate regulation of water intake by animals has been stressed by Adolph (1943). Thus, Bellows (1939) showed that placing water directly into the stomach by catheters ("stomach-loading") reduces water intake during subsequent drinking periods. O'Kelley (1954) found that water intake in rats was decreased roughly in direct proportion to the volume of water preloaded in their stomachs. However, if the animal is allowed to drink immediately after enough water has been placed in its stomach to make up the deficit, it will nevertheless drink; it takes about 15 min. for the stomach preload to be taken up by the blood stream and absorbed by the bodily tissues. This means that it is the state of the bodily tissues, rather than the state of stomach distension, that is crucially related to water intake.

Whether dehydration increases water intake by directly affecting some specific mechanism in the central nervous system or through the sensory feedback from the dehydrated bodily tissues is an important question, but one which cannot be definitely answered at present. It is known that injecting a salt or water solution directly into certain parts of the brain of an animal affects its water intake. Andersson (1953) showed that the injection of a hypertonic salt solution into a certain part of the hypothalamus evoked drinking in goats. Miller (1957) and his collaborators, by means of permanently implanted hypodermic needles, have been able systematically to study the effects of such injections in the third and lateral ventricles on the drinking behavior of cats. They have found that injections of minute amounts (0.15 milliliter) of a 2 per cent salt solution or distilled water, respectively, increase or decrease the water intake of moderately thirsty cats. These results suggest that it may be possible to regulate water intake by manipulating the water and salt contents of certain parts of the brain in the absence of sensory feedback from other (dehydrated) tissues of the body. However, this point is by no means proved. Furthermore, whether such direct central effects constitute the mechanism which normally regulates the water intake of animals also remains to be investigated.

SEXUAL RESPONSES

The occurrence of sexual responses is usually dramatically affected by variations of gonadal hormones in the blood stream. This has been shown by both castration and replacement techniques. The studies of the effects of hormonal variations on sexual behavior have been reviewed by Beach (1947) and Morgan & Stellar (1950).

*Effects of castration.* The following statements, based mostly on research on the rat, seem to be warranted by the reviewed literature. (1) Castration in the postpuberal female (bilateral ovariectomy) abolishes the estrous cycle and makes the animal sexually unreceptive. However, there is considerable variation in the speed and extent of the effects of castration. In the lower mammals, such as rodents and carnivores, postpuberal castration abolishes copulation promptly and completely. In the higher mammals such as monkeys, apes, and man, reduction in sexual responses following castration occurs gradually and does not always lead to complete loss of ability to copulate; the human female may not show any marked reduction in sexual activity following bilateral ovariectomy. This phyletic change is also reflected in the fact that, whereas females of lower mammals engage in copulation and other forms of sexual activity only during estrus, primate females sometimes mate during anestrus as well. (2) The effect of postpuberal castration on male sexual behavior appears to be somewhat less severe than on the female's sexual response. Nevertheless, castration leads to a marked reduction in the copulatory activity. Some carnivores and subhuman primates may continue to copulate successfully for several months after postpuberal castration, but rats show a rapid decline in ability to copulate. Human males may continue copulation for a few years after castration in adulthood. (3) In general, prepuberal castration in both male and female prevents the appearance of normal copulatory activity, though many components of sexual behavior may appear in an adumbrated and weak fashion.

Thus, the occurrence of normal sexual responses is highly dependent upon gonadal hormones; however, in primates, especially in apes and man, factors other than the gonadal-hormone concentration in blood appear to become important enough to lead to the occurrence of apparently normal copulation in the absence, or at least marked reduction, of gonadal hormones.

*Effects of administering gonadal hormones.* Results of experiments on the effects of gonadal hormones on sexual behavior, obtained from studies in the rat and a few other species, may be summarized as follows. (1) Precocious sexual
responsiveness can be produced in both sexes by administering
androgen to the male and estrogen to the female. (2) Normal sexual responses can be reinstated in adult castrates of
both sexes by administering androgen to the male and estrogen
to the female. (3) As phyletic level advances, the effect of
replacement therapy on sexual behavior becomes less predictable; in apes and man, the marked individual differences
(observed also in castration studies) are seen in the effects produced by administering gonadal hormones. (4) Administering androgen to a normal female often leads, in a mating situation, to an increase in the incidence of the masculine sexual
pattern and decrease in that of the normal pattern for the
female. Androgen affects the female castrate in the same way.
(5) Similarly, the administration of estrogen to a normal or
castrate male may decrease the occurrence of the typical
masculine reactions and increase that of the feminine sexual
pattern. It should be emphasized that although the last two results seem to hold for the rat, they may not, and probably do
not, hold for the higher mammals, especially the primates.

The main point that requires discussion here concerns the
effects of androgen on the female and of estrogen on the male.
Beach (1948) has pointed out that the administration of androgen to the female disrupts its hormone balance in such a way as
to decrease or eliminate estrogen secretion; similarly, injections
of estrogen decrease the amount of endogenous androgen in
the male. Such decrease of estrogen in the female and androgen
in the male (a situation much like that produced by female and
male castrations) leads to a decrease in the incidence of the
typical feminine sexual pattern in the female and of the typical
masculine pattern in the male. Beach suggests that another
factor also contributes to the increase in the incidence of the
typical response of the other sex. He postulates that the administration of androgen to the female (besides inhibiting
estrogen production) directly stimulates the mechanism for

masculine response, and the administration of estrogen to the male (besides inhibiting androgen production) stimulates the mechanism for feminine response.

Since the correctness of Beach's explanation still remains to be demonstrated, it may be well to look for alternative interpretations of the phenomena. It seems plausible to propose the following line of speculation. We have noted (Chaps. 2 and 4) that both males and females show the typical masculine and feminine sexual responses. Furthermore, the particular pattern shown by two animals in a given situation depends, among other things, on the relative aggressiveness or dominance of the two animals; the dominant animal, whatever its sex, appears more likely to mount and less likely to be mounted than the submissive one. Thus, it is possible that the observed changes in the incidence of the masculine and feminine patterns in the castrated and hormonally treated animals result from changes in the relative dominance of the animals. As has been noted in an earlier section of this chapter, the administration of androgen to female animals tends to increase their dominance, and the administration of estrogen is likely to decrease dominance in the male. Thus, the problem of the hormone-induced changes in the incidence of masculine and feminine sexual pattern becomes one of the hormone-induced changes in dominance. The mechanism of the latter was discussed earlier. Since the relative dominance of animals is also dependent upon factors other than hormonal variations, it is to be expected that hormone administration will not necessarily change the incidence of masculine and feminine sexual patterns. In the primates, owing to the greater importance of other factors, hormonal variations are less likely to alter the established pattern of response than they are in the case of lower mammals such as the rat. The proposed interpretation can be tested by determining whether factors other than gonadal hormones that affect dominance status also affect the incidence of masculine and feminine patterns of sexual response.

*Hormone-habit strength interaction.* It was noted in Chapter 7 that elimination of certain sensory cues was found by

Beach (1942) to have less disrupting effect on the sexual behavior of sexually sophisticated male rats than on that of sexually naive animals. It is likely that prior sexual experience (habit strength) also determines what the effects of castration and gonadal hormone administration will be. One would expect greater influence of such experimental procedures on the sexual behavior of naive animals than on that of sexually sophisticated animals. However, the above discussion of the effects of hormonal variations on aggressive behavior points to the existence of marked species differences in this area. It may be that precastration sexual experience is more important for the lower than for the higher mammals in determining what the effects of castration will be. However, there appear to be no systematic investigations designed to study such interaction between habit strength and the effects of hormonal variations at various phyletic levels.

*Individual differences.* Grunt & Young (1953) divided a group of male guinea pigs into "high-drive," "medium-drive," and "low-drive" groups on the basis of their performance scores in 10 tests of copulation. Then these animals were castrated. In the postcastration tests of copulation the scores of all the groups declined gradually but steadily, and at about identical rates, until all of them reached the same low score. Subsequently, under androgen therapy, their performance in the copulation tests began to improve. The interesting finding was that, though given identical dosages of androgen, in general each group reached its own precastration level of sexual performance, so that the three groups retained the same order as in the tests at the beginning of the experiment. Furthermore, the groups reached their maximum performance scores at about the same time, so that the rate of improvement in the high-drive group was higher than the rates in the other two groups. Grunt & Young interpret the findings in terms of individual differences in reactivity of sexual tissues to androgen. Although the factor of habit strength or sexual experience at the time of castration was not controlled in this study, the results suggest a possible genetic basis for the determination of individual differences in reactivity to gonadal hormones. Such a genetic interpretation of individual differences is supported by the findings of Goy & Young (1956–57). These investigators found the effects of injections of alpha-estradiol followed by progesterone to be different in the females of each of three strains of guinea pigs. That the three strains were differentially sensitive to equal amounts of the hormones was shown by such measures of sexual responsiveness as latency and duration of estrus, duration of maximum lordosis, and per cent of animals brought into heat. These differences are probably also attributable to the possible differential reactivity of the sexual tissues of the three strains to the hormones.

*Mechanism of hormonal effects on sexual behavior.* We have not yet discussed the possible mechanisms through which hormones affect the occurrence of sexual activities. The obvious questions are: Why does the administration of androgen to the male castrate increase its sexual activity, and why does the administration of estrogen to the female castrate increase its sexual receptivity? Generally speaking, gonadal hormones can affect the incidence of sexual responses either by some direct central effects or by the indirect effects of the sensory feedback from peripheral receptors, or by both these means. It is not possible at present to choose between these alternatives; one can only consider a few relevant points.

Beach & Levinson (1950) studied the effects of castration and subsequent androgen therapy on the integument of the glans penis of rats. They found that castration reduced the number of the cornified papillae between the epithelial folds. The administration of the hormone increased the number of papillae in proportion to the amount administered. The important finding concerned the correspondence between the emergence of papillae and sexual behavior. The frequency of copulation followed closely the anatomical changes. (The deflection of the papillae presumably stimulates touch receptors and causes a sensory discharge.) This finding suggests that the sensory impulses from the genital areas, resulting from the anatomical changes produced by hormonal variations, may form the basis of the hormone-induced changes in sexual behavior. However, we also know (Chap. 7) that, at least in the adult sophisticated animal, the removal or denervation of external genitalia (without castration) does not reduce (attempted) copulatory activity. It remains to be determined whether gonadal hormone variations produced in animals without external genitalia will affect their (attempted) sexual behavior.

If the administration of, for example, androgen to male castrates without external genitalia were to increase their sexual activity, this fact would favor a direct central-effect interpretation of the effects of androgen on male sexual behavior, but would not enable us to reject a peripheral or sensory-feedback interpretation. For it is possible that androgen affects tissues other than those of the genital region, so that the sensory feedback from such other androgen-induced bodily changes may serve to increase the incidence of sexual responses. That is to say, the sensory stimulation arising from a variety of tissues and organs (representing general "tonus" or "health" of the organism) may to a certain extent serve the same function as the sensory feedback from the genital region. Such an influence on sexual activity of events that do not specifically involve the genital organs is suggested by a number of findings. For example, variations in thyroid output which affect the general metabolism of the animal, but appear to have no specific effects on the genital region, may affect sexual behavior. (*See* Stern, 1957, for review.) Similarly, sometimes the administration of androgen to a spayed female may reinstate its sexual receptivity, and the administration of large dosages of estrogen to male castrates may reinstate their normal sexual activity (Beach, 1948, p. 217). Whereas an interpretation of these findings must await exact knowledge of the effects of androgen and estrogen on the various organs and systems of the body, they are consistent with a peripheral-feedback type of interpretation of the effects of hormonal variations on sexual behavior.

## MATERNAL BEHAVIOR

The various activities subsumed under the rubric of "maternal behavior" (*see* Chaps. 2 and 4) are partly under the influence of blood chemistry. The following statements are based mainly on experimental work with rats and, in view of marked species differences, should not be too readily generalized to other mammals.

Of all the maternal activities, nest building appears to be the one that is most dramatically affected by variations in blood chemistry. Richter (1937) has shown that thyroidectomy, adrenalectomy, gonadectomy, or hypophysectomy leads immediately to a marked increase in nest building. As pointed out in Chapter 2, an increase in nest building can be brought about by reduction in body temperature. It is likely that the extirpation of the above endocrine structures decreases metabolic rate and body temperature and thus increases nest building. The thyroid is the most closely associated with metabolic rate, and its extirpation produces the maximum increase.

The main feature of behavior at parturition is that the mother licks and cleans the fetuses. It was noted in Chapter 4 that pregnancy may lead to changes in salt content of the blood stream, and this humoral change may lead to an increase in genital licking and, after parturition, to licking of the fetuses. If this interpretation is correct, it should be possible to control the frequency of occurrence of licking responses by altering the concentration of appropriate salts in the blood stream. Experiments are needed to verify the existence of such a relation.

The nursing activity of the female rat involves crouching over the young and sitting still. This cuddling activity has been shown to depend partly on prolactin, a pituitary hormone which is secreted during pregnancy and stimulates mammary secretion. Riddle, Bates, & Lahr (1935) have shown that the administration of this hormone induces cuddling of pups in about 60 per cent of virgin female rats. The fact that prolactin does not induce cuddling in many females (about 40 per cent), as well as the fact that cuddling often occurs in virgin females and males (Chap. 2) without the administration of this hormone, shows that prolactin is only one of the factors that control the occurrence of nursing behavior. It appears that prolactin, by initiating the secretion of milk and thus increasing the turgor of the mammary glands, provides the type of sensory stimulation which contributes to, but is not crucial to, the occurrence of nursing behavior.

Riddle *et al.* (1941–42) have shown that humoral variations arising from hypophysectomy and injections of other hormones and drugs also affect the occurrence of nursing activity. The factors (e.g. prolactin, progesterone, phenol) that bring about an increase in nursing all appear to be antigonadal. In this connection it is interesting to note that a decrease in estrogen output occurs during pregnancy, and injections of estrogen decrease nursing activity in lactating females. It may be that rate of metabolism and body temperature are involved in nursing activity just as they are in nest building. If the conditions that increase nursing also decrease the output of gonadal hormones, then it can be argued that increased nursing activity results from decreased metabolism associated with decreased gonadal output. Thus, cuddling or sitting still on top of a litter, like nest building (*see* Chap. 4), may be partly a warmth-getting device. The finding of Beach & Jaynes (1956) that rats show preference for retrieving normal rather than refrigerated pups lends some indirect support to the present suggestion. Such an interpretation would also account for the nursing activity that is normally shown by some males and virgin females. According to the speculations presented above, any humoral changes that (1) increase mammary secretion and (2) decrease body temperature will lead to an increase in the occurrence of nursing activity.

### THE GENERAL MECHANISMS OF HUMORAL ACTION

The problem of determining the general mechanisms by which changes in blood chemistry lead to variations in the occurrence of various activities is a complex one and most difficult to unravel. The main difficulty arises from the fact that a change in the concentration of constituents in the blood stream may affect a variety of functions in a way that leads to a further change in blood chemistry. For example, hypophysectomy eliminates the pituitary hormones, and the absence of pituitary hormones from the blood stream in turn affects a number of other endocrine glands (e.g. gonads, thyroid, adrenal) in such a way as to reduce their output too. Similarly, a reduction, in the blood stream, of vitamins, sugar, and other dietary substances may bring about further changes in blood chemistry by damaging the liver or other tissues. In some cases the change in blood chemistry initiates events that produce compensatory changes. Anoxemia leads to an increase in breathing rate which in turn may increase the oxygen content of blood. Thus, the behavioral effects of any experimentally produced humoral change are likely to be obscured by the further changes in blood chemistry brought about as indirect effects of the experimental treatment.

## POTENTIAL MECHANISMS

Whereas the complexity of the problem makes it difficult to state the exact mechanism of the behavioral effects produced by specific humoral changes, it is still possible to consider the general mechanisms. Beach (1948) has enumerated and discussed the possible mechanisms of humoral action: First, changes in blood chemistry may influence behavior through their effects on such general characteristics of the organism as its state of health, rate of metabolism, and muscular strength. Second, humoral variations may affect behavior by altering the morphologic structures employed in the particular response. Thus, hormonally induced changes in the penis, vagina, or mammary tissue are necessary before, respectively, effective copulation or nursing can take place. Third, variations in blood chemistry may influence response by affecting the sensitivity of receptors in various parts of the body. For example, anoxia, changes in the level of blood sugar, vitamin deficiency, and certain drugs seem to alter receptor sensitivity. Fourth, humoral variations may influence behavior through their effects upon the central nervous system. There are various views concerning the exact way in which such a mechanism may operate. The most widely held of such interpretations is the one that postulates a direct effect of a given humoral variation on a specific "center" or neural integration;

the stimulation of a particular neural integration is in turn assumed to increase its responsiveness to certain specific types of external stimulation. Thus, gonadal hormones are said to stimulate the neural integration corresponding to sexual behavior in such a way that its threshold of firing is decreased so that appropriate stimulation is more likely to initiate sexual responses. To this list of possible mechanisms proposed by Beach, one more item should be added. Fifth, humoral variations may influence behavior through their effect on the arousal level of the organism. It has been noted in Chapter 8 that variations in the hormonal and other humoral factors can bring about changes in arousal level and that changes in arousal level do affect the activities of the organism.

In any given instance of a behavioral effect brought about by humoral variations, any one or more of the above mechanisms may be responsible for the change in behavior.

## Peripheral vs. Central Interpretations

A question that is theoretically important concerns the relative importance of the sensory feedback effects (the first three of the mechanisms listed above) and the direct central effects (the fourth mechanism) of a humoral change. When a humoral change alters the responses of an animal, we can assume that the humoral change has somehow altered the firing of neural integrations that correspond to the particular activity. If the hormonal variation produces some direct central effect, we should expect a nonspecific change in the pattern of neural firing in a certain area of the brain. If, on the other hand, hormonal variations act through feedback, we should expect the pattern of neural firing to be altered by the specific cues provided by the sensory stimulation arising from a variety of bodily organs and tissues. At present, there appears to be no evidence that would enable us to decide which one, if either, of the mechanisms is more important in the humoral-behavior relations.

# Chapter 10

# An Overview, a General Problem, and Human Motivation

The purpose of this chapter is to restate the general approach adopted in this book, to summarize the main conclusions derived from the analysis of various motivational phenomena, to discuss a general problem raised by the conclusions, and to show how the present approach can be applied to an analysis of human motivational activities.

## AN OVERVIEW

Let us begin by considering the main features of the approach adopted and the problems raised in this book, and the general conclusions that can be drawn from the various discussions.

### THE APPROACH

Extending the earlier discussion of MacCorquodale & Meehl (1948), Rozeboom (1956) has restated and clarified the distinctions between two types of "mediation" variables or concepts. An intervening or *transformation concept* is one which has been systematically defined in terms of certain (observable) antecedent or independent variables and is derived non-empirically from those variables, so that one can move from antecedent variables to the mediation variable with certainty, without error. A transformation concept has no *excess meaning*, that is, any intuitive or theoretical connotations that are not a part of its formal definition; an example is "volume," which may be defined as, and is interchangeable with, the product of length times width times height. A *hypothetical construct*, on the other hand, is an inferred concept, having excess meaning and, therefore, one for which the passage from the antecedent conditions to the mediation variable must be made with less than logical certainty. These distinctions are relevant to the following discussion.

As pointed out in Chapter 1, the traditional interpretations of motivational phenomena have made use of mediation concepts such as instincts, drives, needs, and motives. Used as nouns, these terms refer to hypothetical constructs that directly correspond to the observed activities they are designed to explain. At the most naive level, the constructs are intuitively and vaguely defined, directly reflecting the various classes of observed activities. Such hypothetical constructs (e.g. maternal instinct, exploratory drive) provide merely redundant descriptions, not systematic interpretations. At the most sophisticated level, an attempt is made somehow to replace hypothetical constructs by transformation variables. Brown & Farber's (1951) definition of "frustration" is an example of the sophisticated use of mediation concepts. They define it as a hypothetical state of the organism which is completely determined by the relative strengths of two opposing response tendencies; the strengths of response tendencies are in turn completely determined by certain manipulable antecedent conditions, such as number of reinforcements and delay of reinforcement. Although the term "frustration" still retains many subjective connotations, in intention and principle Brown & Farber's definition seems to meet the criteria of a transformation variable. In between the two extremes of transformation variables and intuitively derived hypothetical constructs lie most of the mediation variables employed in psychology. That is to say, mediation variables, as at present employed in psychology, typically carry some excess meaning.

As Rozeboom (1956) and others have pointed out, excess meanings are not necessarily a hindrance to research, and such refined hypothetical constructs as Hull's (1943) habit strength can be usefully considered as attributes of the organism whose direct and exact quantitative relations to empirical variables still await experimental clarification. Thus, in deciding upon an approach to the study of behavior, the question is not whether mediation concepts should have any excess meaning at all, but rather how much excess meaning a hypothetical construct can have and still be useful. Skinner (1953) attempts to avoid all excess meaning and, therefore, does not postulate any constructs, preferring to analyze behavior in terms of specific empirical variables. Hebb (1949, 1951), on the other hand, is willing to make his constructs so general that they become far removed from empirically manipulable variables; this is not to deny that his constructs may be neurophysiologically plausible.

The general point of view adopted in the writing of this book lies somewhere between the positions of Skinner and Hebb. This approach seeks to formulate specific questions, as well as general problems, in empirical terms without reference to any hypothetical constructs. It is also empirical and non-theoretical in dealing with the established functional relations between independent and dependent variables. However, it employs constructs (e.g. positive reinforcing mechanism, central effect, sensory feedback) in bringing together and suggesting a common neurophysiological mechanism for a diverse set of empirical findings. When used, such concepts are not presented as explanations but merely as tentative guides for research aimed at linking behavioral with neurophysiological data. The present approach also employs certain other non-empirical concepts, such as habit strength and arousal. A hypothetical construct of this type is used as a general label for a set of specific measures which often (though not necessarily) covary and, therefore, can be presumed to be related to similar neurophysiological processes. In short, this approach does not employ hypothetical mediation concepts that only intuitively reflect observed activities; rather the constructs employed summarize, and are derived from, empirically established functional relations. It is primarily an empirical approach, but one which employs hypothetical constructs to the extent of pointing to such lines for further research as would enable one to interpret behavioral data in terms of antecedent and neurophysiological variables that are also empirical.

## THE PROBLEM

Within the above general framework, the psychological problems presented by motivational phenomena can be stated in the form of two general empirical questions. First, how do the various activities of which an organism is capable develop in its repertoire? Second, what are the factors that determine that one rather than another of these activities will occur at a particular time and place, and the details (e.g. latency, errors, etc.) of the way in which a given activity occurs? The point of view adopted in this book assumes that these two questions incorporate all the problems that have traditionally been considered problems of motivation. The first of the above questions incorporates "the problem of instinct," the discussions of purpose and goal direction, the issue of the nature and number of "primary drive behaviors," and the problem of "pleasure and pain" or reinforcement. The second question above incorporates all the problems that are implied in the traditional phrase "strength of motivation or drive." These problems involve a consideration of the factors that determine the frequency (and some secondary characteristics) of the occurrence of an activity. What this book has attempted to do is to deal systematically with the traditional problems, discussions, and issues in the area of motivation as special cases of the two general questions stated above. Of course, it is not implied that the book has in any sense successfully or definitively answered these questions. Rather this work should be looked upon as an attempt at reformulating the various specific "problems of motivation" within a general systematic framework.

In this book the two general questions, one concerned with the development of activities and the other with their occurrence, have been discussed only with reference to the so-called motivational phenomena. This category of phenomena includes those activities with reference to which the traditional "dynamic" concepts, such as instincts, drives, and primary motives, have been defined. However, a moment's reflection will show that the same two questions can also be legitimately asked in connection with perceptual responses[1] and other cognitive activities such as motor skills, problem solving, and verbal behavior. Thus, by asking about motivational phenomena the same questions as can be asked about "nonmotivational" phenomena, the present approach brings together different behavioral phenomena into a single general scheme. It also suggests how some problems (e.g. goal direction, reinforcement, extinction, stimulus generalization, and humoral control of activities), which have traditionally been discussed only with reference to particular classes of phenomena, are relevant to all classes of activities.

SOME TENTATIVE CONCLUSIONS

The analysis of motivational phenomena undertaken in the preceding chapters suggests the following tentative conclusions:

1. At present there appears to be no precise way of classifying the various activities in which organisms engage. A convenient method is that of categorizing activities conjointly in terms of the responses involved and the objects or events with respect to which they may be said to be directed.

2. The features (e.g. appropriateness, persistence, searching) of behavior which are subsumed under the label "goal direction" are, at least in mammals, acquired through prior experience. This experience involves the selective reinforcement of the component responses that make up the given activity. In general, the motivational activities, such as eating,

[1] Bruner's (1957) analysis of perceptual phenomena in terms of (the development of) perceptual response categories and the factors that determine the "accessibility" (or occurrence) of the categories seems to parallel the present discussion of motivational activities.

escaping, and avoiding, are acquired in the same way as are perceptual motor skills and other abilities. The amount of experience required for the development of motivational activities (e.g. sexual behavior) is quite small in the lower mammals, but seems to increase in the higher species.

3. The fact of the rather sudden emergence of certain activities (e.g. dietary preferences, "imprinting," species-specific activities) is not necessarily inconsistent with the reinforcement interpretation. The necessary reinforcement can occur within the first experimental session; the main problem is that of determining exactly what events serve as reinforcers and what accounts for their great efficacy as reinforcers.

4. The species and strain differences in the readiness with which certain directed activities develop can be attributed to jointly (a) the species and strain differences in the frequency of occurrence of the component responses that make up an activity, and (b) the differences in the efficacy of certain objects and events as reinforcers for members of different species and strains. The precise constitutional, morphological, and experiential factors that determine these species and strain differences remain to be investigated.

5. Neither drive reduction nor the elicitation of consummatory responses is a necessary condition for obtaining positive reinforcing effects; however, each one of them is a sufficient condition, as are also certain instances of increased sensory stimulation and of intracranial stimulation. The exact nature of the positive and negative reinforcing mechanisms still remains a mystery.

6. A smaller percentage of the occurrences of an activity need to be reinforced in order to maintain it at a certain level of performance than are needed to attain that level in the first place. Avoidance responses and responses maintained on intermittent reinforcement are more resistant to extinction than are responses each occurrence of which has been reinforced.

7. Sensory cues provided by the stimulation of sensory organs determine whether a particular response will occur. (Basically, there is no difference between the roles of interoceptive and exteroceptive sensory cues in the control of behavior.) A

response can occur only within a certain range of variation of sensory cues present when the response was acquired or last performed.

8. If sensory cues are varied within their effective range for a given response, the response usually shows minor variations in some of its characteristics (e.g. amplitude, latency). The degree to which the response characteristics change appears to be proportional to the extent to which the sensory cues are altered. The change in sensory cues may facilitate or interfere with a given response. The problems of stimulus generalization, facilitation or "positive transfer," and conflict are special cases of the general question of what happens when sensory cues are varied.

9. The habit strength of a response is related to the effects that alterations in sensory cues will have on it. In general, the greater the habit strength the wider the range of variation of sensory cues within which the response will occur normally.

10. The concept of level of arousal can serve as a unifying construct for referring to the "excitement" feature of a variety of situations and phenomena, such as "emotion," "anxiety," "dynamogenic effect," "irrelevant drive," "frustration," "stress," and "displacement."

11. The level of arousal of an organism is related to the probabilities of occurrence of the activities in its repertoire. A given response can occur only within certain limits of level of arousal. Within these limits, some of the characteristics of the response change as arousal level is varied.

12. The habit strength of a response is related to the effects that alterations in arousal level will have on it. In general, the greater the habit strength the wider the range of arousal level within which the response will occur in its usual form.

13. Variations in the concentrations of the various constituents of the blood stream determine the probabilities of occurrence of the activities in an animal's repertoire. A given response can occur only within a certain range of humoral variation; within this range, some characteristics of the response change as the chemistry of the blood stream is varied.

14. Again, the exact effect on a response of a humoral

change is related to the habit strength of the response. The greater the habit strength the more likely is the response to withstand variations in blood chemistry.

15. The chemistry of the blood stream seems to exert a much more direct effect in the lower than in the higher mammals; the effects of humoral variations become more variable as one moves from the rat to man.

16. Two main classes of mechanisms can account for the effects on behavior of variations in arousal level and blood chemistry. The behavioral effects may be brought about by the sensory feedback (to the brain) from changes in peripheral organs associated with variations in arousal and blood chemistry. Alternatively, or in addition to the feedback mechanism, the behavioral effects may result from some direct action of the arousal and humoral changes on certain special areas or centers in the brain. The evidence available at present does not enable one to decide upon the relative roles of these two mechanisms.

The above conclusions suggest that the traditional problem of "strength of motivation" is essentially a problem of the roles of different factors that determine the occurrence of a given response. The relevant sets of variables represent variations in habit strength, sensory cues, level of arousal, and blood chemistry.[2] As mentioned before (Chap. 1), the present approach seeks to replace the concept of "strength of motivation or drive" by a consideration of the role of the above four sets of variables in determining the occurrence of the various activities that exist in an animal's repertoire.

## A GENERAL PROBLEM

The factor of habit strength seems to occupy a special place among the variables that determine the occurrence of responses. It has been noted that the effects on a response of the three other sets of variables are dependent upon the habit strength of the response. In general, the greater the habit strength the less the effect that variations in the other variables

[2] These categories are not mutually exclusive, although eventually perhaps they can be made so. Further, abnormality of the brain or of other tissues of the body is not considered as a separate factor here.

are likely to have on the response. Thus, with increasing habit strength a response seems to become less variant with respect to changes in the factors that initially could control it. This phenomenon is the one for which Allport (1937) coined the phrase "functional autonomy of motives." In a sense the most general problem posed by the conclusions listed above concerns this phenomenon, and we turn now to a discussion of it.

## The Concept of Functional Autonomy

Allport (1937) argued, essentially, that through practice or repeated performance an activity can become functionally autonomous with respect to the conditions that played a crucial role in the development of the activity. The term "motive" in "functional autonomy of motives" can be omitted from Allport's discussion without altering the gist of his argument; more empirically, one can talk simply in terms of the functional autonomy of certain activities. To Allport this concept implied two things. First, such autonomous activities function independently of their historical antecedents, that is, independently of the conditions that played a crucial part in their acquisition. Second, such autonomous activities are in some sense "self-perpetuating."

Since it was proposed in the heyday of drive doctrine, the concept of functional autonomy was not well received by many psychologists. At the time when motivation was becoming a key concept in psychology, the suggestion that certain activities could be "autonomous" (i.e. without "underlying motives") received much discussion but little support (e.g. Bertocci, 1940). Drive theorists tended to explain away (though apparently seldom in print) the phenomenon by saying that some secondary drives and secondary reinforcers undoubtedly operate to maintain the apparently autonomous activities, for, according to their doctrine, no activity could conceivably be maintained without some drive and some reinforcement. Now that the drive doctrine and the concept of motive have themselves been found to be unsatisfactory, it is time to reconsider the types of activities that Allport described as functionally autonomous, and to ask what specific problem is posed by them. We shall see that such activities cannot be exactly described either as self-perpetuating or as completely autonomous; but, they are autonomous with respect to a limited set of conditions; they are partially autonomous.

## SOME EXAMPLES OF PARTIALLY AUTONOMOUS ACTIVITIES

In Chapter 4 it was noted that once rats have been made to hoard certain materials through some form of deprivation or environmental change they sometimes continue to hoard the materials long after the removal of the conditions that were necessary to initiate the hoarding activity. Ross, Smith, & Nienstedt (1950) describe such persistence of hoarding activity as "hangover effect," Stellar *et al.* (1952) as "potentiating effect," and Licklider & Licklider (1950) as "partial autonomy of the motor system" involved in hoarding. Earl (1957) trained food-deprived mice to dig sand to obtain food. When the animals reached the criterion of digging 3.5 lb. of sand per day for 10 consecutive days, he either fed the animals before the trials or delayed the food reinforcement. In both cases Earl found that the mice kept on digging as before "with no trend toward extinction." He writes, "viewed empirically, it was as if the very act of digging had become demanding or had developed 'invitational character' " (1957, p. 250). Obviously, at a certain stage of performance certain activities may become relatively independent of the conditions that initiated them. Such continuation of an ongoing activity was described by Woodworth (1918) as "mechanisms become drives."

In Chapter 6 it was shown that the reinforcement conditions required for the acquisition of a response are much more stringent than those needed for its maintenance. The difficulty of extinguishing an avoidance response or a response maintained on an intermittent reinforcement schedule also suggests a change from the earlier to the later stages of performance in the conditions that control the response. Chapters 7, 8, and 9 described many experimental findings that point to the same general conclusion. The sensory feedback from autonomic changes in the viscera may contribute to the acquisition of an avoidance response but is not necessary for the maintenance of the response. Sexually experienced animals can continue to copulate adequately in the absence of a certain proportion of sensory cues essential for the initial copulations. Whereas the prepuberal castrate is almost always sexually inactive, the sexually experienced castrate, at least in some primate species, may continue to copulate adequately, thus showing relative independence of the hormonal control of sexual behavior that characterizes the naive animal. Similarly, it appears that, when a task has been well-practiced, normal performance on it can be maintained even at levels of arousal that are far removed from the one at which the task was initially learned.

Allport (1937) described many classes of fully developed symptoms (e.g. obsessions, compulsions) of mental patients as responses that had become autonomous with respect to the historical conditions producing them. Such "fixations" have also been noted in experimental studies. Hunt & Schlosberg (1950) electrified the water supply of rats, so that animals received a shock when they drank water. One of the habits developed by the animals under these conditions was that of drinking in a few quick licks, with a rest after each series of licks. Some of the animals also started to bite and pull at the water bottle. Hunt & Schlosberg noted that these response patterns carried over into days when the shock was off and, in general, were resistant to extinction. Maier & Ellen (1951) have enumerated many instances in which, once animals have acquired a particular response in an insoluble discrimination problem, they may continue to execute the same response even when subsequently given a soluble problem with a predictable reinforcement. As Ellen (1956) points out, such "fixated" behavior has a "compulsive property" which interferes with the acquisition of more adaptive responses.

The above facts only show that, with increase in habit strength, a response may become independent of some of the conditions that played a crucial role in its acquisition. This does not entitle us to say that the response has in some sense become completely autonomous or self-perpetuating, but we can say that the response has become partially autonomous, or independent of some of the conditions that exercised a control over it before. The next obvious question concerns the nature of this partial autonomy. By what process is it brought about? We know that increase in habit strength is a necessary condition for bringing about such autonomy. But the important question is this: What precise changes in the control of the response are brought about by increasing habit strength?

## An Analysis of Behavioral Cycles

The study of cyclic activities, such as eating, drinking, and general activity, provides an approach to unravelling the processes that underlie partially autonomous activities.

*Some properties of cyclic activities.* In the adult animal certain behavioral cycles are well established. The rat, for example, eats and drinks every two or three hours and shows a diurnal activity cycle. These cyclical changes in the behavior of adult animals seem to be fairly independent of the conditions that initially establish them. It is likely that variations in blood chemistry and sensory cues provided by gastric distension play a crucial role in the establishment in infancy of eating and drinking cycles, even though studies show that eating and drinking in adults is relatively independent of these factors. Similarly, the diurnal activity cycle seen in the adult rat is probably initially established in relation to the light-dark cycle and the feeding schedule. There appear to be no investigations bearing directly on the development in infancy of cyclical behavioral changes. However, studies on the development of new cyclical changes in the adult provide some relevant information. Spragg (1940) established cyclical physiological, and corresponding behavioral, changes in chimpanzees by giving them daily injections of morphine. H. D. Beach (1957) has reported similar findings on the rat. In both these studies it was shown that relief of morphine-induced withdrawal symptoms by giving the animals morphine led to the emergence of cycles of morphine-seeking behavior. It appears plausible that cycles of eating and drinking are also initially established through the periodic relief by food and water of the "withdrawal symptoms" (changes in blood chemistry and sensory cues) arising from the depletion of nutritive materials in the body.

That cycles of eating, drinking, and other motivational activities do not represent any specific "endogenous rhythms,"[3] but are acquired through the periodic operation of certain crucial conditions, is also shown by the fact that the established cycles can be altered. It has been noted in Chapter 4 that switching from an *ad libitum* to a limited-time eating schedule gradually alters the pattern of activity and eating until a new cycle is established. The established activity cycles in the rat can also be altered by changing the light-dark cycle. For example, Browman (1937) placed rats under artificial light-dark cycles of 12, 8, and 6 hr. The rats gradually changed from the normal diurnal activity cycle to cycles that conformed to the artificial light-dark periods, always showing their greatest activity in the dark. Human beings often report a disturbance in their sleep and eating cycles after fast travel from one to another markedly different longitude; however, their cycles quickly adjust to their new surroundings. These facts also show that cyclic changes in behavior never become completely autonomous; they can be altered by controlling the conditions which initially establish them.

*An interpretation of behavioral cycles.* In the infant, if eating, drinking, and increase in general activity occur cyclically, it is presumably because the conditions controlling these activities themselves occur in cycles. Insofar as the digestive processes and the shifts from light to dark are fairly stable and regular, the corresponding humoral, gastric, and other bodily changes that control eating, drinking, and general activity in the infant must also be regular.[4] As these activities repeatedly occur at roughly regular intervals, certain extraneous cues, unrelated to the underlying physiological changes, become associated with the activities. The extraneous cues may be environmental (e.g. being moved from the living cage to the feeding stand) or

---

[3] For an interesting discussion of the fallacy of postulating "endogenous rhythms," see Cole (1957).

[4] It should be noted that there appear to be no studies showing conclusively that in the infant the variations in these processes, and the corresponding variation in behavior, are in fact so precisely periodic as to justify the use of the term "cycles."

they may be related to some physiological processes (e.g. changes in muscular tonus) that are not intrinsically involved in the particular response. In Chapter 7 it was postulated that the greater the number of response-associated cues present the more likely is the response to occur. From such a relation it follows that the greater the number of extraneous cues associated with a given activity the more likely it is to occur in the absence of the physiological changes intrinsically involved in it. Thus, the periodic occurrence of the activity gradually comes to be elicited by the extraneous cues; and, if these cues occur at regular periodic intervals, the corresponding activity shows cyclical variations. It is incorrect to say that the behavioral cycles become independent of the underlying processes, for one can always alter the cycles by changing the basic conditions (e.g. light-dark intervals, feeding schedule) on the basis of which the cycles were initially established. In this connection, the only reasonable statement one can make is that the *maintenance* of the cycles comes to be mediated by a variety of extraneous cues; the extraneous cues can continue to be effective only if they remain associated with the underlying physiological changes ultimately determining the activities. So long as the extraneous cues correspond (even roughly) to the basic physiological conditions, the regularity and precision of a behavioral cycle will depend upon the regularity with which the extraneous cues occur.

It follows from the above that, if the intervals between the successive occurrences of the intrinsic determinants are too long, as, for example, in the case of estrual changes, extraneous cues will be less likely to become associated with the determinants and, thus, will be less likely to mediate the particular behavioral cycle. Naturalistic observations in the laboratory suggest that extraneous cues are less important in the maintenance of the estrus-related activity cycles than they are in the more frequent activity cycles associated with feeding and light-dark periods.

When the environmental conditions are kept constant, so that no differential extraneous cues are available for association with an activity, the repeated occurrence of the activity is likely to remain under the control of the basic physiological determinants. Thus, Baker (1953) has shown that the normal eating cycle of the rat is disrupted when the animal is placed under conditions of uniform temperature and illumination and the cues associated with the feeding schedule are minimized. Gilbert & James (1956) also found the normal eating cycles to disappear when the normal (extraneous) interoceptive and environmental cues were interfered with.[5] Similarly, when rats are blinded or are placed in an all-light or all-dark chamber, the normal activity cycle is often disrupted, and the animals show a smaller difference between day and night activity. The animals may reverse the activity cycles (with respect to the preblinding light-dark periods) several times in a few months. They seem to maintain regular alternations of peaks and troughs of activity, but the total period of the cycle may deviate considerably from 24 hr. and may vary from individual to individual. These results stem from the investigations of Hunt & Schlosberg (1939a) and Browman (1942).

MacLeod & Roff (1936) and Heron,[6] in the Bexton, Heron, & Scott (1954) study, have noted similar disruptions of eating and sleeping cycles in human subjects when some of the normally available light and time cues were withheld from them for periods of a few days. Of course, the subjects ate and slept at *approximately* the normal intervals, but the intervals between the successive feeding and sleeping periods were sufficiently different from those prevailing under normal circumstances to lead, in some cases, to a displacement of the feeding and sleeping cycles with respect to the normal times for these activities. For example, in the Bexton, Heron, &

[5] In both these studies the experimenters found eating periods to be completely randomly distributed in time. This suggests either that the basic physiological changes that determine eating are not as cyclic as is sometimes presumed, or that the experimenters did not carry on the experiment sufficiently long for the presumed regularity of the physiological processes to reflect itself in some kind of an eating cycle. It is possible that the regular occurrence of extraneous cues may even be necessary for the emergence of exact cycles, for in the absence of the extraneous cues the fluctuations in the incidence of the activity may be too arhythmic to be called cycles at all.
[6] In a personal communication to the author, from Dr. W. Heron, Department of Psychology, McGill University, Montreal, Canada.

Scott study, after a few days in the experimental chamber, some of the subjects asked for the usual breakfast foods in the evening and for dinner in the morning. All these studies show that certain extraneous cues are normally responsible for the maintenance of behavioral cycles, and that the behavioral cycles may correspond only roughly to the physiological changes on the basis of which the cycles are initially established. It appears that, given the (rough) periodicity of the underlying physiological changes, once a sufficient number of extraneous cues are associated with an activity, the degree of regularity with which it is repeated depends more upon the regularity with which the extraneous cues occur than upon the regularity of the physiological changes themselves. However, a behavioral cycle can be said to be autonomous only in the sense that its maintenance is mediated by factors other than those that initiated it; it is not autonomous in the sense of being self-perpetuating or endogenous.

FACTORS UNDERLYING PARTIAL AUTONOMY

The above discussion suggests certain factors as the basis for the partial autonomy seen in certain activities. First, there appears to be a *substitution* of new or extraneous cues for the cues (and other factors) that initially elicited a given set of responses. It is likely that cue substitution is important in the development of partial autonomy not only in cyclic activities, but also in the various other activities which show some degree of autonomy. The substitute cues seem to become sufficiently effective to maintain the occurrence of a given activity even when the conditions that established it are no longer present. The mechanism of cue substitution itself is not well understood. Bruner, Matter, & Papanek (1955) and Bruner (1957a) have drawn attention to this problem of the range of cues the animal associates with a response beyond the cues that are necessary for the acquisition of the response. They refer to it as the problem of "breadth of learning," and have suggested experimental methods for investigating the conditions that determine the range of cues which become associated with a given response. Pending detailed study of such conditions, one can only say that the cues repeatedly associated with the oc-currence of a given response are likely to become substitute cues, and the greater the number of such substitute cues the more likely is the response to occur in the absence of the con-ditions that operated during acquisition.

A second process possibly responsible for partial autonomy is that of *increased effectiveness* of cues, which shows itself in a reduction in the number of cues required for eliciting a re-sponse. It appears that, as a result of repeated performance, there is a decrease in the number of associated cues required to elicit a response. The experiment of Gilbert & James (1956) showed that the well-established eating cycles are disrupted only when both the environmental and interoceptive cues are eliminated; one of these sets of cues can be eliminated without disrupting the cycles. This process of increased effectiveness of cues in eliciting a response appears to be responsible for the autonomy seen in the occurrence, for example, of sexual responses in animals deprived of various sense modalities. It is likely that such increased effectiveness of cues, brought about by the repeated association of the cues with a response, is a factor that operates in all cases where activities become par-tially autonomous. As suggested by Hebb (1949), neurophysi-ologically, this process is probably related to the increase in the strength of connections involved in the cell assemblies corresponding to a given activity, so that fewer simultaneous nerve impulses are required to fire the assemblies.

Apart from the processes of cue substitution and increased effectiveness suggested by the analysis of cyclic activities, one other factor probably plays a part in some cases of partial autonomy. This is the factor of *reinforcer substitution*. It is likely that the activities that were acquired on the basis of one reinforcer are maintained in the absence of that reinforcer because some other event has come to reinforce the same activity. A habit of maze running acquired with food as the reinforcer can be easily maintained by switching the animal to water deprivation and offering it water in the goal box. Hoarding and play activities are probably maintained in this way. Hoarding is usually acquired under certain specific internal and external conditions, but, once acquired, it seems to become independent of those conditions. It is likely that the activity involved in hoarding itself serves as a reinforcer of response sequences involved in it. (The positive reinforcing effects of activity were discussed in Chap. 5.) Similarly, play activities (e.g. a cat repeatedly chasing, catching, and releasing a ball, chimpanzees "following the leader," or a human being solving a crossword puzzle) may be maintained by the reinforcing effects of the activity involved in the play responses themselves. There is, of course, a danger in postulating such a reinforcer substitution process as a ready explanation for all cases of partial autonomy, but research on the details of operation of this process and caution in postulating it should diminish the danger.

In summary, as a consequence of repetition, the maintenance of a given activity does become independent of some of the conditions that played a crucial role in the development of that activity. The factors of cue substitution, increased effectiveness of cues, and reinforcer substitution can probably account for such partial autonomy whenever it does occur. So far little is known about the conditions that determine the operation of these factors and about their underlying neurophysiological mechanisms.

## APPLICATIONS TO HUMAN MOTIVATIONAL ACTIVITIES

So far the discussions of various problems have been conducted at a level of generality that makes them applicable to mammalian behavior in general (and to the behavior of many other vertebrate species too). In this last section of the book an attempt will be made to show a way, within the general framework adopted here, of dealing with problems of human behavior. This can be done best by considering these problems within the general context of evolutionary changes in behavior.

### PHYLOGENETIC CHANGES IN BEHAVIOR

Exploration, withdrawal, aggression, eating, drinking, copulating, and care of the young are activities that change in some respects with changing evolutionary level. It is not possible to deal with these changes in detail here; only a few general points relevant to the present discussion need be mentioned. First, each of the motivational activities shows increasing variety as one moves from the lower mammals to man. This increasing variety is seen in an increase in the number of alternative response sequences that may be effective with respect to one and the same goal, and the consequent increase in ("personality") differences in the responses of individuals with respect to goals of the same general class.[7] In general, the higher mammals are capable of making many more discrete responses than are lower mammals, and this is accompanied by an increase in the variety of responses that may be associated with food, novel stimuli, a sexual object, or with any other object or event with respect to which an activity is defined. In man, the use of language immensely increases the number of responses that become associated with the different classes of goals. Thus, the variability of responses involved in any given activity depends more upon the species one is dealing with than upon the goal with respect to which the activity is defined. Just because certain activities are shared by all mammals or vertebrates does not mean that they are necessarily, in some sense, "simple" activities; the degree of "complexity" of an activity depends upon the species in which it is studied. Thus, food seeking and eating, for example, is as complex an activity as the species in which it is studied is phyletically advanced.

Second, the number of objects and events which act as reinforcers (primary or secondary) and with respect to which it is meaningful to describe behavior also increases with advancing phyletic level. That is to say, the behavior of higher mammals can be adequately described with respect to a much greater variety of goals than is needed for the description of, for example, rat behavior. A satiated rat will not eat the type of food that it normally eats but will, a moment later, eat a

[7] Since classes of activities are defined partly in terms of goals (*see* Chap. 2), a certain amount of circularity is inherent in this statement. However, the circularity cannot be avoided until a completely objective method of classifying activities, without reference to goals, has been devised.

preferred food. It can differentiate between a number of classes of foods, and its behavior with respect to one class may be quite different from its behavior with respect to another. This "differentiation of goals" has to be multiplied many times in order adequately to describe the behavior of primates with respect to food and other classes of goals. Since experience with objects and events is necessary before they can be considered as goals (see Chap. 3), there is also an increase, with phyletic level, in the differences in the goals that are relevant for the description of the behavior of different (individual) animals. Again, in man, the regular use of language symbols as reinforcers tremendously increases the number of goals and individual differences in the relevance of different goals required for an adequate description of behavior.

Third, another way in which behavior changes with phyletic level is in the relative importance of the factors that control it. In the lower mammals, the various motivational activities seem to be fairly directly under the control of the factors that are crucial in the acquisition of those activities. However, as one ascends the phylogenetic scale, more of what was described as "extraneous cues" come to determine the occurrence of the activities. This does not mean that the behavior of higher species cannot be affected by altering the relevant basic physiological processes and cues; rather, it denotes that extraneous cues assume a degree of control over behavior such that many activities can occur in the absence of the conditions under which they were acquired. Thus, the behavior of the higher mammals appears to be "more autonomous" than that of the lower species.

All the above types of evolutionary changes are relevant to the following discussion of motivational activities in man.

## THE TRADITIONAL APPROACH TO "HUMAN MOTIVATION"

The activities of man are far more numerous and varied than are those of other primates and lower mammals. Man not only explores, withdraws, attacks, eats, drinks, copulates, and takes care of the young, but also shows many activities which cannot, without gross simplification, be classified with respect to the categories of goals that are adequate for describing the behavior of other species. Man influences, persuades, directs, prohibits, restrains, and punishes submissive individuals; he listens to, applauds, emulates, and follows the advice of a dominant person; he makes sexual advances and seduces a sexually appealing object; he examines and comments upon the colors, sounds, and objects around him; he displays himself and makes himself conspicuous by wearing unusual clothing or none at all; he remains aloof and indifferent from, or praises and criticizes the actions of social institutions and persons around him; and he reads and creates works of art and science. Psychologists interested in the area of "human motivation" have been concerned with such classes of activities, in addition to those that man shares with other mammals.

Traditionally, the problems posed by human motivational activities have been approached in the same way as the motivational activities of animals. Certain hypothetical entities, which intuitively reflect or echo the observed activities, are postulated to deal with those activities. The hypothetical entities have been called "instincts" (Freud, 1910; 1st ed., 1905; McDougall, 1912; 1st ed., 1908), "traits" (Allport, 1937), "needs" (Murray, 1938), or, simply, "motives" (e.g. McClelland et al., 1953). Lists of such postulated constructs include items such as sex instinct, maternal instinct, hostility, need dominance, need deference, need play, need exhibition, need homosexuality, and achievement motive.

As observed before, such hypothetical constructs merely provide redundant descriptions of the phenomena while appearing to explain them; and, at best, in the hands of empirical workers, they may serve as constructs that vaguely link the observed activities to certain manipulable antecedent conditions. The usual concern of the latter, more empirical, approach has been with the "strength" of the postulated ("motivational") entities. The strength is estimated by determining the frequency and other characteristics of the occurrence of the corresponding classes of activities. Thus, Murray (1938) estimates the strength of need affiliation by, for example, determining the frequency of occurrence of acts (linguistic as well as the more overt acts) pertaining to making acquaintance, meeting, drawing near, shaking hands, waving, going arm in arm, greeting, and "exchanging sentiments"; and McClelland *et al.* (1953) quantify achievement motive in terms of the frequency of acts pertaining to the accomplishment of difficult, great, and important deeds. The general aim of these approaches is that of interpreting the various human motivational activities in terms of the estimated strength of the postulated constructs.

Undoubtedly, these lines of investigation have been quite fruitful. However, their usefulness is severely limited by the fact that they classify activities according to goals as they are defined by common sense and postulate constructs that only intuitively reflect the activities they are designed to interpret. Furthermore, though these approaches have been practically useful in determining individual differences in "personality," they have tended to place the study of human motivational activities outside the framework of theoretical discussions of motivational phenomena in general.

## APPLICATION OF THE PRESENT APPROACH

The general approach outlined in Chapter 1 and restated in the beginning of this chapter can also be applied to the study of human motivational activities. One of the aims of this approach would be to define the classes of activities in which one is interested. Developing a meaningful definition of an activity itself involves considerable experimentation designed to determine exactly what classes of goals and responses can be legitimately included in the definition, and what classes of goals and responses have to be specifically excluded. In general, an activity can be included in a given class only if the conditions that affect it also affect in a similar way the other activities in the class. However, if the definition is to be useful at all, the conditions (actual or presumed) that affect a given class of activities should not form a part of the definition of that class. If the final statement of the definition of a class includes some reference to the conditions that affect it, then it becomes impossible to raise certain important questions. For example, if one of the defining characteristics of "aggressive activity" is that it is caused by "frustration," it becomes meaningless to ask whether hunger, or alcohol, or brain damage by itself (in the absence of frustration) is related to aggressive activity. Thus, though a meaningful definition of an activity is developed by determining what conditions affect it, the final definition itself must be stated only in terms of responses and goals, without reference to the real or presumed causes of that activity. Also, the various activities must be defined without any reference to subjective states, such as "feelings of anger or anxiety," "desire for affiliation," and "emotion of rivalry." The verbal reports of experiential states are, of course, activities that must be studied like other activities, but such subjective experiences cannot be considered as representing psychologically valid categories for the analysis of behavior.

A second aim of the present approach to human motivational activities would be the study of the development of activities in the repertoires of human beings. This task involves an investigation of the exact roles of the constitutional factors and of different types of experiences in the acquisition of various classes of activities. For example, size and body build may be related to the development (in a particular social setting) of a given class of aggressive activities, and autonomic reactivity may determine the readiness with which avoidance responses are acquired. Both body build and autonomic reactivity appear to be partly determined by constitutional factors. The development of aggressive and avoidance activities would also depend upon the frequency with which aggressive and avoidance responses are or are not reinforced. Successive experiences during development would determine the net result of the reinforcement of such responses. Much remains to be learned about the specific types of constitutional and experiential factors that determine the development of human motivational activities.

The third general aim of the present approach would be the study of the factors that determine the occurrence of the various human motivational activities. It is assumed that the factors of habit strength, sensory cues, arousal level, and the state of blood chemistry completely determine the frequency of occurrence and other characteristics of any given activity. For example, the frequency of greeting and other affiliative acts may decrease under high arousal, and the frequency of aggressive acts or linguistic "achievement acts" may increase under the influence of alcohol. Similarly, the changes in the performance of some creative activity under "stress" may be determined by the changes in sensory cues and arousal level brought about by the new ("stress") situation. Our discussion of the partial autonomy of activities indicates that, besides determining the way in which various activities initially develop in the repertoire of man, it is also important to analyze the particular factors that maintain or determine the repeated occurrences of an activity at a given time. Thus, if one wishes to eliminate or to decrease the frequency of occurrence of a response, it would be more important to know and manipulate the crucial sensory cues and other conditions that currently controlled that response than to unearth the factors under which the response was first acquired.

Finally, if the approach to the study of human motivational activities suggested here is adopted, it is likely that the tendency of postulating ad hoc hypothetical entities will be minimized, and mediation concepts will be employed only for the purpose of summarizing known empirical relations and indicating fruitful lines for further research.

# References

ADLERSTEIN, A., & FEHRER, ELIZABETH. (1955) The effect of food deprivation on exploratory behavior in a complex maze. *J. comp. physiol. Psychol.*, 48, 250–53.

ADOLPH, E. F. (1943) *Physiological regulations.* Lancaster, Pa.: Cattell.

ALLPORT, G. W. (1937) *Personality: a psychological interpretation.* New York: Holt.

AMSEL, A. (1949) Selective association and the anticipatory goal response mechanism as explanatory concepts in learning theory. *J. exp. Psychol.*, 39, 785–99.

AMSEL, A. (1950) The effect upon level of consummatory response of the addition of anxiety to a motivational complex. *J. exp. Psychol.*, 40, 709–15.

AMSEL, A., & COLE, K. F. (1953) Generalization of fear-motivated interference with water intake. *J. exp. Psychol.*, 46, 243–47.

AMSEL, A., & MALTZMAN, I. (1950) The effect upon generalized drive strength of emotionality as inferred from the level of consummatory response. *J. exp. Psychol.*, 40, 563–69.

AMSEL, A., & ROUSSEL, JACQUELINE. (1952) Motivational properties of frustration: I. Effects on a running response of the addition of frustration to the motivational complex. *J. exp. Psychol.*, 43, 363–68.

ANASTASI, ANNE, FULLER, J. L., SCOTT, J. P., & SCHMITT, J. R. (1955) A factor analysis of the performance of dogs on certain learning tests. *Zoologica*, 40, 33–46.

ANDERSON, E. E. (1940) The sex hormones and emotional behavior: I. The effect of sexual receptivity upon timidity in the female rat. *J. genet. Psychol.*, 56, 149–58.

ANDERSON, E. E. (1941) The externalization of drive: III. Maze learning by non-rewarded and by satiated rats. *J. genet. Psychol.*, 59, 397–426.

ANDERSON, E. E., & ANDERSON, SARAH F. (1940) The sex hormones and emotional behavior: II. The influence of the female sex hormone upon timidity in normal and castrated female rats. *J. genet. Psychol.*, 56, 159–68.

ANDERSSON, B. (1953) The effect of injections of hypertonic NaCl solutions into different parts of the hypothalamus of goats. *Acta Physiol. Scand.*, 28, 188–201.

Ax, A. F. (1953) The physiological differentiation between fear and anger in humans. *Psychosom. Med.*, 15, 433–42.

Bailey, C. J. (1955) The effectiveness of drives as cues. *J. comp. physiol. Psychol.*, 48, 183–87.

Bailey, C. J., & Miller, N. E. (1952) The effect of sodium amytal on an approach-avoidance conflict in cats. *J. comp. physiol. Psychol.*, 45, 205–8.

Bailey, C. J., & Porter, L. W. (1955) Relevant cues in drive discrimination in cats. *J. comp. physiol. Psychol.*, 48, 180–82.

Bain, A. (1868) *The senses and the intellect*. (3d Ed.) London: Longmans, Green.

Baker, R. A. (1953) Aperiodic feeding behavior in the albino rat. *J. comp. physiol. Psychol.*, 46, 422–26.

Baker, R. A. (1955) The effects of repeated deprivation experience on feeding behavior. *J. comp. physiol. Psychol.*, 48, 37–42.

Ball, Josephine. (1934) Sex behavior of the rat after removal of the uterus and vagina. *J. comp. Psychol.*, 18, 419–22.

Bancaud, J., Bloch, V., & Paillard, J. (1953) Contribution E.E.G. à l'étude des potentiels évoqués chez l'homme au niveau du vertex. *Rev. Neurologique*, 89, 399–418.

Bard, P. (1935) The effects of denervation of the genitalia on the oestrual behavior of cats. *Amer. J. Physiol.*, 113, 5.

Bare, J. K. (1949) The specific hunger for sodium chloride in normal and adrenalectomized white rats. *J. comp. physiol. Psychol.*, 42, 242–53.

Bartoshuk, A. K. (1955) Electromyographic gradients in goal-directed activity. *Canad. J. Psychol.*, 9, 21–28.

Bash, K. W. (1939) An investigation into a possible organic basis for the hunger drive. *J. comp. Psychol.*, 28, 109–34.

Bass, M. J., & Hull, C. L. (1934) The irradiation of a tactile conditioned reflex in man. *J. comp. Psychol.*, 17, 47–65.

Beach, F. A. (1942) Analysis of the stimuli adequate to elicit mating behavior in the sexually inexperienced male rat. *J. comp. Psychol.*, 33, 163–207.

Beach, F. A. (1945) Current concepts of play in animals. *Amer. Nat.*, 79, 523–41.

Beach, F. A. (1947) Evolutionary changes in the physiological control of mating behavior in mammals. *Psychol. Rev.*, 54, 297–315.

Beach, F. A. (1948) *Hormones and Behavior*. New York: Hoeber.

Beach, F. A. (1951) Instinctive behavior: reproductive activities. In S. S. Stevens (Ed.), *Handbook of experimental psychology*. New York: Wiley. Pp. 387–434.

Beach, F. A. (1955) The descent of instinct. *Psychol. Rev.*, 62, 401–10.

Beach, F. A. (1956) Characteristics of masculine "sex drive." In M. R. Jones (Ed.), *Nebraska symposium on motivation*. Lincoln: Univer. of Nebraska Press. Pp. 1–32.

BEACH, F. A., & JAYNES, J. (1954) Effects of early experience upon the behavior of animals. *Psychol. Bull.*, 51, 239–63.

BEACH, F. A., & JAYNES, J. (1956) Studies of maternal retrieving in rats: III. Sensory cues involved in the lactating female's response to her young. *Behaviour*, 10, 104–25.

BEACH, F. A., & JORDAN, LISBETH. (1956) Effects of sexual reinforcement upon the performance of male rats in a straight runway. *J. comp. physiol. Psychol.*, 49, 105–10.

BEACH, F. A., & LEVINSON, G. (1950) Effects of androgen on the glans penis and mating behavior of castrated male rats. *J. exp. Zool.*, 114, 159–68.

BEACH, H. D. (1957) Morphine addiction in rats. *Canad. J. Psychol.*, 11, 104–12.

BEACH, H. D. (1957a) Some effects of morphine on habit function. *Canad. J. Psychol.*, 11, 193–98.

BEEBE-CENTER, J. G., BLACK, P., HOFFMAN, A. C., & WADE, MARJORIE. (1948) Relative per diem consumption as a measure of preference in the rat. *J. comp. physiol. Psychol.*, 41, 239–51.

BÉLANGER, D. (1957) "Gradients" musculaires et processus mentaux supérieurs. *Canad. J. Psychol.*, 11, 113–22.

BELLOWS, R. T. (1939) Time factors in water drinking in dogs. *Amer. J. Physiol.*, 125, 87–97.

BERKUN, M. M., KESSEN, MARION L., & MILLER, N. E. (1952) Hunger-reducing effects of food by stomach fistula versus food by mouth measured by a consummatory response. *J. comp. physiol. Psychol.*, 45, 550–54.

BERLYNE, D. E. (1950) Novelty and curiosity as determinants of exploratory behaviour. *Brit. J. Psychol.*, 41, 68–80.

BERLYNE, D. E. (1954) A theory of human curiosity. *Brit. J. Psychol.*, 45, 180–91.

BERLYNE, D. E. (1955) The arousal and satiation of perceptual curiosity in the rat. *J. comp. physiol. Psychol.*, 48, 238–46.

BERNARD, L. L. (1924) *Instinct, a study in social psychology*. New York: Holt.

BERSH, P. J., NOTTERMAN, J. M., & SCHOENFELD, W. N. (1956) Extinction of a human cardiac-response during avoidance-conditioning. *Amer. J. Psychol.*, 69, 244–51.

BERTOCCI, P. A. (1940) A critique of G. W. Allport's theory of motivation. *Psychol. Rev.*, 47, 501–32.

BEXTON, W. H., HERON, W., & SCOTT, T. H. (1954) Effects of decreased variation in the sensory environment. *Canad. J. Psychol.*, 8, 70–76.

BINDRA, D. (1947) Water-hoarding in rats. *J. comp. physiol. Psychol.*, 40, 149–56.

BINDRA, D. (1948) The nature of motivation for hoarding food. *J. comp. physiol. Psychol.*, 41, 211–18.

BINDRA, D. (1948a) What makes rats hoard? *J. comp. physiol. Psychol.*, 41, 397–402.

BINDRA, D. (1955) Organization in emotional and motivated behaviour. *Canad. J. Psychol.*, 9, 161–67.

BINDRA, D. (1956) Presentation No. 2. In J. M. Tanner & Bärbel Inhelder (Eds.), *Discussions on child development.* Vol. 2. London: Tavistock. Pp. 75–122.

BINDRA, D. (1957) Comparative psychology. *Annu. Rev. Psychol.*, 8, 399–414.

BINDRA, D., & CAMERON, LOIS. (1953) Changes in experimentally produced anxiety with the passage of time: incubation effect. *J. exp. Psychol.*, 45, 197–203.

BINDRA, D., & THOMPSON, W. R. (1953) An evaluation of defecation and urination as measures of fearfulness. *J. comp. physiol. Psychol.*, 46, 43–45.

BIRCH, H. G. (1956) Sources of order in the maternal behavior of animals. *Amer. J. Orthopsychiat.*, 26, 279–84.

BIRCH, H. G., & CLARK, G. (1946) Hormonal modification of social behavior: II. The effects of sex-hormone administration on the social dominance status of the female-castrate chimpanzee. *Psychosom. Med.*, 8, 320–31.

BIRCH, H. G., & CLARK, G. (1950) Hormonal modification of social behavior: IV. The mechanism of estrogen-induced dominance in chimpanzees. *J. comp. physiol. Psychol.*, 43, 181–93.

BLACK, A. H. (1956) The extinction of avoidance responses under curare. Unpublished Ph.D. thesis, Harvard Univer.

BLOOMBERG, R., & WEBB, W. B. (1949) Various degrees within a single drive as cues for spatial response learning in the white rat. *J. exp. Psychol.*, 39, 628–36.

BORING, E. G. (1915) The sensations of the alimentary canal. *Amer. J. Psychol.*, 26, 1–57.

BRADY, J. V. (1955) Extinction of a conditioned "fear" response as a function of reinforcement schedules for competing behavior. *J. Psychol.*, 40, 25–34.

BROWMAN, L. G. (1937) Light in its relation to activity and oestrus rhythms in the albino rat. *J. exp. Zool.*, 75, 375–88.

BROWMAN, L. G. (1942) The effect of bilateral optic enucleation on the voluntary muscular activity of the albino rat. *J. exp. Zool.*, 91, 331–44.

BROWN, J. S. (1948) Gradients of approach and avoidance responses and their relation to level of motivation. *J. comp. physiol. Psychol.*, 41, 450–65.

BROWN, J. S. (1953) Problems presented by the concept of acquired drives. In *Current theory and research in motivation: a symposium.* Lincoln: Univer. of Nebraska Press. Pp. 1–21.

Brown, J. S. (1955) Pleasure-seeking behavior and the drive-reduction hypothesis. *Psychol. Rev.*, **62**, 169–79.

Brown, J. S., & Farber, I. E. (1951) Emotions conceptualized as intervening variables—with suggestions toward a theory of frustration. *Psychol. Bull.*, **48**, 465–95.

Bruner, J. S. (1957) On perceptual readiness. *Psychol. Rev.*, **64**, 123–52.

Bruner, J. S. (1957a) Comment "Effect of overtraining on subsequent learning of incidental cues." *Psychol. Rep.*, **3**, 317–20.

Bruner, J. S., Matter, Jean, & Papanek, Miriam L. (1955) Breadth of learning as a function of drive level and mechanization. *Psychol. Rev.*, **62**, 1–10.

Brush, F. R. (1956) Acquisition and extinction of avoidance learning as a function of shock intensity. Unpublished Ph.D. thesis, Harvard Univer.

Brush, F. R. (1957) The effects of shock intensity on the acquisition and extinction of an avoidance response in dogs. *J. comp. physiol. Psychol.*, **50**, 547–52.

Bugelski, R. (1938) Extinction with and without sub-goal reinforcement. *J. comp. Psychol.*, **26**, 121–33.

Butler, R. A. (1953) Discrimination learning by rhesus monkeys to visual-exploration motivation. *J. comp. physiol. Psychol.*, **46**, 95–98.

Butler, R. A. (1957) The effect of deprivation of visual incentives on visual exploration motivation in monkeys. *J. comp. physiol. Psychol.*, **50**, 177–79.

Butler, R. A. (1957a) Discrimination learning by rhesus monkeys to auditory incentives. *J. comp. physiol. Psychol.*, **50**, 239–41.

Butler, R. A., & Alexander, H. M. (1955) Daily patterns of visual exploratory behavior in the monkey. *J. comp. physiol. Psychol.*, **48**, 247–49.

Campbell, B. A. (1955) The fractional reduction in noxious stimulation required to produce "just noticeable" learning. *J. comp. physiol. Psychol.*, **48**, 141–48.

Campbell, B. A. (1956) The reinforcement difference limen (RDL) function for shock reduction. *J. exp. Psychol.*, **52**, 258–62.

Campbell, B. A., & Sheffield, F. D. (1953) Relation of random activity to food deprivation. *J. comp. physiol. Psychol.*, **46**, 320–22.

Cannon, W. B. (1927) The James-Lange theory of emotions: a critical examination and an alternative theory. *Amer. J. Psychol.*, **39**, 106–24.

Cannon, W. B. (1929) *Bodily changes in pain, hunger, fear, and rage.* (2d Ed.) New York: Appleton-Century. (1st Ed. 1915.)

Cannon, W. B., & Washburn, A. L. (1912) An explanation of hunger. *Amer. J. Physiol.*, **29**, 441–54.

Carlson, A. J. (1912) The relation between the contractions of the empty stomach and the sensation of hunger. *Amer. J. Physiol.*, 31, 175–92.

CARPENTER, C. R. (1942) Sexual behavior of free ranging rhesus monkeys (Macaca mulatta). I. Specimens, procedures, and behavioral characteristics of estrus. II. Periodicity of estrous, homosexual, autoerotic, and nonconformist behavior. *J. comp. Psychol.*, 33, 113–62.

CARR, W. J. (1952) The effect of adrenalectomy upon the NaCl taste threshold in rat. *J. comp. physiol. Psychol.*, 45, 377–80.

CHAMBERS, R. M. (1956) Effects of intravenous glucose injections on learning, general activity, and hunger drive. *J. comp. physiol. Psychol.*, 49, 558–64.

CHURCH, R. M., & SOLOMON, R. L. (1956) Traumatic avoidance learning: the effects of delay of shock termination. *Psychol. Rep.*, 2, 357–68.

CLARK, G., & BIRCH, H. G. (1945) Hormonal modifications of social behavior: I. The effect of sex-hormone administration on the social behavior of a male-castrate chimpanzee. *Psychosom. Med.*, 7, 321–29.

CLARK, G., & BIRCH, H. G. (1946) Hormonal modifications of social behavior: III. The effects of stilbesterol therapy on social dominance in the female-castrate chimpanzee. *Bull. Canad. psychol. Ass.*, 6, 15–18.

COLE, L. C. (1957) Biological clock in the unicorn. *Science*, 125, 874–76.

CONGER, J. J. (1951) The effects of alcohol on conflict behavior in the albino rat. *Quart. J. Stud. Alcohol*, 12, 1–29.

COPPOCK, H. W., & CHAMBERS, R. M. (1954) Reinforcement of position preference by automatic intravenous injections of glucose. *J. comp. physiol. Psychol.*, 47, 355–57.

COWLES, J. T. (1937) Food-tokens as incentives for learning by chimpanzees. *Comp. Psychol. Monogr.*, 14, No. 5 (Serial No. 71).

CRAWFORD, M. P. (1940) The relation between social dominance and the menstrual cycle in female chimpanzees. *J. comp. Psychol.*, 30, 483–513.

CRESPI, L. P. (1942) Quantitative variation of incentive and performance in the white rat. *Amer. J. Psychol.*, 55, 467–517.

CRUM, JANET, BROWN, W. L., & BITTERMAN, M. E. (1951) The effect of partial and delayed reinforcement on resistance to extinction. *Amer. J. Psychol.*, 64, 228–37.

DARWIN, C. (1859) *On the origin of species.* London: Murray.

DARWIN, C. (1872) *The expression of emotions in man and animals.* London: Murray.

DAVIS, R. C. (1937) The relation of certain muscle action potentials to "mental work." *Indiana Univer. Publ. Sci. Ser.*, No. 5.

DAVIS, R. C. (1948) Motor effects of strong auditory stimuli. *J. exp. Psychol.*, **38**. 257–75.

DAVIS, R. C. (1957) Response patterns. *Trans. New York Acad. Sci.*, **19**, 731–39.

DAVIS, R. C. (1957a) Continuous recording of arterial pressure: an analysis of the problem. *J. comp. physiol. Psychol.*, **50**, 524–29.

DAVIS, R. C., & BUCHWALD, A. M. (1957) An exploration of somatic response patterns: stimulus and sex differences. *J. comp. physiol. Psychol.*, **50**, 44–52.

DAVIS, R. C., BUCHWALD, A. M., & FRANKMANN, R. W. (1955) Autonomic and muscular responses, and their relation to simple stimuli. *Psychol. Monogr.*, **69**, No. 20 (Whole No. 405).

DAVIS, R. C., GARAFOLO, LORAZE, & GAULT, F. P. (1957) An exploration of abdominal potentials. *J. comp. physiol. Psychol.*, **50**, 519–23.

DAVIS, R. C., LUNDERVOLD, A., & MILLER, J. D. (1957) The pattern of somatic response during a repetitive motor task and its modification by visual stimuli. *J. comp. physiol. Psychol.*, **50**, 53–60.

DAVIS, R. C., & VAN LIERE, D. W. (1949) Adaptation of the muscular tension response to gunfire. *J. exp. Psychol.*, **39**, 114–17.

DELGADO, J. M. R., ROBERTS, W. W., & MILLER, N. E. (1954) Learning motivated by electrical stimulation of the brain. *Amer. J. Physiol.*, **179**, 587–93.

DEMBER, W. N., EARL, R. W., & PARADISE, N. (1957) Response by rats to differential stimulus complexity. *J. comp. physiol. Psychol.*, **50**, 514–18.

DEUTSCH, J. A. (1956) The inadequacy of the Hullian derivations of reasoning and latent learning. *Psychol. Rev.*, **63**, 389–99.

DEWEY, J. (1917) The need for social psychology. *Psychol. Rev.*, **24**, 266–77.

DINSMOOR, J. A. (1950) A quantitative comparison of the discriminative and reinforcing functions of a stimulus. *J. exp. Psychol.*, **40**, 458–72.

DINSMOOR, J. A. (1954) Punishment: I. The avoidance hypothesis. *Psychol. Rev.*, **61**, 34–46.

DINSMOOR, J. A. (1955) Punishment: II. An interpretation of empirical findings. *Psychol. Rev.*, **62**, 96–105.

DIVEN, K. (1937) Certain determinants in the conditioning of anxiety reactions. *J. Psychol.*, **3**, 291–308.

DOLLARD, J., & MILLER, N. E. (1950) *Personality and psychotherapy.* New York: McGraw-Hill.

DOLLARD, J., MILLER, N. E., DOOB, L. W., MOWRER, O. H., & SEARS, R. R. (1939) *Frustration and aggression.* New Haven: Yale Univer. Press.

DUFFY, ELIZABETH. (1934) Emotion: an example of the need for reorientation in psychology. *Psychol. Rev.*, **41**, 184–98.

DUFFY, ELIZABETH. (1941) The conceptual categories of psychology: a suggestion for revision. *Psychol. Rev.*, **48**, 177–203.

DUFFY, ELIZABETH. (1941a) An explanation of "emotional" phenomena without the use of the concept "emotion." *J. gen. Psychol.*, **25**, 283–93.

DUFFY, ELIZABETH. (1951) The concept of energy mobilization. *Psychol. Rev.*, **58**, 30–40.

DUFFY, ELIZABETH. (1957) The psychological significance of the concept of "arousal" or "activation." *Psychol. Rev.*, **64**, 265–75.

DUFORT, R. J., & KIMBLE, G. A. (1956) Changes in response strength with changes in the amount of reinforcement. *J. exp. Psychol.*, **51**, 185–91.

DUNLAP, K. (1919) Are there any instincts? *J. abnorm. Psychol.*, **14**, 307–11.

EARL, R. W. (1957) Motivation, performance, and extinction. *J. comp. physiol. Psychol.*, **50**, 248–51.

EDMONSON, BARBARA W., & AMSEL, A. (1954) The effects of massing and distribution of extinction trials on the persistence of a fear-motivated instrumental response. *J. comp. physiol. Psychol.*, **47**, 117–23.

ELLEN, P. (1956) The compulsive nature of abnormal fixations. *J. comp. physiol. Psychol.*, **49**, 309–17.

EPSTEIN, A. N., & STELLAR, E. (1955) The control of salt preference in the adrenalectomized rat. *J. comp. physiol. Psychol.*, **48**, 167–72.

ESTES, W. K. (1944) An experimental study of punishment. *Psychol. Monogr.*, **57**, No. 3 (Whole No. 263).

ESTES, W. K. (1950) Toward a statistical theory of learning. *Psychol. Rev.*, **57**, 94–107.

ESTES, W. K., & SKINNER, B. F. (1941) Some quantitative properties of anxiety. *J. exp. Psychol.*, **29**, 390–400.

FANTZ, R. L. (1957) Form preferences in newly hatched chicks. *J. comp. physiol. Psychol.*, **50**, 422–30.

FERSTER, C. B. (1953) Sustained behavior under delayed reinforcement. *J. exp. Psychol.*, **45**, 218–24.

FINCH, G., & CULLER, E. (1935) Relation of forgetting to experimental extinction. *Amer. J. Psychol.*, **47**, 656–62.

FINGER, F. W. (1951) The effect of food deprivation and subsequent satiation upon general activity in the rat. *J. comp. physiol. Psychol.*, **44**, 557–64.

FINGER, F. W., & REID, L. S. (1952) The effect of water deprivation and subsequent satiation upon general activity in the rat. *J. comp. physiol. Psychol.*, **45**, 368–72.

FINGER, F. W., REID, L. S., & WEASNER, M. H. (1957) The effect of reinforcement upon activity during cyclic food deprivation. *J. comp. physiol. Psychol.*, **50**, 495–98.

FINK, J. B., & PATTON, R. M. (1953) Decrement of a learned drinking response accompanying changes in several stimulus characteristics *J. comp. physiol. Psychol.*, **46**, 23–27.

FISHER, A. E., & HALE, E. B. (1956–57) Stimulus determinants of sexual and aggressive behavior in male domestic fowl. *Behaviour*, **10**, 309–23.

FLYNN, J. P., & JEROME, E. A. (1952) Learning in an automatic multiple-choice box with light as incentive. *J. comp. physiol. Psychol.*, **45**, 336–40.

FORD, C. S., & BEACH, F. A. (1951) *Patterns of sexual behavior.* New York: Harper.

FREEMAN, G. L. (1940) The relationship between performance level and bodily activity level. *J. exp. Psychol.*, **26**, 602–8.

FREEMAN, G. L. (1948) *The energetics of human behavior.* Ithaca: Cornell Univer. Press.

FREUD, S. (1910) Three contributions to the theory of sex. Translated by A. A. Brill. *Nerv. and ment. Dis. Monogr. Ser.*, No. 7. (1st Ed., German, 1905.)

FRICK, F. C. (1953) The effect of anxiety—a problem in measurement. *J. comp. physiol. Psychol.*, **46**, 120–23.

FULLER, J. L. (1951) Genetic variability in some physiological constants of dogs. *Amer. J. Physiol.*, **166**, 20–24.

GELLHORN, E. (1943) *Autonomic regulations.* New York: Interscience.

GESELL, A. et al. (1934) *An atlas of infant behavior.* New Haven: Yale Univer. Press.

GHENT, LILA. (1951) The relation of experience to the development of hunger. *Canad. J. Psychol.*, **5**, 77–81.

GILBERT, T. F., & JAMES, W. T. (1956) The dependency of cyclical feeding behavior on internal and external cues. *J. comp. physiol. Psychol.*, **49**, 342–44.

GOODSON, F. E., & BROWNSTEIN, A. (1955) Secondary reinforcing and motivating properties of stimuli contiguous with shock onset and termination. *J. comp. physiol. Psychol.*, **48**, 381–86.

GOY, R. W., & YOUNG, W. C. (1956–57) Strain differences in the behavioral responses of female guinea pigs to alpha-estradiol benzoate and progesterone. *Behaviour*, **10**, 340–54.

GRANDINE, L., & HARLOW, H. F. (1948) Generalization of the characteristics of a single learned stimulus by monkeys. *J. comp. physiol. Psychol.*, **41**, 327–38.

GRICE, G. R. (1948) The relation of secondary reinforcement to delayed reward in visual discrimination learning. *J. exp. Psychol.*, **38**, 1–16.

GRICE, G. R. (1948a) The acquisition of a visual discrimination habit following response to a single stimulus. *J. exp. Psychol.*, **38**, 633–42.

GRICE, G. R. (1949) Visual discrimination learning with simultaneous and successive presentation of stimuli. *J. comp. physiol. Psychol.*, **42**, 365–73.

GRICE, G. R. (1951) The acquisition of a visual discrimination habit following extinction of response to one stimulus. *J. comp. physiol. Psychol.*, 44, 149–53.

GRICE, G. R., & SALTZ, E. (1950) The generalization of an instrumental response to stimuli varying in the size dimension. *J. exp. Psychol.*, 40, 702–8.

GRINKER, R. R., & SPIEGEL, J. P. (1945) *Men under stress.* Philadelphia: Blakiston.

GRUNT, J. A., & YOUNG, W. C. (1953) Consistency of sexual behavior patterns in individual male guinea pigs following castration and androgen therapy. *J. comp. physiol. Psychol.*, 46, 138–44.

GUTHRIE, E. R. (1935) *The psychology of learning.* New York: Harper.

GUTTMAN, N. (1953) Operant conditioning, extinction, and periodic reinforcement in relation to concentration of sucrose used as reinforcing agent. *J. exp. Psychol.*, 46, 213–24.

GUTTMAN, N. (1954) Equal-reinforcement values for sucrose and glucose solutions compared with equal-sweetness values. *J. comp. physiol. Psychol.*, 47, 358–61.

GUTTMAN, N., & KALISH, H. I. (1956) Discriminability and stimulus generalization. *J. exp. Psychol.*, 51, 79–88.

GWINN, G. T. (1951) Resistance to extinction of learned fear-drives. *J. exp. Psychol.*, 42, 6–12.

HAGGARD, E. A. (1943) Experimental studies in affective processes: I. Some effects of cognitive structure and active participation on certain autonomic reactions during and following experimentally induced stress. *J. exp. Psychol.*, 33, 257–84.

HALL, C. S. (1938) The inheritance of emotionality. *Sigma Xi Quart.*, 26, 17–27.

HALL, J. F. (1955) Experimental extinction as a function of altered stimulating conditions. *J. genet. Psychol.*, 87, 155–58.

HALL, J. F. (1955a) Activity as a function of a restricted drinking schedule. *J. comp. physiol. Psychol.*, 48, 265–66.

HALL, J. F. (1956) The relationship between external stimulation, food deprivation, and activity. *J. comp. physiol. Psychol.*, 49, 339–41.

HALL, J. F., & HANFORD, P. V. (1954) Activity as a function of a restricted feeding schedule. *J. comp. physiol. Psychol.*, 47, 362–63.

HALL, J. F., SMITH, K., SCHNITZER, S B., & HANFORD, P. V. (1953) Elevation of activity level in the rat following transition from ad libitum to restricted feeding. *J. comp. physiol. Psychol.*, 46, 429–33.

HALL, JULIA C. (1955) Some conditions of anxiety extinction. *J. abnorm. soc. Psychol.*, 51, 126–32.

HARLOW, H. F. (1949) The formation of learning sets. *Psychol. Rev.*, 56, 51–65.

HARLOW, H. F. (1953) Motivation as a factor in the acquisition of new responses. In *Current theory and research in motivation: a symposium*. Lincoln: Univer. of Nebraska Press. Pp. 24–49.

HARLOW, H. F. (1953a) Mice, monkeys, men, and motives. *Psychol. Rev.*, 60, 23–32.

HARLOW, H. F., HARLOW, MARGARET K., & MEYER, D. R. (1950) Learning motivated by a manipulation drive. *J. exp. Psychol.*, 40, 228–34.

HARLOW, H. F., & McCLEARN, G. E. (1954) Object discrimination learned by monkeys on the basis of manipulation motives. *J. comp. physiol. Psychol.*, 47, 73–76.

HARRIMAN, A. E., & MacLEOD, R. B. (1953) Discriminative thresholds of salt for normal and adrenalectomized rats. *Amer. J. Psychol.*, 66, 465–71.

HAVELKA, J. (1956) Problem-seeking behaviour in rats. *Canad. J. Psychol.*, 10, 91–97.

HAYES, K. J., & HAYES, CATHERINE. (1952) Imitation in a home-raised chimpanzee. *J. comp. physiol. Psychol.*, 45, 450–59.

HAYWARD, S. C. (1957) Modification of sexual behavior of the male albino rat. *J. comp. physiol. Psychol.*, 50, 70–73.

HEBB, D. O. (1945) The forms and conditions of chimpanzee anger. *Bull. Canad. psychol. Ass.*, 5, 32–35.

HEBB, D. O. (1946) Behavioral differences between male and female chimpanzees. *Bull. Canad. psychol. Ass.*, 6, 56–58.

HEBB, D. O. (1946a) On the nature of fear. *Psychol. Rev.*, 53, 259–76.

HEBB, D. O. (1949) *The organization of behavior*. New York: Wiley.

HEBB, D. O. (1951) The role of neurological ideas in psychology. *J. Pers.*, 20, 39–55.

HEBB, D. O. (1953) Heredity and environment in mammalian behaviour. *Brit. J. animal Behav.*, 1, 43–47.

HEBB, D. O. (1954) If man is a mammal, why doan he act like a mammal? You tell me dat. *Amer. Psychologist*, 9, 502 (Abstract).

HEBB, D. O. (1955) Drives and the C.N.S. (Conceptual Nervous System). *Psychol. Rev.*, 62, 243–54.

HEBB, D. O., & MAHUT, H. (1955) Motivation et recherche du changement perceptif chez le rat et chez l'homme. *J. de Psychol. norm. et path.*, 48, 209–21.

HEBB, D. O., & RIESEN, A. H. (1943) The genesis of irrational fears. *Bull. Canad. psychol. Ass.*, 3, 49–50.

HERON, W. (1957) The pathology of boredom. *Scientific Amer.*, 196, 52–56.

HERON, W. T. (1949) Internal stimuli and learning. *J. comp. physiol. Psychol.*, 42, 486–92.

HERRNSTEIN, R. J., & MORSE, W. H. (1957) Some effects of response-independent positive reinforcement on maintained operant behavior. *J. comp. physiol. Psychol.*, 50, 461–67.

HESS, E. H. (1957) Effects of meprobamate on imprinting in waterfowl. *Ann. New York Acad. Sci.*, 67, 724–32.

HILGARD, E. R., & MARQUIS, D. G. (1940) *Conditioning and learning.* New York: Appleton-Century.

HILL, WINFRED F. (1956) Activity as an autonomous drive. *J. comp. physiol. Psychol.*, 49, 15–19.

HINDE, R. A. (1954) Factors governing the changes in strength of a partially inborn response, as shown by the mobbing behaviour of the chaffinch (Fringilla coelebs): I. The nature of the response, and an examination of its course. *Proc. Royal Soc., B.*, 142, 306–31.

HINDE, R. A. (1954a) Factors governing the changes in the strength of a partially inborn response, as shown by the mobbing behaviour of the chaffinch (Fringilla coelebs): II. The waning of the response. *Proc. Royal Soc., B.*, 142, 331–58.

HINDE, R. A. (1956) Ethological models and the concept of 'drive.' *Brit. J. Phil. Sci.*, 6, 321–31.

HINDE, R. A., THORPE, W. H., & VINCE, M. A. (1956) The following response of young coots and moorhens. *Behaviour*, 9, 214–42.

HIRSCH, J., LINDLEY, R. H., & TOLMAN, E. C. (1955) An experimental test of an alleged innate sign stimulus. *J. comp. physiol. Psychol.*, 48, 278–80.

HOLLISTER, L. E., TRAUB, L., & BECKMAN, W. G. (1956) Psychiatric use of reserpine and chlorpromazine: results of double-blind studies. In N. S. Kline (Ed.), *Psychopharmacology.* Washington, D. C.: Amer. Ass. Advancement of Science. Pp. 65–74.

HOLMES, J. H. (1941) A study of thirst. Unpublished thesis for the degree of Doctor of Medical Science, Columbia Univer.

HOPKINS, C. O. (1955) Effectiveness of secondary reinforcing stimuli as a function of the quantity and quality of food reinforcement. *J. exp. Psychol.*, 50, 339–42.

HOVLAND, C. I. (1937) The generalization of conditioned responses: I. The sensory generalization of conditioned responses with varying frequencies of tone. *J. gen. Psychol.*, 17, 125–48.

HOVLAND, C. I. (1937a) The generalization of conditioned responses: II. The sensory generalization of conditioned responses with varying intensities of tone. *J. genet. Psychol.*, 51, 279–91.

HUGHES, L. H. (1957) Saccharine reinforcement in a T maze. *J. comp. physiol. Psychol.*, 50, 431–35.

HULL, C. L. (1933) Differential habituation to internal stimuli in the albino rat. *J. comp. Psychol.*, 16, 255–73.

HULL, C. L. (1943) *Principles of behavior.* New York: Appleton-Century.

HULL, C. L., LIVINGSTON, J. R., ROUSE, R. O., & BARKER, A. N. (1951) True, sham, and esophageal feeding as reinforcements. *J. comp. physiol. Psychol.*, 44, 236–45.

HUNT, H. F., & BRADY, J. V. (1951) Some effects of electro-convulsive shock on a conditioned emotional response ("anxiety"). *J. comp. physiol. Psychol.*, 44, 88–98.

HUNT, J. McV. (1941) The effects of infant feeding-frustration upon adult hoarding behavior. *J. abnorm. soc. Psychol.*, 36, 336–60.

HUNT, J. McV., & SCHLOSBERG, H. (1939) General activity in the male white rat. *J. comp. Psychol.*, 28, 23–38.

HUNT, J. McV., & SCHLOSBERG, H. (1939a) The influence of illumination upon general activity in normal, blinded and castrated male white rats. *J. comp. Psychol.*, 28, 285–98.

HUNT, J. McV., & SCHLOSBERG, H. (1950) Behavior of rats in continuous conflict. *J. comp. physiol. Psychol.*, 43, 351–57.

HUNT, J. McV., SCHLOSBERG, H., SOLOMON, R. L., & STELLAR, E. (1947) Studies of the effects of infantile experience on adult behavior in rats. I. Effects of infantile feeding frustration on adult hoarding. *J. comp. physiol. Psychol.*, 40, 291–304.

HURWITZ, H. M. B. (1956) Conditioned responses in rats reinforced by light. *Brit. J. animal. Behav.*, 4, 31–33.

HURWITZ, H. M. B., & CUTTS, J. (1957) Discrimination and operant extinction. *Brit. J. Psychol.*, 48, 90–92.

HUTT, P. J. (1954) Rate of bar pressing as a function of quality and quantity of food reward. *J. comp. physiol. Psychol.*, 47, 235–39.

JAMES, W. (1890) *The principles of psychology.* New York: Holt.

JAMES, W. T. (1953) Social facilitation of eating behavior in puppies after satiation. *J. comp. physiol. Psychol.*, 46, 427–28.

JASPER, H. H. (1941) Electroencephalography. In W. Penfield & T. C. Erickson (Eds.) *Epilepsy and cerebral localization.* Springfield, Ill.: Thomas. Pp. 380–454.

JAYNES, J. (1956) Imprinting: the interaction of learned and innate behavior: I. Development and generalization. *J. comp. physiol. Psychol.*, 49, 201–6.

JENKINS, J. J., & HANRATTY, JACQUELINE A. (1949) Drive intensity discrimination in the albino rat. *J. comp. physiol. Psychol.*, 42, 228–32.

JENKINS, W. O., & STANLEY, J. C. (1950) Partial reinforcement: a review and critique. *Psychol. Bull.*, 47, 193–234.

JOHN, E. R., WENZEL, B. M., & TSCHIRGI, R. D. (1958) Differential effects of reserpine on conditioned responses in cats. *Science*, 127, 25–26.

KAGAN, J., & BEACH, F. A. (1953) Effects of early experience on mating behavior in male rats. *J. comp. physiol. Psychol.*, 46, 204–8.

KAGAN, J., & BERKUN, M. (1954) The reward value of running activity. *J. comp. physiol. Psychol.*, 47, 108.

KAMIN, L. J. (1956) The effects of termination of the CS and avoidance of the US on avoidance learning. *J. comp. physiol. Psychol.*, 49, 420–24.

KAMIN, L. J. (1957) The gradient of delay of secondary reward in avoidance learning. *J. comp. physiol. Psychol.*, 50, 445–49.

KAMIN, L. J. (1957a) The gradient of delay of secondary reward in avoidance learning tested on avoidance trials only. *J. comp. physiol. Psychol.*, 50, 450–56.

KAPLAN, M. (1952) The effects of noxious stimulus intensity and duration during intermittent reinforcement of escape behavior. *J. comp. physiol. Psychol.*, 45, 538–49.

KAPLAN, M. (1956) The maintenance of escape behavior under fixed-ratio reinforcement. *J. comp. physiol. Psychol.*, 49, 153–57.

KENDLER, H. H. (1949) An experimental examination of the non-selective principle of association of drive-stimuli. *Amer. J. Psychol.*, 62, 382–91.

KIMBLE, G. A. (1955) Shock intensity and avoidance learning. *J. comp. physiol. Psychol.*, 48, 281–84.

KINDER, ELAINE F. (1927) A study of the nest-building activity of the albino rat. *J. exp. Zool.*, 47, 117–61.

KINSEY, A. C., POMEROY, W. B., MARTIN, C. E., & GEBHARD, P. H., et al. (1953) *Sexual behavior in the human female.* Philadelphia: Saunders.

KISH, G. B. (1955) Learning when the onset of illumination is used as reinforcing stimulus. *J. comp. physiol. Psychol.*, 48, 261–64.

KISH, G. B., & ANTONITIS, J. J. (1956) Unconditioned operant behavior in two homozygous strains of mice. *J. genet. Psychol.*, 88, 121–29.

KLING, J. W. (1952) Generalization of extinction of an instrumental response to stimuli varying in the size dimension. *J. exp. Psychol.*, 44, 339–46.

KLING, J. W. (1956) Speed of running as a function of goal-box behavior. *J. comp. physiol. Psychol.*, 49, 474–76.

KLING, J. W., HOROWITZ, L., & DELHAGEN, J. E. (1956) Light as a positive reinforcer for rat responding. *Psychol. Rep.*, 2, 337–40.

KOBRICK, J. L. (1956) The relationship among three measures of response strength as a function of the numbers of reinforcements. *J. comp. physiol. Psychol.*, 49, 582–85.

KOCH, S. (1956) Behavior as "intrinsically" regulated: work notes towards a pre-theory of phenomena called "motivational." In M. R. Jones (Ed.), *Nebraska symposium on motivation.* Lincoln: Univer. of Nebraska Press. Pp. 42–87.

KOHN, M. (1951) Satiation of hunger from food injected directly into the stomach versus food ingested by mouth. *J. comp. physiol. Psychol.*, 44, 412–22.

KOSMAN, MARY E., & GERARD, R. W. (1955) The effect of adrenaline on a conditioned avoidance response. *J. comp. physiol. Psychol.*, 48, 506–8.

KRECH, D. (1950) Dynamic systems, psychological fields, and hypothetical constructs. *Psychol. Rev.*, 57, 283–90.

Kuo, Z. Y. (1928) The fundamental error of the concept of purpose and the trial and error fallacy. *Psychol. Rev.*, 35, 414–33.

Lacey, J. I. (1950) Individual differences in somatic response patterns. *J. comp. physiol. Psychol.*, 43, 338–50.

Lacey, J. I. (1956) The evaluation of autonomic responses: toward a general solution. *Ann. New York Acad. Sci.*, 67, 123–64.

Lacey, J. I., Bateman, Dorothy E., & Van Lehn, Ruth. (1953) Autonomic response specificity: an experimental study. *Psychosom. Med.*, 15, 8–21.

Lacey, J. I., & Van Lehn, Ruth. (1952) Differential emphasis in somatic response to stress: an experimental study. *Psychosom. Med.*, 14, 71–81.

Lange, C., & James, W. (1922) *The emotions.* Baltimore: Williams & Wilkins.

Lashley, K. S. (1938) Experimental analysis of instinctive behavior. *Psychol. Rev.*, 45, 445–71.

Lashley, K. S., & Wade, Marjorie (1946) The Pavlovian theory of generalization. *Psychol. Rev.*, 53, 72–87.

Lawrence, D. H., & Mason, W. A. (1955) Intake and weight adjustments in rats to changes in feeding schedule. *J. comp. physiol. Psychol.*, 48, 43–46.

Lawrence, D. H., & Mason, W. A. (1955a) Food intake in the rat as a function of deprivation intervals and feeding rhythms. *J. comp. physiol. Psychol.*, 48, 267–71.

Lawson, R. (1957) Brightness discrimination performance and secondary reward strength as a function of primary reward amount. *J. comp. physiol. Psychol.*, 50, 35–39.

Lazarus, R. S., & McCleary, R. A. (1951) Autonomic discrimination without awareness: a study of subception. *Psychol. Rev.*, 58, 113–22.

Leeper, R. W. (1935) The role of motivation in learning: a study of the phenomenon of differential motivational control of the utilization of habits. *J. genet. Psychol.*, 46, 3–40.

Leeper, R. W. (1948) A motivational theory of emotion to replace "emotion as disorganized response." *Psychol. Rev.*, 55, 5–21.

Lehrman, D. S. (1953) A critique of Konrad Lorenz's theory of instinctive behavior. *Quart. Rev. Biol.*, 28, 337–63.

Lehrman, D. S. (1956) The organization of maternal behavior and the problem of instinct. In *L'instinct dans les comportement des animaux et de l'homme.* Paris: Masson. Pp. 475–520.

Levine, S. (1953) The role of irrelevant drive stimuli in learning. *J. exp. Psychol.*, 45, 410–16.

Levy, D. M. (1941) The hostile act. *Psychol. Rev.*, 48, 356–61.

Lewis, D. J., & Cotton, J. W. (1957) Learning and performance as a function of drive strength during acquisition and extinction. *J. comp. physiol. Psychol.*, 50, 189–94.

LICHTENSTEIN, P. E. (1950) Studies of anxiety: I. The production of a feeding inhibition in dogs. *J. comp. physiol. Psychol.*, 43, 16–29.

LICKLIDER, LOUISE C., & LICKLIDER, J. C. R. (1950) Observations on the hoarding behavior of rats. *J. comp. physiol. Psychol.*, 43, 129–34.

LINDSLEY, D. B. (1951) Emotion. In S. S. Stevens (Ed.), *Handbook of experimental psychology.* New York: Wiley. Pp. 473–516.

LORENZ, K. (1935) Der Kumpan in der Umwelt des Vogels. *J. Ornithol. Lpz.*, 83, 137–213, 289–413.

LORENZ, K. (1937) Ueber den Begriff der Instinkthandlung. *Folia biotheor.*, Leiden, 2, 17–50.

LORENZ, K. (1941) Vergleichende Bewegungsstudien an Anatinen. *J. Ornithol.*, 89, 194–294.

LORENZ, K. (1950) The comparative method in studying innate behavior patterns. *Symp. Soc. exp. Biol.*, 4, 221–68.

LORENZ, K., & TINBERGEN, N. (1938) Taxis und Instinkthandlung in der Eirollbewegung der Graugans. I. Z. *Tierpsychol.*, 2, 1–29.

LUBORSKY, L. (1945) Aircraft recognition: I. The relative efficiency of teaching procedures. *J. appl. Psychol.*, 29, 385–98.

LURIA, A. R. (1932) *The nature of human conflicts: or emotion, conflict, and will.* New York: Liveright.

MACCORQUODALE, K., & MEEHL, P. E. (1948) On a distinction between hypothetical constructs and intervening variables. *Psychol. Rev.*, 55, 95–107.

MACLEOD, R. B., & ROFF, M. F. (1936) An experiment in temporal disorientation. *Acta Psychol.*, 1, 381–423.

MAHUT, HELEN. (1955) Breed differences in the dog's emotional behavior. Unpublished Ph.D. thesis, McGill University.

MAIER, N. R. F. (1931) Reasoning in humans. II. The solution of a problem and its appearance in consciousness. *J. comp. Psychol.*, 12, 181–94.

MAIER, N. R. F., & ELLEN, P. (1951) Can the anxiety-reduction theory explain abnormal fixations. *Psychol. Rev.*, 58, 435–45.

MALMO, R. B. (1957) Anxiety and behavioral arousal. *Psychol. Rev.*, 64, 276–87.

MALMO, R. B., & DAVIS, J. F. (1956) Physiological gradients as indicants of "arousal" in mirror tracing. *Canad. J. Psychol.*, 10, 231–38.

MALMO, R. B., & SHAGASS, C. (1949) Physiologic studies of reaction to stress in anxiety and early schizophrenia. *Psychosom. Med.*, 11, 9–24.

MALMO, R. B., & SHAGASS, C. (1949a) Physiologic study of symptom mechanisms in psychiatric patients under stress. *Psychosom. Med.*, 11, 25–29.

MALMO, R. B., SHAGASS, C., & DAVIS, F. H. (1950) Specificity of bodily reactions under stress. In *Life stress and bodily disease.* (Volume 29 of the 1949 Proceedings of the Association for Research in Nervous and Mental Disease.) Pp. 231–61.

MALMO, R. B., SHAGASS, C., & DAVIS, J. F. (1951) Electromyographic studies of muscular tension in psychiatric patients under stress. *J. clin. exp. Psychopath.*, 12, 45–66.

MALMO, R. B., WALLERSTEIN, H., & SHAGASS, C. (1953) Headache proneness and mechanisms of motor conflict in psychiatric patients. *J. Pers.*, 22, 163–87.

MARINESCO, G., & KREINDLER, A. (1933) Des réflexes conditionnels: 1. l'organisation des réflexes conditionnels chez l'enfant. *J. de Psychol.*, 30, 855–86.

MARSHALL, S. L. A. (1947) *Men against fire.* New York: Morrow.

MARX, M. H. (1950) A stimulus-response analysis of the hoarding habit in the rat. *Psychol. Rev.*, 57, 80–93.

MARX, M. H. (1950a) Experimental analysis of the hoarding habit in the rat: I. Preliminary observations. *J. comp. physiol. Psychol.*, 43, 295–308.

MARX, M. H. (1950b) Note on depression of spontaneous running activity by the appetite depressant gossypol in rats. *J. comp. physiol. Psychol.*, 43, 396–97.

MARX, M. H. (1951) Experimental analysis of the hoarding habit in the rat: II. Terminal reinforcement. *J. comp. physiol. Psychol.*, 44, 168–77.

MARX, M. H. (1952) Infantile deprivation and adult behavior in the rat: retention of increased rate of eating. *J. comp. physiol. Psychol.*, 45, 43–49.

MARX, M. H. (1957) Experimental analysis of the hoarding habit in the rat: III. Terminal reinforcement under low drive. *J. comp. physiol. Psychol.*, 50, 168–71.

MARX, M. H., & BROWNSTEIN, A. J. (1957) Experimental analysis of the hoarding habit in the rat: IV. Terminal reinforcement followed by high drive at test. *J. comp. physiol. Psychol.*, 50, 617–20.

MARX, M. H., HENDERSON, R. L., & ROBERTS, C. L. (1955) Positive reinforcement of the bar-pressing response by a light stimulus following dark operant pretests with no after effect. *J. comp. physiol. Psychol.*, 48, 73–76.

MASSERMAN, J. H. (1943) *Behavior and neurosis.* Chicago: Univer. of Chicago Press.

McBRIDE, A. F., & HEBB, D. O. (1948) Behavior of the captive bottlenose dolphin, *Tursiops truncatus*. *J. comp. physiol. Psychol.*, 41, 111–23.

McCLEARY, R. A., & MORGAN, C. T. (1946) Food hoarding in rats as a function of environmental temperature. *J. comp. Psychol.*, 39, 371–78.

McCLELLAND, D. C. (1951) *Personality.* New York: Sloane.

McCLELLAND, D. C., ATKINSON, J. W., CLARK, R. A., & LOWELL, E. L. (1953) *The achievement motive.* New York: Appleton-Century-Crofts.

McDougall, W. (1912) *An introduction to social psychology.* (5th ed.) London: Methuen. (1st Ed., 1908)

McDougall, W. (1932) *The energies of men.* London: Methuen.

McKelvey, R. K., & Marx, M. H. (1951) Effects of infantile food and water deprivation on adult hoarding in the rat. *J. comp. physiol. Psychol.,* 44, 423–30.

Meehl, P. E. (1950) On the circularity of the law of effect. *Psychol. Bull.,* 47, 52–75.

Melzack, R. (1952) Irrational fears in the dog. *Canad. J. Psychol.,* 6, 141–47.

Melzack, R. (1954) The effects of early experience on the emotional responses to pain. Unpublished Ph.D. thesis, McGill Univer.

Melzack, R. (1954a) The genesis of emotional behavior: an experimental study of the dog. *J. comp. physiol. Psychol.,* 47, 166–68.

Melzack, R., & Scott, T. H. (1957) The effects of early experience on the response to pain. *J. comp. physiol. Psychol.,* 50, 155–61.

Metzger, R., Cotton, J. W., & Lewis, D. J. (1957) Effect of reinforcement magnitude and of order of presentation of different magnitudes on runway behavior. *J. comp. physiol. Psychol.,* 50, 184–88.

Meyer, D. R. (1952) The stability of human gustatory sensitivity during changes in time of food deprivation. *J. comp. physiol. Psychol.,* 45, 373–76.

Miles, R. C. (1956) Secondary-reinforcement stimulation throughout a series of spontaneous recoveries. *J. comp. physiol. Psychol.,* 49, 496–98.

Miller, G. A., & Frick, F. C. (1949) Statistical behavioristics and sequences of responses. *Psychol. Rev.,* 56, 311–24.

Miller, G. A., & Viek, P. (1944) An analysis of the rat's response to unfamiliar aspects of the hoarding situation. *J. comp. Psychol.,* 37, 221–31.

Miller, N. E. (1944) Experimental studies of conflict. In J. McV. Hunt (Ed.), *Personality and the behavior disorders.* New York: Ronald, Vol. 1. Pp. 431–65.

Miller, N. E. (1951) Learnable drives and rewards. In S. S. Stevens (Ed.), *Handbook of experimental psychology.* New York: Wiley. Pp. 435–72.

Miller, N. E. (1957) Experiments on motivation. *Science,* 126, 1271–78.

Miller, N. E., & Dollard, J. (1941) *Social learning and imitation.* New Haven: Yale Univer. Press.

Miller, N. E., & Kessen, Marion L. (1952) Reward effects of food via stomach fistula compared with those of food via mouth. *J. comp. physiol. Psychol.,* 45, 555–64.

Miller, N. E., Sampliner, R. I., & Woodrow, P. (1957) Thirst-reducing effects of water by stomach fistula vs. water by mouth measured by both a consummatory and an instrumental response. *J. comp. physiol. Psychol.*, **50**, 1–5.

MILLER, W. C., & GREENE, J. E. (1954) Generalization of an avoidance response to varying intensities of sound. *J. comp. physiol. Psychol.*, **47**, 136–39.

MILNER, P. M. (1957) The cell assembly: Mark II. *Psychol. Rev.*, **64**, 242–52.

MIRA, E. (1943) *Psychiatry in war.* New York: Norton.

MIRSKY, A. F. (1955) The influence of sex hormones on social behavior in monkeys. *J. comp. physiol. Psychol.*, **48**, 327–35.

MOGENSON, G. J., & EHRLICH, D. J. (1958) The effects of gentling and shock on growth and behaviour in rats. *Canad. J. Psychol.*, **12**, 165–70.

MONTGOMERY, K. C. (1951) The relation between exploratory behavior and spontaneous alternation in the white rat. *J. comp. physiol. Psychol.*, **44**, 582–89.

MONTGOMERY, K. C. (1953) Exploratory behavior as a function of "similarity" of stimulation situations. *J. comp. physiol. Psychol.*, **46**, 129–33.

MONTGOMERY, K. C. (1953a) The effect of the hunger and thirst drives upon exploratory behavior. *J. comp. physiol. Psychol.*, **46**, 315–19.

MONTGOMERY, K. C. (1953b) The effect of activity deprivation upon exploratory behavior. *J. comp. physiol. Psychol.*, **46**, 438–41.

MONTGOMERY, K. C. (1955) The relation between fear induced by novel stimulation and exploratory behavior. *J. comp. physiol. Psychol.*, **48**, 254–60.

MONTGOMERY, K. C., & MONKMAN, J. A. (1955) The relation between fear and exploratory behavior. *J. comp. physiol. Psychol.*, **48**, 132–36.

MONTGOMERY, K. C., & SEGALL, M. (1955) Discrimination learning based upon the exploratory drive. *J. comp. physiol. Psychol.*, **48**, 225–28.

MOON, L. E., & LODAHL, T. M. (1956) The reinforcing effect of changes in illumination on lever-pressing in the monkey. *Amer. J. Psychol.*, **69**, 288–90.

MORGAN, C. T. (1943) *Physiological psychology.* New York: McGraw-Hill.

MORGAN, C. T. (1947) The hoarding instinct. *Psychol. Rev.*, **54**, 335–41.

MORGAN, C. T., & MORGAN, J. D. (1940) Studies in hunger: I. The effects of insulin upon the rat's rate of eating. *J. genet. Psychol.*, **56**, 137–47.

MORGAN, C. T., & MORGAN, J. D. (1940a) Studies in hunger: II. The relation of gastric denervation and dietary sugar to the effect of insulin upon food in-take in the rat. *J. genet. Psychol.*, **57**, 153–63.

MORGAN, C. T., & STELLAR, E. (1950) *Physiological psychology.* (2d ed.) New York: McGraw-Hill.

MORGAN, C. T., STELLAR, E., & JOHNSON, O. (1943) Food-deprivation and hoarding in rats. *J. comp. Psychol.*, 35, 275–96.

MORUZZI, G., & MAGOUN, H. W. (1949) Brain stem reticular formation and activation of the EEG. *EEG clin. Neurophysiol.*, 1, 455–73.

MOWRER, O. H. (1939) A stimulus-response analysis of anxiety and its role as a reinforcing agent. *Psychol. Rev.*, 46, 553–65.

MOWRER, O. H. (1946) The law of effect and ego psychology. *Psychol. Rev.*, 53, 321–34.

MOWRER, O. H. (1948) Learning theory and the neurotic paradox. *Amer. J. Orthopsychiat.*, 18, 571–610.

MOWRER, O. H., & JONES, HELEN M. (1943) Extinction and behavior variability as functions of effortfulness of task. *J. exp. Psychol.*, 33, 369–86.

MOWRER, O. H., & LAMOREAUX, R. R. (1942) Avoidance conditioning and signal duration—a study of secondary motivation and reward. *Psychol. Monogr.*, 54, No. 5 (Whole No. 247).

MOWRER, O. H., & LAMOREAUX, R. R. (1946) Fear as an intervening variable in avoidance conditioning. *J. comp. Psychol.*, 39, 29–50.

MUNN, N. L. (1950) *Handbook of psychological research on the rat.* Boston: Houghton Mifflin.

MUNN, N. L. (1955) *The evolution and growth of human behavior.* Boston: Houghton Mifflin.

MURPHY, J. V., & MILLER, R. E. (1955) The effect of adrenocorticotrophic hormone (ACTH) on avoidance conditioning in the rat. *J. comp. physiol. Psychol.*, 48, 47–49.

MURPHY, J. V., & MILLER, R. E. (1956) The manipulation of dominance in monkeys with conditioned fear. *J. abnorm. soc. Psychol.*, 53, 244–48.

MURRAY, H. A., et al. (1938) *Explorations in personality.* New York: Oxford Univer. Press.

NEFZGER, M. D. (1957) The properties of stimuli associated with shock reduction. *J. exp. Psychol.*, 53, 184–88.

NISSEN, H. W. (1953) Instinct as seen by a psychologist. *Psychol. Rev.*, 60, 291–94.

NISSEN, H. W. (1954) The nature of the drive as innate determinant of behavioral organization. In M. R. Jones (Ed.), *Nebraska symposium on motivation.* Lincoln: Univer. of Nebraska Press. Pp. 281–321.

O'KELLY, L. I. (1954) The effect of preloads of water and sodium chloride on voluntary water intake of thirsty rats. *J. comp. physiol. Psychol.*, 47, 7–13.

OLDS, J. (1955) Physiological mechanisms of reward. In M. R. Jones (Ed.), *Nebraska symposium on motivation.* Lincoln: Univer. of Nebraska Press. Pp. 73–139.

OLDS, J. (1956) A preliminary mapping of electrical reinforcing effects in the rat brain. *J. comp. physiol. Psychol.*, 49, 281–85.

OLDS, J., & MILNER, P. (1954) Positive reinforcement produced by electrical stimulation of septal area and other regions of rat brain. *J. comp. physiol. Psychol.*, 47, 419–27.

OSGOOD, C. E. (1953) *Method and theory in experimental psychology.* New York: Oxford Univer. Press.

PAVLOV, I. P. (1928) *Lectures on conditioned reflexes.* Translated by W. H. Gantt. New York: International.

PAYNE, R. B., HAUTY, G. T., & MOORE, E. W. (1957) Restoration of tracking proficiency as a function of amount and delay of analeptic medication. *J. comp. physiol. Psychol.*, 50, 146–49.

PERKINS, C. C., JR. (1947) The relation of secondary reward to gradients of reinforcement. *J. exp. Psychol.*, 37, 377–92.

PETERSON, L. R. (1956) Variable delayed reinforcement. *J. comp. physiol. Psychol.*, 49, 232–34.

PFAFFMAN, C., & BARE, J. K. (1950) Gustatory nerve discharges in normal and adrenalectomized rats. *J. comp. physiol. Psychol.*, 43, 320–24.

POSTMAN, L. (1947) The history and present status of the law of effect. *Psychol. Bull.*, 44, 489–563.

PRECHTL, H., & SCHLEIDT, W. M. (1951) Auslösende und steuernde Mechanismen des Saugaktes. *Z. vergl. Physiol.*, 33, 53–62.

RAMSAY, A. O., & HESS, E. H. (1954) A laboratory approach to the study of imprinting. *Wilson Bull.*, 66, 196–206.

RASMUSSEN, E. W. (1955) Experimental homosexual behavior in male albino rats. *Acta Psychol.*, 11, 303–34.

RAZRAN, G. (1949) Stimulus generalization of conditioned responses. *Psychol. Bull.*, 46, 337–65.

RAZRAN, G. (1956) Extinction re-examined and re-analyzed: a new theory. *Psychol. Rev.*, 63, 39–52.

REID, L. S., & FINGER, F. W. (1955) The rat's adjustment to 23-hour food-deprivation cycles. *J. comp. physiol. Psychol.*, 48, 110–13.

RESTLE, F. A. (1955) A theory of discrimination learning. *Psychol. Rev.*, 62, 11–19.

RHEINGOLD, HARRIET L., & HESS, E. H. (1957) The chick's "preference" for some visual properties of water. *J. comp. physiol. Psychol.*, 50, 417–21.

RICHTER, C. P. (1922) A behavioristic study of the activity of the rat. *Comp. Psychol. Monogr.*, 1, No. 2.

RICHTER, C. P. (1927) Animal behavior and internal drives. *Quart. Rev. Biol.*, 2, 307–43.

RICHTER, C. P. (1936) Increased salt appetite in adrenalectomized rats. *Amer. J. Physiol.*, 115, 155–61.

RICHTER, C. P. (1937) Hypophyseal control of behavior. *Cold Spring Harbor Symp. Quant. Biol.*, 5, 258–68.

RICHTER, C. P. (1939) Salt taste thresholds of normal and adrenalecto-mized rats. *Endocrinology*, 24, 367–71.

RICHTER, C. P., & BRAILEY, M. E. (1929) Water intake and its relation to the surface area of the body. *Proc. nat. Acad. Sci.*, 15, 570–78.

RIDDLE, O., BATES, R. W., & LAHR, E. L. (1935) Maternal behavior induced in virgin rats by prolactin. *Proc. Soc. exp. Biol. & Med.*, 32, 730–34.

RIDDLE, O., HOLLANDER, W. F., MILLER, R. A., LAHR, E. L., SMITH, G. C., & MARVIN, H. N. (1941–42) Endocrine studies. *Carnegie Inst. Wash. Yearb.* 41, 203–11.

RIESS, B. F. (1950) The isolation of factors of learning and native behavior in field and laboratory studies. *Ann. New York Acad. Sci.*, 51, 1093–102.

RIGBY, W. K. (1954) Approach and avoidance gradients and conflict behavior in a predominantly temporal situation. *J. comp. physiol. Psychol.*, 47, 83–89.

ROCKETT, F. C. (1955) A note on "An experimental test of an alleged innate sign stimulus" by Hirsch, Lindley, and Tolman. *Percept. motor Skills*, 5, 155–56.

ROSS, S., & ROSS, JEAN G. (1949) Social facilitation of feeding behavior in dogs: I. Group and solitary feeding. *J. genet. Psychol.*, 74, 97–108.

ROSS, S., & ROSS, JEAN G. (1949a) Social facilitation of feeding behavior in dogs: II. Feeding after satiation. *J. genet. Psychol.*, 74, 293–304.

ROSS, S., SMITH, W. I., & NIENSTEDT, C. W., JR. (1950) The hoarding of non-relevant material by the white rat. *J. comp. physiol. Psychol.*, 43, 217–25.

ROSVOLD, H. E., MIRSKY, A. F., & PRIBRAM, K. H. (1954) Influence of amygdalectomy on social behavior in monkeys. *J. comp. physiol. Psychol.*, 47, 173–78.

ROZEBOOM, W. W. (1956) Mediation variables in scientific theory. *Psychol. Rev.*, 63, 249–64.

SCHLOSBERG, H. (1947) The concept of play. *Psychol. Rev.*, 54, 229–31.

SCHLOSBERG, H. (1954) Three dimensions of emotion. *Psychol. Rev.*, 61, 81–88.

SCHLOSBERG, H., & PRATT, CORNELIA H. (1956) The secondary reward value of inaccessible food for hungry and satiated rats. *J. comp. physiol. Psychol.*, 49, 149–52.

SCHNORE, M. M. (1957) Individual differences in patterning and level of physiological activity: a study of arousal. Unpublished Ph.D. thesis, McGill Univer.

SCHOENFELD, W. N. (1950) An experimental approach to anxiety, escape and avoidance behavior. In P. H. Hoch, & J. Zubin (Eds.), *Anxiety.* New York: Grune & Stratton. Pp. 70–99.

SCOTT, E. D., & WIKE, E. L. (1956) The effect of partially delayed reinforcement and trial-distribution on the extinction of an instrumental response. *Amer. J. Psychol.*, 69, 264–68.

SCOTT, W. W., SCOTT, C. C., & LUCKHARDT, A. B. (1938) Observations on the blood-sugar level before, during, and after hunger periods in humans. *Amer. J. Physiol.*, 123, 243–47.

SEARS, R. R. (1943) *Survey of objective studies of psychoanalytic concepts.* New York: Social Science Research Council.

SEWARD, J. P. (1950) Secondary reinforcement as tertiary motivation: a revision of Hull's revision. *Psychol. Rev.*, 57, 362–74.

SEWARD, J. P. (1953) How are motives learned? *Psychol. Rev.*, 60, 99–110.

SEWARD, J. P. (1956) Drive, incentive, and reinforcement. *Psychol. Rev.*, 63, 195–203.

SEWARD, J. P. (1956a) A neurological approach to motivation. In M. R. Jones (Ed.), *Nebraska symposium on motivation.* Lincoln: Univer. of Nebraska Press. Pp. 180–208.

SEWARD, J. P., & PEREBOOM, A. C. (1955) A note on the learning of "spontaneous" activity. *Amer. J. Psychol.*, 68, 139–42.

SHARPLESS, S. K. (1954) Role of the reticular formation in habituation. Unpublished Ph.D. thesis, McGill Univer.

SHEFFIELD, F. D., & CAMPBELL, B. A. (1954) The role of experience in the "spontaneous" activity of hungry rats. *J. comp. physiol. Psychol.*, 47, 97–100.

SHEFFIELD, F. D., & ROBY, T. B. (1950) Reward value of a non-nutritive sweet taste. *J. comp. physiol. Psychol.*, 43, 471–81.

SHEFFIELD, F. D., ROBY, T. B., & CAMPBELL, B. A. (1954) Drive reduction versus consummatory behavior as determinants of reinforcement. *J. comp. physiol. Psychol.*, 47, 349–54.

SHEFFIELD, F. D., WULFF, J. J., & BACKER, R. (1951) Reward value of copulation without sex drive reduction. *J. comp. physiol. Psychol.*, 44, 3–8.

SHERMAN, M. (1927) Differentiation of emotional responses in infants. *J. comp. Psychol.*, 7, 265–84, 335–51.

SHOBEN, E. J., JR. (1949) Psychotherapy as a problem in learning theory. *Psychol. Bull.*, 46, 366–92.

SIDMAN, M. (1953) Avoidance conditioning with brief shock and no exteroceptive warning signal. *Science*, 118, 157–58.

SIDMAN, M. (1955) On the persistence of avoidance behavior. *J. abnorm. soc. Psychol.*, 50, 217–20.

SIDMAN, M. (1956) Drug-behavior interaction. *Ann. New York Acad. Sci.*, 65, 282–302.

SIDMAN, M., BRADY, J. V., BOREN, J. J., CONRAD, D. J., & SCHULMAN, A. (1955) Reward schedules and behavior maintained by intracranial self-stimulation. *Science*, 122, 830–31.

SIEGEL, P. S. (1947) The relationship between voluntary water intake, body weight loss, and number of hours of water privation in the rat. *J. comp. physiol. Psychol.*, 40, 231–38.

SIEGEL, P. S., & BRANTLEY, J. J. (1951) The relationship of emotionality to the consummatory response of eating. *J. exp. Psychol.*, **42**, 304–6.

SIEGEL, P. S., & DORMAN, L. B. (1954) Food intake of the rat following the intragastric administration of "hungry" and "satiated" blood. *J. comp. physiol. Psychol.*, **47**, 227–29.

SIEGEL, P. S., & SIEGEL, HELEN S. (1949) The effect of emotionality on the water intake of the rat. *J. comp. physiol. Psychol.*, **42**, 12–16.

SIEGEL, P. S., & STEINBERG, M. (1949) Activity level as a function of hunger. *J. comp. physiol. Psychol.*, **42**, 413–16.

SIEGEL, P. S., & STUCKEY, HELEN L. (1947) An examination of some factors relating to the voluntary water intake of the rat. *J. comp. physiol. Psychol.*, **40**, 271–74.

SIEGEL, P. S., & STUCKEY, HELEN L. (1947a) The diurnal course of water and food intake in the normal mature rat. *J. comp. physiol. Psychol.*, **40**, 365–70.

SIEGEL, P. S., & TALANTIS, BILLIE S. (1950) Water intake as a function of privation interval when food is withheld. *J. comp. physiol. Psychol.*, **43**, 62–65.

SIEGEL, P. S., & TAUB, D. V. (1952) A "hunger hormone"? *J. comp. physiol. Psychol.*, **45**, 250–53.

SKINNER, B. F. (1938) *The behavior of organisms: an experimental analysis.* New York: Appleton-Century.

SKINNER, B. F. (1948) "Superstition" in the pigeon. *J. exp. Psychol.*, **38**, 168–72.

SKINNER, B. F. (1953) *Science and human behavior.* New York: Macmillan.

SMITH, A. A. (1953) An electromyographic study of tension in interrupted and completed tasks. *J. exp. Psychol.*, **46**, 32–36.

SMITH, A. A., MALMO, R. B., & SHAGASS, C. (1954) An electromyographic study of listening and talking. *Canad. J. Psychol.*, **8**, 219–27.

SMITH, M., & DUFFY, M. (1955) The effects of intragastric injection of various substances on subsequent bar-pressing. *J. comp. physiol. Psychol.*, **48**, 387–91.

SOLOMON, R. L. (1948) Effort and extinction rate: a confirmation. *J. comp. physiol. Psychol.*, **41**, 93–101.

SOLOMON, R. L., & BRUSH, ELINOR S. (1956) Experimentally derived conceptions of anxiety and aversion. In M. R. Jones (Ed.), *Nebraska symposium on motivation.* Lincoln: Univer. of Nebraska Press. Pp. 212–305.

SOLOMON, R. L., KAMIN, L. J., & WYNNE, L. C. (1953) Traumatic avoidance learning: the outcomes of several extinction procedures with dogs. *J. abnorm. soc. Psychol.*, **48**, 291–302.

SOLOMON, R. L., & WYNNE, L. C. (1953) Traumatic avoidance learning: acquisition in normal dogs. *Psychol. Monogr.*, **67**, No. 4 (Whole No. 354).

SOLOMON, R. L., & WYNNE, L. C. (1954) Traumatic avoidance learning: the principles of anxiety conservation and partial irreversibility. *Psychol. Rev.*, 61, 353–85.

SOMMERHOFF, G. (1950) *Analytical biology.* London: Oxford Univer. Press.

SPENCE, K. W. (1944) The nature of theory construction in contemporary psychology. *Psychol. Rev.*, 51, 47–68.

SPENCE, K. W. (1947) The role of secondary reinforcement in delayed reward learning. *Psychol. Rev.*, 54, 1–8.

SPENCE, K. W., & LIPPITT, R. O. (1940) "Latent" learning of a simple maze problem with relevant needs satiated. *Psychol. Bull.*, 37, 429.

SPENCER, H. (1872–73) *The principles of psychology.* 2 vols. New York: Appleton.

SPRAGG, S. D. S. (1940) Morphine addiction in chimpanzees. *Comp. Psychol. Monogr.*, 15, No. 7.

STELLAR, E., & HILL, J. H. (1952) The rat's rate of drinking as a function of water deprivation. *J. comp. physiol. Psychol.*, 45, 96–102.

STELLAR, E., HUNT, J. McV., SCHLOSBERG, H., & SOLOMON, R. L. (1952) The effect of illumination on hoarding behavior. *J. comp. physiol. Psychol.*, 45, 504–7.

STENNETT, R. G. (1957) The relationship of performance level to level of arousal. *J. exp. Psychol.*, 54, 54–61.

STERN, MURIEL H. (1957) The relation between thyroid function and human temperament. Unpublished Ph.D. thesis, McGill Univer.

STEWART, JANE, & HURWITZ, H. M. B. (1958) Studies in light-reinforced behaviour III. Continuous, zero and fixed-ratio reinforcement. *Quart. J. exp. Psychol.* 1958, 10, 56–61.

SURWILLO, W. W. (1956) Psychological factors in muscle-action potentials: EMG gradients. *J. exp. Psychol.*, 52, 263–72.

THOMPSON, W. R. (1953) Exploratory behavior as a function of hunger in "bright" and "dull" rats. *J. comp. physiol. Psychol.*, 46, 323–26.

THOMPSON, W. R., & HERON, W. (1954) The effect of early restriction on activity in dogs. *J. comp. physiol. Psychol.*, 47, 77–82.

THORNDIKE, E. L. (1905) *The elements of psychology.* New York: Seiler.

THORNDIKE, E. L. (1911) *Animal intelligence: experimental studies.* New York: Macmillan.

THORNDIKE, E. L. (1913) *Educational psychology.* Vol. 2. *The original nature of man.* New York: Teachers Coll., Columbia Univer.

THORPE, W. H. (1956) *Learning and instinct in animals.* London: Methuen.

TINBERGEN, N. (1948) Social releasers and the experimental method required for their study. *Wilson Bull.*, 60, 6–51.

TINBERGEN, N. (1951) *The study of instinct.* London: Oxford Univer. Press.

TINBERGEN, N. (1957) On anti-predator responses in certain birds—a reply. *J. comp. physiol. Psychol.,* 50, 412–14.

TOLMAN, E. C. (1925) Purpose and cognition: the determiners of animal learning. *Psychol. Rev.,* 32, 285–97.

TOLMAN, E. C. (1932) *Purposive behavior in animals and men.* New York: Century.

TSANG, Y. C. (1938) Hunger motivation in gastrectomized rats. *J. comp. Psychol.,* 26, 1–17.

TYHURST, J. S. (1951) Individual reactions to community disaster. *Amer. J. Psychiat.,* 107, 764–69.

TYHURST, J. S., & RICHMAN, A. (1955) Clinical experience with psychiatric patients on reserpine—preliminary impressions. *Canad. Med. Assoc. J.,* 72, 458–59.

VERPLANCK, W. S., & HAYES, J. R. (1953) Eating and drinking as a function of maintenance schedule. *J. comp. physiol. Psychol.,* 46, 327–33.

WALLACE, A. F. C. (1956) *Human behavior in extreme situations.* Washington, D. C.: National Acad. of Sciences, National Research Council Publication No. 390.

WALLERSTEIN, H. (1954) An electromyographic study of attentive listening. *Canad. J. Psychol.,* 8, 228–38.

WARDEN, C. J., *et al.* (1931) *Animal motivation.* New York: Columbia Univer. Press.

WARREN, ROSLYN P., & ARONSON, L. R. (1957) Sexual behavior in adult male hamsters castrated-adrenalectomized prior to puberty. *J. comp. physiol. Psychol.,* 50, 475–80.

WATSON, J. B. (1914) *Behavior: an introduction to comparative psychology.* New York: Holt.

WATSON, J. B. (1919) *Psychology from the standpoint of a behaviorist.* Philadelphia: Lippincott.

WATSON, J. B. (1930) *Behaviorism.* (Rev. ed.) New York: Norton.

WEININGER, O. (1956) The effects of early experience on behavior and growth characteristics. *J. comp. physiol. Psychol.,* 49, 1–9.

WELKER, W. I. (1956) Some determinants of play and exploration in chimpanzees. *J. comp. physiol. Psychol.,* 49, 84–89.

WELKER, W. I. (1956a) Variability of play and exploratory behavior in chimpanzees. *J. comp. physiol. Psychol.,* 49, 181–85.

WELKER, W. I. (1956b) Effects of age and experience on play and exploration of young chimpanzees. *J. comp. physiol. Psychol.,* 49, 223–26.

WENDT, G. R. (1936) An interpretation of inhibition of conditioned reflexes as competition between reaction systems. *Psychol. Rev.,* 43, 258–81.

WENGER, M. A. (1948) Studies of autonomic balance in Army Air

Forces personnel. *Comp. Psychol. Monogr.*, **19**, No. 4 (Serial No. 101).

WHITE, R. W. (1956) *The abnormal personality* (2d ed.) New York: Ronald. [1st ed., 1948.]

WHITING, J. W. M., & CHILD, I. L. (1953) *Child training and personality*. New Haven: Yale Univer. Press.

WIESNER, B. P., & SHEARD, NORAH M. (1933) *Maternal behaviour in the rat*. Edinburgh: Oliver and Boyd.

WILLIAMS, S. B. (1938) Resistance to extinction as a function of the number of reinforcements. *J. exp. Psychol.*, **23**, 506–22.

WILLINGHAM, W. W. (1956) The organization of emotional behavior in mice. *J. comp. physiol. Psychol.*, **49**, 345–48.

WILSON, M. P. (1954) Periodic reinforcement interval and number of periodic reinforcements as parameters of response strength. *J. comp. physiol. Psychol.*, **47**, 51–56.

WOLFE, J. B. (1936) Effectiveness of token-rewards for chimpanzees. *Comp. Psychol. Monogr.*, **12**, No. 5 (Serial No. 60).

WOLFLE, D. L. (1935) The relative efficiency of constant and varied stimulation during learning. *J. comp. Psychol.*, **19**, 5–27.

WOLPE, J. (1950) Need-reduction, drive-reduction, and reinforcement: a neurophysiological view. *Psychol. Rev.*, **57**, 19–26.

WOODBURY, C. B., & WILDER, D. H. (1954) The principle of selective association of drive stimuli. *J. exp. Psychol.*, **47**, 301–2.

WOODWORTH, R. S. (1918) *Dynamic psychology*. New York: Columbia Univer. Press.

WYNNE, L. C., & SOLOMON, R. L. (1955) Traumatic avoidance learning: acquisition and extinction in dogs deprived of normal peripheral autonomic function. *Genet. Psychol. Monogr.*, **52**, 241–84.

YERKES, R. M. (1940) Social behavior of chimpanzees: Dominance between mates in relation to sexual status. *J. comp. Psychol.*, **30**, 147–86.

YERKES, R. M. (1943) *Chimpanzees: a laboratory colony*. New Haven: Yale Univer. Press.

YERKES, R. M., & DODSON, J. D. (1908) The relation of strength of stimulus to rapidity of habit-formation. *J. comp. Neurol. Psychol.*, **18**, 458–82.

YOUNG, P. T. (1936) *Motivation of behavior*. New York: Wiley.

YOUNG, P. T. (1943) *Emotion in man and animal*. New York: Wiley.

YOUNG, P. T. (1944) Studies of food preference, appetite and dietary habit. I. Running activity and dietary habit of the rat in relation to food preference. *J. comp. Psychol.*, **37**, 327–70.

YOUNG, P. T. (1948) Appetite, palatability and feeding habit: a critical review. *Psychol. Bull.*, **45**, 289–320.

YOUNG, P. T. (1949) Food-seeking drive, affective process, and learning. *Psychol. Rev.*, **56**, 98–121.

YOUNG, P. T. (1949a) Emotion as disorganized response—A reply to Professor Leeper. *Psychol. Rev.*, 56, 184–91.

YOUNG, P. T. (1955) The role of hedonic processes in motivation. In M. R. Jones (Ed.), *Nebraska symposium on motivation*. Lincoln: Univer. of Nebraska Press. Pp. 193–238.

YOUNG, P. T., & ASDOURIAN, D. (1957) Relative acceptability of sodium chloride and sucrose solutions. *J. comp. physiol. Psychol.*, 50, 499–503.

YOUNG, P. T., & CHAPLIN, J. P. (1945) Studies of food preference, appetite and dietary habit. III. Palatability and appetite in relation to bodily need. *Comp. Psychol. Monogr.*, 18, No. 3 (Serial No. 95).

YOUNG, P. T., HEYER, A. W., & RICHEY, H. W. (1952) Drinking patterns in the rat following water deprivation and subcutaneous injections of sodium chloride. *J. comp. physiol. Psychol.*, 45, 90–95.

YOUNG, P. T., & RICHEY, H. W. (1952) Diurnal drinking patterns in the rat. *J. comp. physiol. Psychol.*, 45, 80–89.

YOUNG, P. T., & SHUFORD, E. H., JR. (1954) Intensity, duration, and repetition of hedonic processes as related to acquisition of motives. *J. comp. physiol. Psychol.*, 47, 298–305.

YOUNG, P. T., & SHUFORD, E. H., JR. (1955) Quantitative control of motivation through sucrose solutions of different concentrations. *J. comp. physiol. Psychol.*, 48, 114–18.

ZIMMERMAN, D. W. (1957) Durable secondary reinforcement: method and theory. *Psychol. Rev.*, 64, 373–83.

# Name Index

# Subject Index